100 Master Speeches

Speeches for Special Occasions

I0676160

100 Master Speeches

Speeches for Special Occasions

FOR THE USE OF

Orators, Teachers and Students, Officers and Members of
Clubs, Societies, and Organization, and
Business and Professional Men

BY

WILLIAM HOMER AMES, Ph.B.

AND

PAUL A. MILLER, B.D.

WILDSIDE PRESS

Copyright, 1923
PUBLIC SPEAKERS' SOCIETY.
Rights Reserved in All Foreign Countries.

Evangelical Press, Harrisburg, Pa.

PREFACE

The immediate popular favor which was accorded the preceding volume of *One Hundred Master Speeches*, on topics connected with the various phases of education, convinced the publishers that a definite need existed for such a work, and at the same time suggested the desirability of following the initial volume with others, in which the same topical grouping should be continued.

It will be seen by the table of contents that the present volume is made up of speeches for special occasions, including holidays; civic, religious, patriotic and fraternal celebrations and events; literary and club programs, and social gatherings. The comprehensive scope of this book will give it a wide appeal, and it is believed that among its one hundred model speeches, each written for a special occasion, every reader will find much helpful illustrative material.

Like its predecessor, this volume is not a compilation of material previously published, but every one of the speeches included in its pages is an original production, written within the twelve months immediately preceding the date of publication of the book, and has never before appeared in print. This fact, which will be made evident by the most casual examination, gives this work a unique character and value, and places it in a class by itself.

In the breathless rush and feverish activity of a commercial and industrial age, the art of public speaking in America has for a time suffered a neglect that can be seen in our dearth of orators and public speakers qualified to be classed with the great names associated with the early history of our nation. There are positive indications, however, that this condition is passing away, and that oratory is again coming into its own. If this humble contribution shall aid in this desired end, the purpose of the authors and publishers will have been achieved.

WILLIAM HOMER AMES.

CONTENTS

CONTENTS　　　　　　7

FOURTH OF JULY ADDRESS

Among all holidays of the year, one stands out as preëminently American; one appeals especially to the sentiment of patriotism and national pride that glows in every loyal American breast. Independence Day—the Fourth of July—is observed in every state in the Union as our distinctive national holiday; for the event which it celebrates is by far the most important in American history—an event, indeed, no less than the birth of a nation.

To all true men the birth of a nation must always be a sacred thing. For the nation is the place where men are made, and by its fitness to make men, to mould and perfect human character, and to give to the world leaders of thought and action,—by this alone each nation must be judged.

Today memory carries us back one hundred and forty-seven years to an immortal gathering of patriots in Independence Hall, Philadelphia, where a document was signed that was destined to have a profound effect upon the history of the world.

The Declaration of Independence was the first solemn declaration, by a nation, of the only legitimate foundation of civil government. It was the corner stone of a new fabric, destined to cover the surface of the globe. It demolished at a stroke the lawlessness of all governments founded upon conquest. It swept away the rubbish of accumulated centuries of servitude.

From the day of this declaration, the people of North America were no longer children, appealing to the sympathies of a heartless mother; no longer subjects, leaning upon the shattered columns of royal promises, and invoking the faith of parchment to secure their rights; they were a nation, asserting as a right, and maintaining by force of arms, their own existence.

The Declaration of Independence was an epoch-making transaction in human affairs. As such it will keep its place in human history as long as the institutions of civilization shall endure. For the vast influence which they exerted upon the world, the scene and the actors were indebted to no stage trappings or dramatic effects. There was nothing wonderful or elaborate to impress the eye in the setting of that great world-drama. Imagination and art gave no studied grace or decoration to the persons, the place, or the performance that made up the business of the day. It was an assembly at which Destiny herself seemed to preside, and the Muse of History to poise her recording pen.

The value and force which belong to the actors in that event rest wholly on the wisdom, the courage and the faith that formed and executed their great design, and the potency and permanence of its influence upon the affairs of the world which followed as a legitimate consequence.

The dignity of the act was the deliberate, serene and fearless performance of these men, in the clear light of day and by a unanimous purpose, of a civic duty which embraced the greatest hazards to themselves and to all the people to whom they owed their discretionary power, but which to their sober judgment promised benefits to that people and to posterity far outreaching those perils, and greater than human vision could discern.

This immortal state paper was the genuine effusion of the soul of the country at that time, the revelation of its mind, when, in its youth, its enthusiasm, its sublime disregard for danger, it rose to the supreme height of its creative powers. The bill of rights which it promulgates is of rights that are older than human institutions, and spring from the eternal justice which is superior to the State.

Two political theories at that time divided the world: one founded the commonwealth on the reason of the State, the policy of expediency; the other based it on the immutable principle of justice and moral right. The new Republic, as it took its place among the powers of the world, proclaimed its faith in the truth and reality and unchangeableness of freedom, virtue, and right.

The heart of Jefferson, in writing the Declaration, and of Congress in adopting it, beat for all humanity. The assertion of right was made for the entire world and all coming generations. Put forth in the name of the ascendant people at that time, it made the circuit of the world, passing everywhere through the despotic countries of Europe; and the astonished nations, as they read that all men are created free and equal, started out of their lethargy.

To the patriots it gave strength and courage. It gave them a definite purpose, and a name and object commensurate with its cost. When it was formally read from the halls of justice and in the public marts by the officers of the army at the head of their divisions, and by the clergy from their pulpits, its dignity and grandeur impressed the public imagination. The American people pronounced it a fit instrument, clothed in worthy language. The public enthusiasm burst forth, and the echoes of the first Independence Day made thrones tremble to their foundations.

We celebrate today no idle tradition, the deeds of no fabulous race; for we tread in the scarcely obliterated footsteps of an earnest and valiant generation of men, who dared to stake life and fortune and sacred honor upon a declaration of rights, whose promulgation shook tyrants on their thrones, gave hope to fainting freedom, and reformed the political ethics of the world.

America is democracy—tested and triumphant. The foundation of democracy is the spiritual equality of man. There is no other possible equality. Individuals differ in mental and moral endowment. Variety is the law of all life, but in the essence of the soul, every man is like every other man. Here, and here alone, we find equality.   Men, spiritually, are brothers, because all men, spiritually, are sons of one Father. Democracy, therefore, is religion—a religion which transcends sectarianism and sectionalism; which is, in fact, the very essence of communion with the eternal.

ARBOR DAY.

In 1872, J. Sterling Morton, of Nebraska, once Secretary of the United States Department of Agriculture, originated in that State the movement which has since become almost national in its scope, and which has resulted in the general observance of Arbor Day. Nebraska, like many other western States, was in large part almost treeless, and the movement to encourage tree-planting has been so beneficial in its results that its originator is recognized as one of the greatest benefactors of his State. Nebraska figured in the old geographies as ''The Great American Desert,'' but tree-planting has transformed it into a garden spot. Nebraskans are justly proud of this achievement and are determined to perpetuate its results.

In 1876, B. G. Northrup advocated tree planting by children, and offered a dollar prize to every boy and girl who should plant or aid in planting five ''centennial trees,'' but the idea of designating a certain day when all should be invited to unite in this work belongs solely to ex-Governor Morton.

The project sprang at once into popular favor, and over a million trees were planted in Nebraska the first year. Other States soon followed the lead of the ''Tree Planter's State,'' so that now Arbor Day is observed in nearly every state and territory throughout the United States.

The time of its observance is of course not at all uniform, but is selected in each case with reference to climate and local conditions. In the North and West, April and May are the months usually selected. In the South, late autumn and early winter are more favored.

In its origin Arbor Day was more material than sentimental.   The reckless spoilation of the great forests alarmed far-sighted and public-spirited men, who saw in it a great and direct loss to national wealth as well as an even greater menace to climate, and, as a consequence, to agriculture.

In the treeless prairie States of Nebraska and Kansas the lack of forests was severely felt, both in the scarcity of native timber for building purposes, and in the irregularity of rainfall.   Trees were needed to conserve and increase material wealth. States more favored by nature saw in the examples of the prairie states a peril of similar nature should they fail to keep what they already possessed. For them the observance of Arbor Day was in the nature of insurance against the future.

But the planting and care of trees soon became popular not for material reasons alone. In pioneer days a forest seemed an obstacle to agricultural development rather than an aid. Trees were regarded too often as enemies to progress and civilization, useful only as firewood. Their beauty was not appreciated until, with the development of towns and cities, men ceased to think only of material development and began to care for the appearance of their surroundings. Then it was seen that trees were beautiful and contributed much to the attractiveness of any community. In the light of this awakened perception, trees were planted as ornaments, and it is to this belief in the beauty of trees that Arbor Day appeals.

Arbor Day has been adopted by the public schools and is usually thought of as a school holiday. In nearly all of the States the superintendents of public instruction issue pamphlets of programs and suggestions for use in the observance of Arbor Day in the schools. There it takes its place with Washington's and Lincoln's Birthdays and other occasions of national observance.

One difference there is, however, between Arbor Day and all other recognized holidays. Arbor Day is the only occasion which is devoted to the future rather than to the past. It does not seek to commemorate dead heroes and statesmen, but it seeks to accomplish something which, in years to come, will be of increasing benefit to the community at large. Its returns are not immediate and are, therefore, the more unselfish.

That great and many-sided American, Theodore Roosevelt, whose birthday on October 27th will recall his vast contributions to the the welfare of the nation, was an ardent and indefatigable advocate of the preservation of the national forests. Memorials of marble and bronze have been erected in his memory, but by far the most beautiful and appropriate means of commemorating his character and public services is the extension of the Sequoia National Park, to be known as the Roosevelt National Park.

Picture to yourself a tract of land larger than the State of Rhode Island, situated in southern California just west of the summit ridge of the Sierras, embracing within its limits the highest mountain in the United States, with river canyons far surpassing in grandeur any of Europe's scenic features, and all this thrown open by the Government as a national playground.

Mount Whitney, Mount Langley, Mount Tyndall, and Mount Williamson, ranging in height from 14,000 to 14,550 feet, and Mount Brewer, Thunder Mountain, and the Kawaah Peaks, all over 13,500 feet in elevation, are the outstanding features of the park landscape, which also includes the great sequoias, the "Big Trees" that Roosevelt loved so well, in a setting of mountain and cascade extending for seventy-five miles from north to south. What could be more fitting than to dedicate these sixteen hundred square miles of magnificent mountain scenery to the American President who in his lifetime rejoiced unceasingly in his love of the great outdoors?

It is because Arbor Day has other values than the merely commercial, and because it has ceased to stand narrowly for the planting of trees, though that is still its primary object, that it is of such great significance in the growing movement for civic betterment. Arbor Day now allies itself with the general movement which makes for improvement in civic conditions, a movement in behalf of more beautiful surroundings, and children trained to study trees and flowers, and to take delight in their cultivation, will in time see to it that city streets and country highways are also made attractive.

MEMORIAL DAY ADDRESS.

We have gathered here today to review the memories and to honor the fallen heroes of four American wars. About the middle of the last century we engaged in a war with Mexico, and twelve years later marked the beginning of our long and bloody Civil War. In 1898 we were drawn into an armed conflict with Spain, and in 1917 the cry of the endangered representative governments of Europe brought us face to face with the serried ranks of autocracy.

To pay loving tribute to all of these gallant men who offered their lives in defence of country and of principles vital to liberty, we, in common with millions of our fellow-citizens throughout the length and breadth of the land are gathered here in this peaceful spot to testify with speech and song, with silent tears and fragrant flowers, our appreciation of what they did.

Some of them sleep in marble cities of the dead, guarded by a nation's faithful vigils; some in old fields and beside quiet streams; some in Flanders fields where the poppies grow red as the blood that was shed upon the hard-fought fields of France; and some lie in unknown graves. Wherever they sleep, a nation's love is with them today, and their memory will ever be cherished.

The surviving soldiers of the Civil War are rapidly passing away. They are making their last march, moving steadily onward to the silent portals of the West. Slowly, inevitably, the members of the Grand Army of the Republic are nearing the frontiers of the great beyond, and soon the last one must pass over. Let us leave nothing undone to prove to them that the citizens of the great nation which they preserved are not lacking in gratitude, and will never cease to cherish the memory of their noble deeds.

Just as in the crucible the shining metal is separated from the dross, so from the fires and bitter trials of that titanic struggle a greater and nobler nation was to emerge. From that memorable hour at Appomattox when Lee sheathed his sword and Grant said to the shattered Southern regiments, "Go in peace, my brethren," this nation began a new life. In time the gray clouds that followed the hideous night of war rolled away and the clear light of the new day cheered a mourning and stricken people on to new endeavor.

And how fruitful those endeavors have been! Never in the history of nations has there been such marvellous growth as that witnessed in the United States since the Civil War. Great, free and glorious, our nation is the haven for the oppressed of every land, and her institutions typify the highest aspirations of mankind. The story of her progress is a wonderful narrative which thrills the heart of every true American. God bless the soldiers, living and dead, who fought to preserve the Union.

The heroism of the sacrifices of 1863-5 can never be forgotten, but to most of us who are living today they have not the poignant vividness of personal experience. But the year 1918 brought the significance of Memorial Day directly home to the present generation. After that memorable year, there were few Americans who had not suffered personal loss or bereavement. The real meaning of "dying for one's country" was impressed on the consciousness of the people. The succeeding Memorial Days have found the nation honoring the memory of the young heroes who gave their lives in France and Flanders, and revering, with new sincerity and fervor, the men who more than half a century ago offered their lives on the altar of patriotism.

Two outstanding facts of the World War are universally conceded. America's participation and America's sacrifices were small in comparison with the labor and sacrifices of the nations which fought through all the bloody years of the struggle. Yet, during the brief period of American participation, America fought as hard as any other belligerent nation, bore her full share of responsibility and burdens, and thus, coming to the front when the other nations were exhausted, actually won the war.

It is generally believed that but for the American army, the German offensives of March-June, 1918, would have carried Prussianism to victory. America, therefore, without boasting, and with full realization that her sacrifice was small in comparison with the sacrifices of France and England and Belgium and Serbia and Roumania, and even of Russia, can cherish the gratification of having actually won the war by intervention at the most critical moment. Belgium's immortal heroism saved civilization in 1914; American altruism and devotion saved democracy in 1918.

But the story was not begun at Chateau-Thierry. It was not even begun in 1917, when the United States, driven beyond the extreme limit of patience, formally declared the existence of a state of war. It was begun more than fifty years before, when the young manhood of the North marched forth at Lincoln's call. What was done in 1861-5 made possible the culmination of 1918. It is all a part of the same glorious story. Without Chickamauga there would have been no Cantigny; the campaign of the Wilderness paved the way for the battles of the Argonne.

The mantle of the fathers has fallen upon the sons. It has fallen upon them sanctified by the new fraternalism that has brought about a broader charity, a deeper understanding, and has healed the wounds of war.

All over the United States today the graves of true American men, graves new and still unclaimed by nature, and graves of long ago, leveled, perhaps by time's obliterating hand, are honored today by those whose lives have been made livable by the nobility and heroism of those who have died.

They gave their all and today we give our very little. Life was as precious to them as it is to us; nothing that we can give can be more than a weak beginning of their stupendous gift. Nor do they demand great recompense: gratitude and homage and a moment's pause in the mad whirl of life to bestow a thought and a flower on the graves of those whose lives were the price of our security and happiness. Sleep in peace, beloved heroes, "until the day break, and the shadows pass away."

AMERICANISM.

By no means the least result of the Great War is the clarity it has brought to our definition of Americanism. Nineteen-twentieths of our foreign population came from the countries engaged in that epochal struggle. They contributed one-fourth of the fighting strength of this country. You will need no formal definition of Americanism when you consider this simple statement in all its implications. The loyalty of these foreigners to the country of their adoption proves the existence of a vital, living force that in an hour of national emergency can transform a day laborer into a hero.

The war revealed them Americans every one. Before the registration board; on the way to camp, in the cantonment, on the ocean voyage, in the trenches, across no-man's-land, high or low, rich or poor, learned or illiterate, Russian, Pole, Italian, Syrian, Austrian, Magyar, Greek, Irish, Swede, German or what not, they all learned the spirit of America, its ideals and aspirations.

The voluntary gift of their sons on the part of non-English speaking fathers and mothers, their magnanimous response to the call to conserve food, to aid Red Cross, Liberty Loan, War Camp Community Service, and other war activities, was such as to set an example to those who were inclined to look upon them as aliens. The fact is that the great majority of these people are Americans to the core and we have not recognized our brethren. It seems that the war was in this respect another blessing in disguise, because it served to lay bare the great heart-beat of America.

The public school has long been recognized as the melting-pot in which the child of the immigrant is Americanized. This is especially so here in the middle West, where other agencies of a social and educational nature are not so numerous as in the great cities of the East. If the child of foreign-born parents completes his education in the public schools, he cannot be distinguished from the offspring of native stock, whom in fact he frequently outstrips in his educational achievements. We do not begrudge him his success. Here rewards are based on merit and not on the accidental advantage of birth or influence. This is cosmopolitanism. This is Americanism.

We now know that the foreigner in our midst cannot be exploited to our local or national advantage. The adult must be reached through personal extension of the right hand of fellowship. The sincerity of our motives will be tested again and again in the furnace of the suspicion caused by the sharp practices of those who have misinterpreted America to him. The neighbor, the employer, the civic forum, the press, the church, the school, must show him the plane of our best thought and action.

If we hope to reach the foreign element in our midst, we must know the personnel to the last individual and seek him out to give him a personal welcome, not for patronage, but for companionship in a common heritage. Our civic leaders, our social workers, our employers, our religious leaders, the teachers in our schools, must be imbued with the same spirit.

No people are more appreciative of your coöperation. As much joy comes to them when they can speak, read or write the English language as comes to the child beginner when he gains for the first time a mastery over oral or written speech. These new achievements are to them the open door to opportunities previously denied them.

The field of Americanism includes all in our midst. It affords opportunity for our best thought and effort, for the utilization of every agency we can command to weld a cosmopolitan population into a homogeneously helpful and loyal American citizenship.

In America the ancient tyrannies and oppressions under which Europe groans cannot be. In America humanity has its chance to make a new start. Here it can begin again with a clean slate. The men and women who have come from other lands to people it have learned the lesson of Time. By experience of old historic errors, they have learned in what human happiness consists, and on virgin soil, cumbered with no rotting foundations of decayed feudal and ecclesiastical systems, they can build a new state of freshly quarried stone, and beams and rafters smelling sweet of the forest. If ever men had a chance to build a new heaven upon a new earth, it is here in America.

If America is but true to her founders, and the pure and stalwart traditions they have bequeathed, it will be merely the fulfillment of her natural destiny that she shall become not merely in name but in actual fact, the guardian of all the liberties thus far evolved from the travail of the ages, and the patient evolver of yet purer and more complete forms of liberty.

Here in America all the races of the world are gathered together to work, and may it be to pray also. Here all the varied problems of mankind are brought as to one vast council board. Never was there such an opportunity for their solution, and surely America will not fail to take it.

Shall she not constitute herself a vast clearing-house for the wrongs of mankind? Nursed herself in liberty, is it not her manifest destiny, beyond that of any other nation, to evolve a world whose humblest inhabitant shall be joyously free, and in whose remotest corner the winds of Liberty shall blow?

And with that gift of Liberty shall she not bring, too, ideals of "the pursuit of happiness" finer and purer than those too often followed by her citizens today? With fullness of Liberty may there be also a return to that old noble simplicity of American life, when an American gentleman was the first of aristocrats, while remaining the simplest of democrats as well, and an American lady sought no diadem but that of her queenly womanhood.

ADDRESS ON ABRAHAM LINCOLN'S BIRTHDAY.

Our country today does honor not only to one of the greatest Americans, but to one of the greatest men of all time. In his fifty-six years of life, Abraham Lincoln played many parts, for he was in his youth farm hand, store clerk, mill superintendent, stump speaker, rail splitter, boat builder, trader, inventor, grocer, surveyor, postmaster, steamboat pilot, captain of volunteers, and Indian fighter; and in later life he was state legislator, lawyer, presidential elector, congressman, lecturer, debater, candidate for United States senator and Vice President, orator of national fame, President, commander-in-chief of vast armies and fleets, emancipator, hero and martyr. In short, for ingrained versatility, native power, homespun worth and lofty steadfastness, Abraham Lincoln stands supreme.

Yet there is one aspect in which he appears to us that comprehends all others—that of "the first American"—the first man distinctly of our race, born on American soil, bred from the cradle under American institutions, who rose from the rude conditions of the humblest

2

American life to be the embodiment of the highest aspirations, and the realization of the loftiest national ideals of his fellow-countrymen—American in his virtues. American in his imperfections, and superlatively American in all that went to make him great.

Abraham Lincoln was born on February 12th, one hundred and fourteen years ago, in a log cabin among the mountains of the State of Kentucky. He came into a frontier life of comparative poverty, labor, hardship, and rude adventure. He had little instruction and few books. He had no friends among the great and powerful of his time. An equal among equals in the crude simplicity of scattered communities on the border of the wilderness, he rose above the common level by the sheer force of his own qualities.

Even the slight advantages that might have been derived from a settled location were denied Lincoln, for he was taken at the age of seven years from the rude Kentucky neighborhood where he was born to the still ruder wilderness of Indiana, and later into the primeval forests of Central Illinois. In brief, his origin and surroundings were like those of thousands of other Americans who were then growing up to be the brawn and brains of the great, undeveloped West.

But a thirst for learning as a means of rising in the world was born in him. Each day when his work was ended, his studies became the chief pleasure of his life. He read, wrote, and ciphered incessantly. He would sit in the twilight and read a dictionary as long as he could see. He would go to the town constable's cabin, four and a half miles away and devour the Revised Statutes of Indiana.

With such a spirit and with such indomitable persistence, Lincoln became the leader in his community. He was sent to Congress at Washington, where he broadened his conceptions to national scope. He was admitted to the bar, and won a high place as a successful and distinguished advocate.

He became convinced of the wickedness of African slavery, that baleful institution which the defective humanity of our fathers permitted to be established in the American colonies; and with power and insistence that compelled public attention he declared his conviction that human slavery was eternally wrong. He gave voice to the awakened conscience of the North. He led in the struggle for freedom from slavery.

Upon that issue he was elected President. In that cause, as President, he conducted a great war of four years' duration, in which millions of armed men were engaged. When in his wise judgment the time was ripe for it, on his own responsibility in the exercise of his authority as commander-in-chief, invoking the support of his country, the considerate judgment of mankind, and the blessing of God upon his act, he set free the 3,000,000 slaves by his official proclamation, and dedicated the soil of America forever as the home of a united, liberty-loving people.

It was not chance or favorable circumstances that achieved Lincoln's success. The struggle was long and desperate, and often appeared hopeless. He won through the possession of the noblest qualities of manhood. He was simple, honest, sincere and unselfish. He had high courage for action and fortitude in adversity. Never for an instant did the thought of personal advantage compete with the interests of the public cause. He never faltered in the positive and unequivocal declaration of the wrong of slavery, but his sympathy with all his fellowmen was so genuine, his knowledge of human nature was so just, that he was able to lead his countrymen without dogmatism or imputation of assumed authority.

He carried the Civil War to its successful conclusion with inflexible determination; but the many evidences of his kindness of heart toward the people of the South and of his compassion for distress and suffering were the despair of many of his subordinates, and the effect of his humanity and considerate spirit upon the conduct of the war became one of the chief reasons why, when the war was over, the North and South were able during the same generation to join again in friendship as citizens of one united country.

The time has long been here when in solemn awe and reverence we pronounce the name of Lincoln with that of Washington, and in their silent, deathless splendor leave them both shining on.

MOTHER.

The greatest human love is that of a mother, and its divine meaning is God. From the moment when the promise of maternity strikes the chords of heavenly music in a woman's heart until the time when darkness holds the closing eyes, a love is manifest in motherhood the meaning of which no man can fully understand, and the like of which finds no analogy except in divine love that always and everywhere embraces His creatures.

Hers it is to love the child because the child is hers. The life she begat at the pain and peril of her own she nourishes and cherishes without care or thought of her own. Toil, weariness, privation, suffering, are to her the chords of a chorus of hallowed glory and heavenly joy when they serve the well-being and happiness of the child of her heart.

She asks no reward, nor expects any, but the privilege of lavishing her maternal affection where the instinct of her heart directs. In the simple word mother is a mystery of unselfish and unending affection which no coarser soul or grosser mind can solve. Men stand amazed at the presence of its manifestations, and angels gaze with admiration upon the outpourings of a mother's love, while only God can fathom the meaning of its sweetness and its strength.

There is an enduring tenderness in the love of a mother for her son that transcends all other affections of the heart. It is neither to be chilled by selfishness, nor daunted by danger, nor weakened by worthlessness, nor stifled by ingratitude. She will sacrifice every comfort to his convenience, she will surrender every pleasure to his enjoyment; she will glory in his fame and exult in his prosperity; and if misfortune overtake him, he will be the dearer to her for his misfortune; and if disgrace settle upon his name, she will still love and cherish him in spite of his disgrace; and if all the world beside cast him off, she will be all the world to him.

Mother! What a world of meaning is contained in that one little word! Its magnitude is wonderful. Consider its height and breadth, its duties and obligations. Who can measure its possibilities or gauge its meanings?

Confucius, the great philosopher; Alexander, the victorious general; Moses, the prophet of God; Shakespeare, the author; Scott, the novelist and poet; Washington, McKinley, and scores of other great figures in the world's history, owe a great measure of their success to the teachings of a noble mother. It is to the early environment of the hearthstone, to the aspirations of noble women, and to the devotion of worthy mothers, that the world is indebted for its greatest men.

Abraham Lincoln, standing on the pinnacle of success as a statesman, declared, "All that I am or ever expect to be, I owe to my angel mother."

John Quincy Adams said of his mother, "My mother was an angel upon earth. She was a minister of blessing to all human beings within her sphere of action. Her heart was the abode of heavenly purity. She had known sorrow, but her sorrow was silent. If there is existence and reward beyond the grave, my mother is happy."

The mother of Daniel Webster influenced her husband to sell their old homestead that they might devote the proceeds to the education of their two boys. This act of self-sacrificing love and parental solicitude has already and will forever affect the American nation for good, and, indirectly, the entire world.

Cowper, the poet, expressed in the most impressive language the warmth of his affection for the memory of his mother, when, long after her death, his cousin presented him with her picture. "I had rather," said he, "possess that picture than the richest jewel in the British crown; for I love her with an affection that her death fifty-two years since has not the least abated."

The mother of President Garfield was a woman of large gifts and deep piety. She taught her children the Bible, temperance, the love of liberty, and loyalty to their country. Just after President Garfield delivered his inaugural address, while tens of thousands of his countrymen were cheering him, he turned and kissed his aged mother, and then he kissed his wife. Again the vast multitude applauded his action, honoring the tribute to his mother and his wife in the one supreme moment of his life. When the news came to the mother that her son was shot, she cried out in her agony: "The Lord help me! How could anyone be so cold-hearted as to want to kill my baby?"

How true are the words of Jean Paul Richter, who said: "To a man who has had a mother, all women are sacred for her sake!"

In the days of Rome's greatest splendor, there stood on one of her seven hills a temple dedicated to "Fortune"; and over its magnificent portal was written the name of Volumnia, for whose honor the temple had been built, to perpetuate the memory of a matron who had saved Rome by her influence over her son. Not far distant from it arose a column on which was inscribed, "Cornelia, the mother of the Gracchi," in acknowledgment of her worth as the mother of two sons whom she had trained to be ornaments and defenders of the nation. Such was the respect paid to mothers who acted well their part in pagan Rome.

"God could not be everywhere," says a Hebrew proverb, "therefore He made mothers." No language can express the power and beauty and heroism and majesty of a mother's love. It shrinks not where man cowers, and grows stronger where man faints, and over the wastes of worldly fortune sends the radiance of its quenchless fidelity like a star in heaven.

> "All other love is mockery and deceit,
> 'Tis like the mirage of the desert that appears
> A cool refreshing water, and allures
> The thirsty traveller, but flies anon
> And leaves him disappointed, wondering
> So fair a vision should so futile prove.
> A mother's love is like unto a well,
> Sealed and kept secret, a deep-hidden fount
> That flows when every other spring is dry."

"THE FATHERS."

If the sweetest and most enduring thing in the world is a mother's love, then the noblest thing in the world is a father's self-sacrificing toil for his wife and children. It is our fathers who have gone out from the shelter of home and wrested from the world the means by which we have lived. It is our fathers' hands that have compelled the elements to yield the things we have needed to perpetuate our lives and to achieve any degree of success. And while he has done this rugged work, he has not in any degree taken from mother the glory that has rested on her.

If our fathers have done nothing more than this, they have done well. But they have done more than labor that we might live in comfort and a degree of luxury. They have had their part in planting in our bosoms those aspirations that are wholesome and uplifting; in leading our feet into right paths; and by the example of manly virtues, placing before our eyes a model to which we have unconsciously bent and conformed our natures.

Our fathers have taught us industry, the gift of tongues, that makes a man understood and valued in all countries; the philosopher's stone, that turns all metals into gold, and nature's physician, that cures disorders of both the body and the mind.

They have taught us honesty, the shortest and surest way to live with honor in the world, the highest wisdom and the best counsel in all the affairs of life, the virtue which Socrates said could best be cultivated by studying to be what you wish to seem.

They have taught us thrift, the guardian and preserver of the other virtues, the handmaiden of education and enlightenment, and the foundation of the State. The habit of saving is in itself an education; it fosters every virtue, teaches self-denial, cultivates the sense of order, trains to forethought, and so broadens the mind.

Our fathers have taught us fidelity. They have taught us never to betray a friend, much less one of our own household. Fidelity is the sister of justice, and one of the most excellent endowments of the human mind.

They have taught us regard for law, respect for woman, and reverence for things that are high and holy. They have shielded us from the influences that contaminate our youthful lives and lead them astray in forbidden paths.

They have sought to bless us with things material. What father is there who does not seek to provide his own son material things better than he himself has enjoyed?

They have sought to place us in positions of responsibility and trust in the community beyond those which they themselves have occupied.

They have sought to put into our lives aspirations that are noble and true, to the end that in good works we might be carried beyond the point that they have been able to reach.

In all these things our fathers have earnestly sought that we might be more earnest, efficient and valuable members of society than they have been.

To be a father in the highest sense is to be a companion of God; it is to be associated with a noble woman in watching over and directing the destiny of another life in which there is planted an immortal spirit whose end is to be union with the divine.

This conviction is the inspiration of the following beautiful lines by Richard Watson Gilder, entitled ''Father and Child'':

"Beneath the deep and solemn midnight sky,
   At the last verge and boundary of time,
   I stand and listen to the starry chime
That sounds to the inward sense and will not die.
Now do the thoughts that daily hidden lie,
   Arise and live in a celestial clime—
   Unutterable thoughts, most high, sublime,
Crossed by one dread that frights mortality.
Thus as I muse, I hear my little child
   Sob in its sleep within the cottage near—
   My own dear child!—Gone is that mortal doubt!
The Power that drew our lives forth from the wild
   Our Father is: we shall to Him be dear,
   Nor from His universe be blotted out."

Responding to the impulses which the heavenly Father has implanted in their bosoms, our Fathers have led us onward to achieve the highest of which we are capable. Mortality touched by divinity in the making of men—they have helped us to comprehend God, our heavenly Father. So it is that to a degree at least our fathers in the light of their love for us have interpreted God's great love for us, and have inspired us to achieve for our own selves and for the race.

All honor then to our fathers, who through the divine opportunity of parenthood have reached out beyond the material and laid hold on eternal principles of thought and action with which to embody their highest aspirations in the young lives entrusted to their care.

THE ART OF CHRISTMAS.

Many of the most beautiful paintings of the world are closely associated with the Christmas season. Especially is this true of the paintings of the Madonna, the Holy Family, and the Christ child. Medieval art is particularly rich in these subjects, as at that period the religious element was the leading motive in painting.

Among the innumerable pictures in which the world's great religious painters have represented the scenes of the earthly life of Christ, it is amazing to note the large proportion of subjects relating to His infancy. What else can that mean than that the hearts of worshippers ever yearn toward that which they can understand and love, and that thus, of all the varied aspects of Christ's character, it appeals to us most forcibly that he was once a babe in the manger at Bethlehem.

To find the earliest delineations of the Christ-child, we must go to the Catacombs of Rome, and on the walls of their strange subterranean chapels retrace the fading features of the Divine Babe as painted there centuries ago to cheer the hearts of Christians. Two of these primitive frescoes are in the Greek chapel of the Catacomb of Saint Praxedes, where they are a constant object of interest to art pilgrims.

Considered aesthetically, they have of course no intrinsic beauty; but to the thoughtful mind they stand for the beginnings of a great art movement which culminated in the canvases of Raphael and Titian.

From the frescoes of the Catacombs, the next step in the progress of Christian art was to the mosaics ornamenting the basilicas; and here the Christ-child again appears as a conspicuous figure. Some of the most interesting of these mosaics represent the Babe receiving the gifts of the Magi—as at Santa Maria Maggiore in Rome and at St. Apollinare in Ravenna. In others, as at Capua, the Child shares with the enthroned Virgin the adoration of a surrounding group of saints. Still another of peculiar interest is at Santa Maria in Trastevere at Rome, where the Babe is nourished at his mother's breast.

When we enter that strange period of history known as the Dark Ages, we find the art products few and uninteresting; but even then the Christ-child is not forgotten, and again and again he appears sculptured in marble over the portals of cathedrals, or painted in stiff Byzantine style over their altars.

Thus it was that in the new birth of art in Italy, when Niccolo Pisano in sculpture, and Cimabue in painting, awakened the sleeping world to a love of beauty, the Madonna, with her heaven-born Babe, was the first subject to arouse enthusiasm; and it was for a picture of this sort that all Florence went mad with joy, as it was borne along the Street of Rejoicing.

It was then that Italy was transformed into a paradise of art, and all the important cities were full of great painters whose hearts were aglow with the sacred fire of genius. In the host of beautiful works which were produced in the next three centuries, every type of treatment was exemplified, varying from the most simple naturalism to the loftiest idealism. The naive simplicity of Filippino Lippi's chubby baby, placidly sucking his thumb as he looks out from the picture, is matched in the frolicsome boys of Andrea del Sarto's many paintings of the Christ-child, smiling mischievously from the Madonna's arms.

When it would seem that every conceivable type of infancy had already been realized on the canvas, Raphael arose to create an entirely new ideal, and all predecessors paled before his rapidly increasing glory. His conception of the Christ-child ranges from the sleeping Babe from whose innocent face the Madonna softly lifts a veil, to the grave boy whom the Madonna of the Chair clasps in her arms. Every shade of playfulness, of affection, of dignity, and of contemplation, is mirrored in the long series of pictures in which the great artist embodied his ever-changing ideal of the Divine Infant.

The Christ-child of the Madonna of the Casa Tempi, one of Raphael's finest works, is a dimpled baby nestling shyly against his mother's breast; the Sistine Child is a royal messenger lightly enthroned upon the Madonna's arm. In one conception, Mother and Son are absorbed entirely in each other; in the other, they think only of humanity, their wide eyes searching the future with far-seeing gaze, and their thoughts intent upon the coming of the heavenly kingdom.

The gem among Corregio's pictures is an "Adoration of the Shepherds" called "The Holy Night," or "La Notte." It is night—the scene is the manger. The Mother holds the Babe. His body is illuminated with a heavenly radiance that shines from it up into the Mother's face. It falls, also, upon the shepherds and shepherdess. The latter, with one graceful hand, shades her face, while with the other she brings to the Christ-child her offering— a little basket holding two turtle-doves. A group of angels hovers above in softened radiance.

The cold morning light is just breaking, and Joseph in the distance is caring for the donkey upon which Mary rode to Bethlehem. The picture is touched by three lights—the transparent loveliness irradiating from the Christ-child, the softer tints of the angelic host, and the grey morning dawn. "La Notte," with its rare grace and beauty, ranks with Raphael's "Sistine Madonna" as one of the gems of the Dresden Gallery.

We have followed the development of the art of Christmas from the gloomy shadows of the Catacombs to the brilliant glory of the golden age of painting under the great Italian masters. More modern artists have responded to the same tender and beautiful inspiration, but time will not permit to take up in detail these later achievements. Suffice it to say that wherever the Cross sheds its radiance upon believers, the Christ-child and his holy Mother will call forth the most sublime conceptions of the artist, and the most sincere admiration of his followers.

ADDRESS FOR ODD FELLOWS ANNIVERSARY.

For one hundred and four years American citizenship has been enriched, American patriotism has been fostered, and American liberties have been protected by a fraternal order which may rightfully claim a high place of honor among American institutions. Supported by its great army of 2,676,582 members, the principles and ideals of Odd Fellowship have woven themselves into the very fabric of our nation, and have supplied strength and permanence to the foundations of national character.

Have you stood on some sultry day in August, when the parched earth cried to the pitiless skies for life-giving showers, and have you watched some tiny cloud appear on the horizon, and rapidly expand until it filled all the heavens and descended upon the fields in grateful rain? It was from such small beginnings that Odd Fellowship took its origin.

It is quite well established that the first permanent lodge of Odd

Fellows was organized by Thomas Wiley in the city of Baltimore, Maryland, on April 26, 1819. Thomas Wiley was born in London in 1782, and on reaching manhood was initiated into an English lodge of Odd Fellows, in which he became an enthusiastic worker.

He came to this country in 1817, and shortly afterward settled in Baltimore. There he met John Welch, who had also been initiated into the order in England. Not knowing any others who belonged to the order, they inserted the following advertisement in the *Baltimore American* on March 27, 1819: "A few members of the Society of Odd Fellows will be glad to meet their brethren for the purpose of forming a Lodge, on Friday evening, 2nd April, at Seven Stars, Second Street, at the hour of seven p. m."

On that historic night, there assembled, in the little tavern on Second Street, Thomas Wiley, John Welch, Richard Rushworth, John Duncan, and John Cheatham, who there organized Washington Lodge, No. 1, which is still in existence. After the formal opening of the Lodge, Thomas Wiley was installed as Noble Grand and John Welch as Vice Grand.

And so this now great and powerful Order was started on its mission to fraternalize the world and to spread abroad among all mankind its triune principles of Friendship, Love, and Truth. How well it has carried out those principles the vast army that today marches under its banners can testify.

In 1835, Thomas Wiley was elected Traveling Agent of the Grand Lodge of the United States, and traveled all over the country establishing new lodges and encouraging the members. The monuments of his labors may be seen in institutions more lasting than bronze and marble—the living, vitalizing principles of brotherhood practiced by a mighty and progressive Order.

Thomas Wiley died at the age of eighty years in the city of Baltimore, on October 19, 1861, and his body lies in Greenwood Cemetery. But few men have received such tribute of worth as did Thomas Wiley when he was laid at rest, yet his greatest praise is that shown in the tender memory in which he is held by each succeeding generation of Odd Fellows.

The interests that hold our organization together are the highest and noblest that ever animated human beings. The Independent Order of Odd Fellows is founded upon three cardinal principles, Friendship, Love, and Truth.

Friendship between man and man is a most precious possession, a thing infinite and immortal, which improves happiness, abates misery, and divides our grief. Love is an image of God, and not a lifeless image, but the living essence of the divine nature which beams full of all goodness. Truth is the foundation of all knowledge and the cement of all societies: the property of no individual, but the treasure of all men. Friendship, Love, and Truth,—these are the three bright stars that shed their divine radiance over the dark ocean of human existence. Without their guidance, earth would be a prison pen from which we would long to escape to other homes, and man would be nothing more than a brother of the clod.

An order that teaches a higher ideal of life, that gives men a new and abiding faith in charity, virtue, and love, assuredly deserves considerate study by those who are interested in the welfare of the human race.

The Independent Order of Odd Fellows has become one of the most powerful agencies in the warfare against ignorance, vice, intolerance, bigotry, and the host of evils that beset man at every step of his earthly career. It exists in response to the cravings of the human soul for a domain of brotherhood, a fraternity wherein sweet and congenial companionship and mutual offices of kindness and regard may soften the rigors of existence and give mankind an earnest and foretaste of the life beyond.

The cry for companionship is the natural expression of the highest within the heart of man. It is only in mingling with his fellow man that the most beautiful and lasting elements of character in the mind and soul may be developed. Alone, man degenerates; his high ideals and lofty aspirations disappear, and he reverts to the primitive savagery of the beast.

Thus, with Truth as our guide and Friendship and Love as our animating principles, our banner proudly floats on the breezes of every clime as a welcome beacon to the tempest-tossed mariner on the troubled waves.

"Then up with our banner: a standard more fair
Never flashed in the sunshine nor waved in the air;
A precept more holy ne'er came from above,
Than our beautiful legend—'Truth, Friendship, and Love.' "

THANKSGIVING DAY.

Thanksgiving Day is a holiday distinctly American, but similar festivals are found in the history of the Greeks and Romans, who had a day in honor of the goddess Ceres or Demeter, the patron deity of agriculture, which was celebrated yearly on the fourth of October. The Jews also had their Feast of Tabernacles lasting a week in celebration of the harvest.

The Ancient Egyptians feasted and offered sacrifices to their goddess Isis after gathering in their crops, and the English have their harvest home celebration, but America is the only nation to have a regular day set apart each year to give thanks to God for His goodness.

The first thanksgiving in North America of which there is any record was on the shores of Newfoundland in 1578 and was conducted by an English minister. Another similar ceremony was held in the Popham colony in Maine in 1607.

But the two thanksgivings to which we generally trace our holiday were held by the Pilgrims in Plymouth. The festival began about a year after the landing of the Pilgrims on Plymouth Rock, for it was on November 21, 1620, that the "Mayflower" with one hundred and two Pilgrims cast anchor off Cape Cod.

Their voyage had occupied about ten times the number of days that a crossing of the Atlantic now consumes, and after their landing on the edge of an unbroken wilderness, their first year had been filled with hardships, deaths and danger.

Their devoted little band would probably have been doomed to destruction from starvation had not the people planted some corn which they found in the Indian huts. The friendly Indians taught the Pilgrims how to plant and fertilize corn with the bones of fish which abounded along the coast.

The harvest of 1621 was so bountiful that Governor Bradford ordered a three days' feast in October, to which Chief Massasoit and other Indian friends of the colony were invited.

Edward Winslow, third signer of the original "Mayflower" compact, and later Governor of the colony, writes an account of it, supposedly to George Morton under date of December 11, 1621, as follows:

"We set the last spring some twenty acres of Indian corn and sowed some six acres of barley and peas, and, according to the manner of the Indians, manured our ground with herrings or rather shads, which we had in great abundance, and take with great ease at our doors.

"Our corn did prove well; and, God be praised, we had a good increase of Indian corn, and our barley indifferent good, but our peas not worth gathering, for we feared they were too late down. They came up very well and blossomed, but the sun parched them in the blossom.

"Our harvest being gotten in, our Governor sent four men on fowling, that so we might, after a special manner, rejoice together after we had gathered the fruit of our labors.

"They four in one day killed as many fowl as, with a little help beside, served the company almost a week, at which time, amongst other recreations, we exercised our arms, many of the Indians coming amongst us, and among the rest their greatest king, Massasoit, with some ninety men, whom for three days we entertained and feasted; and they went out and killed five deer, which they brought to the plantation, and bestowed on our governor, and on the captain and the others.

"And although it is not always so plentiful as it was at this time with us, yet by the goodness of God, we are so far from want, that we wish you to be partakers of our plenty."

This feast is generally considered the start of our Thanksgiving, but as there was no religious ceremony, the one in July, 1623, was more really typical of our present holiday.

The winter had been very long and hard, then came a long drought from May to July, and a fast day was appointed to pray for rain, which fell after nine hours' prayer.

Then the ship "Fortune" was sighted by Miles Standish, and Governor Bradford appointed a public Thanksgiving Day for July 30th. But it was not until 1677 that the first regular Thanksgiving proclamation was made in Massachusetts.

During the Revolutionary War, there were eight Thanksgiving days appointed by the Continental Congress, and General Washington held two for his officers in the field at Valley Forge.

When he was President, Washington appointed two more Thanksgiving days, in 1789 and 1795.

But our national Thanksgiving as we know it today is due to Abraham Lincoln, who appointed the last Thursday in November, 1864, as a time of thanksgiving for the entire nation.

The Thanksgiving Day which followed the conclusion of the World War in 1919 was memorable for the deep sense of gratitude felt by all the people that the liberties of the world had been preserved and that further sacrifice of our gallant soldiers was made unnecessary.

As a nation we have every reason to be thankful for the many blessings and advantages which are ours, and Thanksgiving Day is the natural expression of the gratitude of a great and free people for the countless evidences of divine favor and protection.

APPROACH OF THE NEW YEAR.

They have a quaint old custom in Scandinavia: the people open their doors five minutes before midnight on the last night of the year and wait in silence until the last stroke of twelve tells each of the assembled families that the old year has gone out and the new year has come in. Here in our own country many of us repair to our churches and wait in prayerful silence, or sit musingly before the fire in our homes until the magic moment comes.

But whatever the custom of whatever the clime, the same mysterious charm surrounds the last hour of the old year and the coming in of the first fresh hour of the new. Every heart alive to hope and fear is impressed by the strange and inevitable division of time. If ever we like to be left alone to our thoughts it is in the last moments of the year. We feel, as it were, suspended between a year slipping out and another being quietly ushered in. Behind us is the past; before us the inscrutable future.

The young look forward to the new; the old would fain linger over the past. In the heart of the son looking into the fire grow the vigorous hopes of the new year. Into the memory of the father comes a picture of the time when he started to take up the burden of self-support. Into the eyes of the daughter, only waiting for the roses to bloom again, comes the love-light as she thinks of the next old year's night when she and another will together watch at the fireside of their own home.

Into the mind of the mother at her side comes also the picture of the next old year's night when she too will watch at the fireside—and alone! The young wife and husband, alone for the first time in their own home watching the old year out, see in the flicker of the flame a little white vision which the future will bring out of the unknown. The aged couple sitting at the fireside see also in the flame a little white vision—only it is in the past. The visions are the same. Only one fills the eyes with joy, the other with grief.

A strange division of time it is. We look at the hands of the clock as they mark the last second of the hour of twelve, and the first of the new hour of one. We feel as if something ought to happen to mark the going of the old and the coming of the new. But nothing happens. The seconds tick on as at any other time of the year, and before the clock ceases to strike the midnight hour we are already several seconds out of the old and into the new.

Then as some one jumps up and some loving voice says cheerily, "A happy New Year," we shake off the old, and the sense of freshness, the feeling of something new, the fascination of thinking that we have embarked upon something which a moment ago seemed dim and unknown takes possession of us. And so fear and joy and hope come nearer together within those few seconds than at any other time of the year.

And so with hope millions stand on the closing day of the year with faces toward the future. "What will it bring to me?" each one asks himself.

No one knows. And how well it is that we do not. It requires sober thought to realize that what we are and what we do are along the lines of a wise creation. It is often very easy for us to feel that we might change things for the better if the power and opportunity were ours. But the most astute cleverness of man is a poor affair when compared with the simplest wisdom of God.

Into the merriment of New Year's Eve, as in all hours of surrender to the impulse for pleasure and diversion, there come unbidden these sober second thoughts which wait on the gayest moments and are guests at every festival. There is a natural reluctance to counting up the years when the apex has been reached; a little sadness in the afternoon, even when it holds the deepest beauty of the day.

Time enriches us with one hand and despoils us with the other; it brings those choice gifts that gain their value from ripeness; and takes from us those possessions into which the fullness of our own years has gone. The inward ripening is constantly attended with the outward loss of things dear with sweet association and ancient use.

The fire that smoulders on the hearth at midnight when the bells are ringing in the New Year knows many lonely figures, brooding over the ravages time has made in the fair estate of life, and counting all that has vanished as loss.

There is but one refuge against the sadness which the years inevitably bring, and that is the deep and abiding consciousness that all life is one, and that in the invisible mansions in which the spirits of men have their homes there is greater safety than in the fortresses of stone which they build to protect their bodies.

Those whom we love go from room to room, and we remain before the fire and mourn as if they had gone out of the house instead of passing into another of its many chambers. We miss not only dear faces, but places and conditions and things to which we have grown used during happy hours, and are burdened with a sense of impoverishment because changes are wrought in our surroundings; and we forget that immortality is in us, not in the things about us, and that when they have served their purpose of sustaining, nourishing, helping us, that which was enduring in them has already become ours beyond the touch of time and change.

And as the strength fails and the senses lose their keenness and the pathos of physical age touches life with its peculiar sadness, there comes also the great hope of passing, not out of a strong house into a lonely waste, but out of a little room into the freedom of that home the happiness of which "eye hath not seen nor ear heard;" for as the homes of the body decay, the spirit which has found refuge in it for a brief space on its journey, emerges into the clear light of God's perpetual presence, and we know that all things are well.

ARMISTICE DAY ADDRESS.

Ladies and Gentlemen:

Memories crowd fast upon the mind as the circling months bring us again to this memorable anniversary. There is not one in this presence who does not have some personal interest in the great events upon which the occasion it commemorates placed the seal of finality.

For some of those who are here today, that interest is tinged with a profound sadness, that yet is a proud sorrow and borders on the realms of joy. For since all must die, how noble and beautiful a thing it is to die for an undying cause and under the approving eye of history. So fell those for whom our hearts mourn to-day, and history has no fairer or more inspiring page than that which records the splendor of their devotion and the completeness of their sacrifice.

They thus are the subject not only of our pride and love, and even of our envy. For it is not given to us so to close the volume of our years and to write our names high upon the imperishable scroll of fame. Chateau Thierry, Belleau Wood and the Forest of the Argonne,—these are names that will forever stand as synonyms for the splendid courage and irresistible energy of the American soldier, —for a courage that stormed up to the very gates of death and snatched the fruits of victory from the jaws of defeat.

Memory follows these sleeping heroes today as we pause for a moment and draw the curtains upon the insistent clamor of the present to wander for a space in the picture galleries of the past. We see them as with impetuous eagerness they seek the registration offices to enlist in that great army of knights errant in the cause of human freedom.

We see them as they take solemn and tender leave of those they love. Some are walking for the last time in quiet sheltered paths where sweet vows are told. Others are bending over cradles, kissing babes that sleep in blessed ignorance of moments heavily freighted with destiny. Some are receiving the blessings of aged fathers. Some are parting with mothers who press them to their hearts again and again and try to speak but can only weep. Kisses and tears, tears and kisses: divine mingling of agony and love! And some are holding subdued and sober converse with wives, and endeavoring with brave words to drive from their hearts the too insistent fear.

We see them part. We see the wife standing in the door-way with the babe in her arms. At a turn of the road a hand waves a last good-bye. She answers by holding the child high in her loving arms. We see them as they march proudly away under the rippling folds of the flag, keeping step to the wild, grand music of war—marching down the streets of the great cities—through the towns and across the gang-ways of steamers—down to the fields of glory, to do and die for the eternal truth and right.

We go with them in memory on their weary marches, into the trenches and on the shell-torn fields, where at night the tortured earth between the lines is carpeted with pain, where death rides whistling in every wind, and even the mists are charged with fiendish and deadly peril, where of all things spent and squandered so lavishly, young human life is held least precious.

We see them in the whirlwind of the charge, where men become iron with nerves of steel; where wounds are received unheeded, and only the ebbing strength gives notice of the ravages of shot and shell.

We are with them in the hospital of pain and in the prisons of hatred and famine; but human speech can never tell the story of what they endured. Among those who came back, a silence falls when all the truth would be known—a silence more eloquent than words.

But the American soldier went forth to battle for the cause of human justice and freedom with no hatred in his heart for any people, but hating war and the things that lead to war. He held in reverence the blood-bought rights of our free nation and defied the threat of armed domination. He died for his country without question or complaint, with faith in his heart and hope on his lips, that his country should triumph and its civilization survive. As a representative soldier of the world's greatest democracy, he offered his life as a sacrifice for the victory of her principles of right and justice over the armed forces of autocratic and military rule.

War, at its best, is horrible. Yet this can be said even for war—it reveals elemental and eternal things. In peace, men reckon action, plan and purpose from the central point of self-interest. War comes, and the same men are conscious of a thing which cannot be measured by yardsticks, nor weighed in scales, nor listed on the stock market; and yet a thing for which they go to the grave as to a bride—glad, grand, masterful, in a savage unselfishness. That wonderful thing which makes men welcome death is principle. In war's light they see it. And as we to-day realize the same truth, how transient and foolish seem men's plans for power and place! How they dissolve into nothingness and only the true, the beautiful and the good remain!

For us who remain in the world of opportunity, with our characters still plastic as clay in the hands of the sculptor, the message of these young lives sacrificed to duty and principle is too plain to be disregarded. The golden bars of sunset, though tender in their softness, are impenetrable, impassable. They mark God's record of a day past recall. They are the lower signal lights warning youth of the danger of delay. They are beacon fires, set in the blue of the western heavens as our call to duty. They urge a full statured manhood and womanhood, the product of a worthy and noble creed:

"To love justice, to long for the right, to love mercy, to pity the suffering, to assist the weak, to forget wrongs and remember benefits, to love the truth, to be sincere, to utter honest words, to love liberty, to wage relentless war against slavery in all its forms, to love wife and child and friend, to make a happy home, to love the beautiful in art, in nature, to cultivate the mind, to be familiar with the mighty thoughts that genius has expressed, the noble deeds of all the world, to cultivate courage and cheerfulness, to make others happy, to fill life with the splendor of generous acts, the warmth of loving words, to discard error, to destroy prejudice, to receive new truths with gladness, to cultivate hope, to see the calm beyond the storm, the

3

dawn beyond the night, to do the best that can be done and then to be resigned.''

ADDRESS OF A NEW PRESIDENT OF A WOMAN'S CLUB.

I most cordially thank you for the honor bestowed upon me and for the expression of your uttermost confidence. It is always a special privilege to preside at a woman's club, particularly since our efforts for greater recognition have not been in vain.

There was a time when organizations promoted and maintained by women were ridiculed; when an extension of the facilities to educate women and train them for responsible duties in public life, was almost universally considered useless. Now that all the larger towns and cities of Great Britain, France, Canada, and the United States have numerous clubs, either to promote research in literature, arts, and social development, or to further the extension of political influence, the general attitude towards organizations such as ours has greatly changed, and admiration and coöperation have taken the place of ridicule and scorn.

And why should it be otherwise? Are women not interested in the solution of public questions? Do the women of our country not show, day after day, their ability to organize and work for the realization of their aims?

Somebody has said that women are to politics and the art of government like the mechanic looking at stock quotations or the broker standing helpless over his car. Such a statement is at total variance of the facts, and the result of misapprehension or ignorance.

Long before our last constitutional amendment placed us on equal footing with men, there have been women who engaged in politics and influenced the fate of nations. There was, for instance, Maria Theresa, of Austria, who in spite of many reverses, made great financial reforms, greatly increased the national revenue, and diminished the burdens of her people by the impetus given by her to agriculture, manufacturers and commerce. Or, to come down to more recent times, Queen Victoria of England surely demonstrated that a woman may be well able to be a successful politician. Every student of history well knows that a remarkable feature of the Victorian era has been the rapid growth and extension of British power and influence.

But it is not in politics alone that women show their abilities. They have made, and are still making, good in education, in business, in all the professions. It seems that even in inventions women have not been without influence. For not a few inventions for which credit is generally given to men are wholly or partially products of feminine genius. For instance, Mm. Jacquard did more to make the wonderful Jacquard loom a success than her husband did. Eli Whitney is generally understood to be the inventor of the cotton gin, but in reality it was a Mrs. Green, at whose home Whitney stayed, while teaching school, who conceived the idea.   Cyrus McCormick probably would have been obliged to abandon the idea of constructing a reaper if a woman had not rigged up for him a modified scissors.   It is as if the vast majority of women have adopted the beautiful motto of Mrs. Browning:

"Get leave to work, 'tis the best you get at all,
    For God in cursing gives better gifts than men in benediction."

It is thus that I "get leave to work." In entering upon my responsibilities as president, my principal wish is that I may prove myself as capable an executive as the retiring president did.   Her refinement, culture, and exquisite tastes have endeared her to all of us, and to be a worthy successor of hers is a task which I can not accomplish without your helping hands, your coöperation, and your kind indulgence.

You have always proved yourselves friends indeed.   It is for this reason that I undertake my work "without fear and trembling," but with confidence in your support.   I know you will often remember the words of T. M. Talfourd, the dramatist:

"It is a little thing to speak a phrase
    Of common comfort, which by daily use
    Has almost lost its sense;
            Yet on the ear
    Of him who thought to die unmourned, 'twill fall
    Like choicest music, fill the glazing eye
    With gentle tears, relax the knotted hand,
    To know the bonds of fellowship again."

Seneca, in his work, "A Happy Life," says: "He that has dedicated his mind to virtue and to the good of human society, whereof he is a member, has consumated all that is either profitable or necessary for him to know or to do towards the establishment of his peace."

Paraphrasing the passage, I might say that I propose to dedicate my mind to the cause you have entrusted to me, to the good of the society of which I have the honor to be a member, and to consecrate my hours to virtuous effort in behalf of all.

Let us then attack our problems boldly, but unitedly.   We shall not find them so difficult, after all.   It is faith that gives charms to life. Faith and love are one.   These are the powers that shall incite us. As Lowell says:

"What thou thinkest, that thou art."

To yourself be true, said the wise and sang the poets of all ages.   To advance we must have faith in ourselves.

I once more wish to express my appreciation of your kindness by bestowing upon me the highest honor this society can confer.   May I

come up to your expectations in the fulfillment of the duties assigned
to me.

Again, I thank you.

<hr />

WHAT THE WOMAN VOTER SHOULD KNOW AND THE RESPONSIBILITY OF THE BALLOT.

Today millions of American women feel an uncertainty which they
find it difficult to express in words, but which is really an absence of
definite purpose regarding the exercise of their new privilege of the
franchise. They realize that a gigantic task confronts them, and that
having the vote imposes upon them a grave responsibility for wise
action. But exactly what to do at the moment to achieve their ideals
they do not know.

The election of the fall of 1920 and the campaign preceding it
found a large number of American women strangely indifferent to the
high privilege of voting. Most of them cast their ballots because they
were expected to do so, and some because a visit to the polls was a new
experience. But these women had as yet no public interests. It had
not yet occurred to them that they could affect the politics in their
local environments. Least of all did it impress them that they needed
training as a preparation for their new responsibility. They smiled
when they were told that the State and National Leagues of Women
Voters were sending political teachers throughout the country to give
brief, intensive courses in the art of voting. Their fathers, husbands,
and brothers had taken no such courses. Why should they, the women,
have to be taught how to vote?

The political teachers, however, changed much of this sentiment and
still are changing it. They changed it by teaching women the personal, practical home value of political education by making them
realize the importance of local politics. The White House may be far
away, but the board of aldermen of one's home town meets just around
the corner; and in many instances it can well stand some local and
intelligent supervision.

The new women voters also learned that citizenship in a democracy
is the greatest and most thrilling experience in coöperation that the
human race has yet made; that rural government is the countryside's
experiment in the art of living together, village government, the
village's experiment; and so on and on in widening circles, until the
great experiment embraces the races of the earth and fulfills the immemorial hope of the brotherhood of man.

They also grasped why it was important to find out how a ballot
should be marked, how a candidate should be nominated, why it was
important to insist that every candidate for office should declare himself plainly upon the questions in which his community was vitally
interested.

They learned another thing—that no matter how intelligently and energetically they might work, only failure would result unless the whole of their community was intelligent and energetic with them,—unless citizenship—suffrage—was widely, wisely and universally taught. What were the schools doing toward that end? Practically nothing.

It is this discovery, made by women throughout the country, which is one of the most surprising features of the new situation. For years America was aware that woman suffrage was coming. What have the schools and colleges of the United States done to prepare students for the duties that await them, duties upon whose thoughtful, unselfish performance hangs the future of democracy, the future, perhaps, of the civilization we have known?

As for the formal work of preparing students for suffrage, there has indeed been an enormous increase since the war revealed our menacing shortcomings in civic education. Massachusetts passed a law making a course in American history and civics obligatory for high school pupils. Other states passed similar laws. The colleges enlarged their work in political science, in history and the allied subjects. A few colleges made courses in government obligatory.

The latter course undertakes a systematic discussion of fundamentals. Consideration is given to the underlying ideals of liberty, equality, fraternity and justice, as expressed by leaders of American political thought; also of individual and group rights growing out of these ideals as found incorporated in American law.

After consideration of the rights and concepts of citizenship, it discusses the need for organization as an essential of group achievement; to the need for leadership as an essential for policy determination as well as of organization for service; and to popular control as a means of making the leadership and the organized agencies for service, public and private, square with the aims and ideals of the citizenry.

It considers also the reasons for and against proposal before Congress and state legislatures and under discussion in the current press; the necessity for the maintenance of law and order; the use and abuse of the constitutional right of free speech, free press, and freedom of assembly; the admission or refusal to admit representatives of socialist constituencies into the councils of state and nation; the right of collective bargaining; workmen's representation in the management of industry; the right and limitation of right to strike for higher wages and better working conditions; the reasons and remedies for the high cost of living, etc.

These are the questions upon which the woman voter should seek, through study and public discussion, to become informed. These women have the courage and the spirit to change untoward conditions. All they need is the education.

Women are encountering exactly the same feelings in practicing politics that they have found obstructing their progress everywhere. Women must prove themselves before they will be trusted in politics either by men or women.

It is true of the masses of women, as of the masses of men, that they find it easier to follow than to direct. They must be sure that the directions that are spoken to them are not dictated by the hope of profit or by the voice of intolerance.

It is of the utmost importance for all women to draw closely together, regardless of parties or political traditions or any other dividing lines, so that those who are able to formulate constructive programs for political action may give to their groups, their communities, the highest interpretation of the women's point of view which shall best serve the aims of representative government.

POVERTY AND CRIME.

In the greatest novel of all time, the epic of the poor, painted upon a stretch of canvas so vast that the best description of the Battle of Waterloo ever written forms but an incident in the march of its events, Victor Hugo depicted the life-long persecution of Jean Valjean for the theft of a loaf of bread taken to satisfy the cravings of hunger.

That great moving drama, "Les Miserables," is the story of the evolution of a human soul, tortured and hounded by the relentless power of the law, yet rising to such god-like heights of forgiveness and self-sacrifice that his inveterate persecutor finally breaks beneath the weight of remorse and prefers death for himself rather than the lashings of an awakened conscience.

It is poverty in the sense of economic insufficiency—its wide extent, its tragic consequence—that forms the real mainspring of modern social unrest and the predominant incentive to la wbreaking. As never before, the world's conscience is stirred that there should be vast numbers of people both in town and country who are brought up with insufficient food, clothing, and house room, whose education is broken off early in order that they may go to work for wages; who thenceforth are engaged for long hours in exhausting toil with imperfectly nourished bodies. Overworked and under-taught, weary and careworn, without quiet and without leisure, they have no chance of making the best of their mental faculties, or of developing the habits of thought and the personal associations which in the more fortunate are the chief deterrents from wrong doing.

Little need be said as to the amount of such poverty. Twenty years ago Robert Hunter estimated that about ten million people in the United States were living in poverty. The social implications of such figures are unmistakable. They mean that a great mass of those whom we are accustomed to regard as the earth's most highly civilized people are habitually under-supplied with the things, physical and spiritual, which the human structure requires, and that this inadequate provision involves not only joyless life but imperfect existence, destined, if unchecked, to result in under-vitalization and degenerate stock, with a predisposition to criminal tendencies.

Two elements go to make a man a criminal—act and intent. The criminal act may have its origin in accident, ignorance, weakness, or viciousness. To the first three of these causes of crime, poverty is undoubtedly one of the main contributing factors.

The poor are peculiarly liable to those lapses into crime which may be classed as accidental. Thrown among companions of inferior mentality, and constantly tempted by the displays of wealth and extravagance, a sudden unreasoning impulse or spirit of social rebellion may carry them into an act involving heavy and often disproportionate penalty. The man who is a criminal as the result of accident cannot be said to have criminal intent in the action, which may, nevertheless, be criminal by the statutes, and such a victim of the law claims our utmost sympathy.

Ignorance is one of the universally prevailing concomitants of crime, and poverty is the mother of ignorance. Those who become criminals through ignorance are to be pitied. It is often a question whether they have any really criminal intent in the things they do; and in some cases of dense ignorance or youthful inexperience, it is absolutely wanting.

Some years ago an old German groceryman in a little town in Illinois refused to pay a boy of fourteen years the weekly salary which was due him as an errand boy. The boy wanted to go to the circus. The old German did not want him to spend his money on what was, in his eyes, foolish extravagance. The boy went to the till and took out what was due him for his week's salary. The groceryman had him arrested. He was tried, convicted, sentenced and delivered to the superintendent of the Pontiac Reformatory. He ate his supper in the superintendent's private office, went back to his home on the next train, paroled to his own grief-stricken father, who had accepted sponsorship of him by telegraph. The only thing *technically illegal* in this case was the wise and kind-hearted superintendent's action—but who shall say it was not just?

Two Sioux Indians stole a steer in preference to starving to death in the fury of a Wyoming blizzard. Through the rapacity of some Shylock they each served a year at Joliet penitentiary. Unable to comprehend anything spoken to them in English, they endured a year's punishment in the darkness of complete bewilderment. Who committed the real crime in this instance? A suspended sentence or parole would have been the means of rendering justice to these poor unfortunates.

Weakness, the third source of crime, may be either mental, moral, or physical, and in the majority of cases coming under either of these heads, the condition may be traced, directly or indirectly, to poverty. Through mental weakness, a man may disregard warning and conscience and imagine that he may do a wrong act and escape the law. Through moral weakness, though realizing the probability of punishment, he may deliberately choose dishonor and disgrace. Through physical weakness, unable to cope with poverty, and seeing those he loves in distress for material comforts, he may rebel at the fate that makes others successful where he fails, and thus be led into crime.

What is the conclusion of the whole matter? Poverty is a disease of society, and for the crime that results from poverty, society is collectively responsible until it finds and applies the remedy. Universal education is the hope of civilization in removing the baneful results of poverty. And with it must go Christian tolerance and forgiveness, which says to the penitent wrong-doer, "Neither do I condemn thee: go and sin no more."

FREEMASONRY—A TEACHER OF TOLERANCE.

From somewhere in the misty depths of a mysterious civilization, Freemasonry has come down to us, scattering along her pathway fragrant flowers of Brotherly Love, Charity, Tolerance, and Truth. She has ever stood for the home, country, the brotherhood of man, and the dissemination of knowledge, constantly bringing mankind into closer communion with the Great Architect of the Universe.

When we consider the antiquity of Masonry, the dangers through which she has successfully passed, the persecutions of bigotry, superstition and fanaticism which she has met and repelled, and behold her to-day with the glory of the centuries clustering about her brow, and the years of useful labor resting so lightly upon her unbowed form, standing upright and stately with all the vigor of early youth—her feet as quick to run errands of mercy, knees as supple to bend in prayer for a brother's need, breasts as faithful to receive and keep a brother's confidence, hands as strong and ready to support a falling brother, and lips ever whispering words of cheer and comfort to the ear of distress—we stand with unshod feet and bared head at her mystic portals, and fain would lay the laurel wreath of well-earned fame upon her brow.

The flight of time has not dulled her ardor nor made sluggish the blood that richly courses through her veins. The finger of the ages has been powerless to mark the flight of years upon her beautiful face. Her form unbent by the burdens she has borne, her eyes are quick to catch the sign of distress, and her ears to hear the plaintive cry of need.

The pathway of Masonry all down through the ages may readily be traced by the magnificent monuments of her glorious achievements in the uplift of humanity. Her brilliant gems of truth glitter and sparkle in every clime where her banner has been unfurled. The cry of distress from the masses brought Masonry into the world to help and assist mankind by the silent influence of her moral teachings. She came without pomp or display, like the dew that fell upon Mount Hermon, a gift of the Grand Architect to aid humanity to throw off. the shackles of mental, physical, and spiritual bondage.

Masonry has been the world's teacher of tolerance. The spirit of Masonry is the Gulf Stream that warms and tempers the current of modern civilization by relieving human suffering and eliminating class distinctions, superstition and falsehood, inspiring men "always to live and move on the plane of the Square and Level, under the law of Love."

When Christopher Columbus discovered this continent, the period was that of the Renaissance, the era of new birth. All over Europe there had been a revival of learning and art. With this had come a new impulse of liberty. Monarchy in order to continue thereafter must change its attitude and limit its arbitrary powers. In time there came to this country settlers from England, France, Holland, and the other countries of the old world, and civilization advanced with rapid strides.

When the time came to lay the corner-stone of this great national structure, there was witnessed in Philadelphia a spirit of liberty combined with tolerance such as the world had never seen. Where did these men learn tolerance? There were churchmen there; and Puritans who hated the Church; there were Calvinists there, and Armenians who were antagonistic to Calvinists; and there were Quakers who had little in common with any of these in religious faith and practice.

But a new force had arisen; a new idea had come into control. The adoption of the American Constitution signalized the coming into flower and fruit of that tolerance of which the Renaissance in Europe was the bud and blossom. The spirit of tolerance took enduring form in the immortal words:

"Congress shall make no law respecting an establishment of religion, or prohibiting the free exercise thereof; or abridging the freedom of speech or of the press; or the right of the people peaceably to assemble, and to petition the government for a redress of grievance."

If ever the sun should go down for the last time upon this nation, the greatest glory of our people would be left in these imperishable words. Then, for the first time in the history of the world, tolerance was written in the fundamental law of a nation, now grounded and guided by that priceless principle.

It is not strange that among those worthy forefathers who incorporated tolerance into our charter of liberties, both as signers of the Declaration of Independence and as voters for the adoption of our Constitution, a large majority were Freemasons. Freemasonry taught tolerance to those men who laid so solidly the foundations of this great Republic.

Fifty-two of the fifty-five immortals who signed the Declaration of Independence had worn the lamb-skin apron and felt the points of the compass upon their breasts. Our first president—as have been many presidents since—was a faithful and active Mason. Every commanding general from Lexington to Yorktown had sought the Lost Word in the lodges of the Widow's Son.

Freemasonry is the most tolerant of all institutions in the world today. In all of its degrees, under whatever name or by whatever body conferred, this spirit of tolerance is emphasized and constantly encouraged. It teaches the obligation to live justly, to love mercy and walk humbly with God, to have common interests both beneficial and protective, to kneel together and spend hours before the open Word of God, to sit in the lodge room with men of every Christian faith, cultivating genuine virtue, eschewing all things mean and low, and above all learning the beauty of Christian charity and tolerance.

AFTER-DINNER ADDRESS AT A MASONIC BANQUET.

There was once an Indiana judge who was proud of two things: his zeal in upholding the law and his belief in the fighting ability of his son. These two hobbies came into violent conflict once, but the problem was happily solved.

It happened that the judge's farm was on the Ohio boundary, and one day he was sitting on a fence that separated the two states. As he sat there, his son and a neighbor's boy came along, quarelling violently, and when they came up to the judge, they began to fight.

The judge straightened himself to his full official dignity, and cried: "In behalf of the majesty of the law, and in the name of the sovereign State of Indiana, I command you to keep the peace."

Just that moment, the rail on which the judge was sitting gave way and dropped him on the Ohio side of the fence. Instantly recovering himself and leaping to his feet, he shouted, "Give him h——, Jim, I'm out of my jurisdiction!"

I sometimes feel out of my jurisdiction when it comes to speaking on an occasion such as this, but Masonry touches life at so many points and so constantly reveals new meanings and applications, that the true Mason finds his inspiration wherever brothers gather around the board of friendship and fraternal love.

The crowning glory of the teachings of our order is to make good workmen of us all. Not only men, but workmen, men who labor for the good of humanity. We must always hold this distinct motive in view, otherwise the symbolism and mysteries of our order would be useless, and our organization would have no right to existence.

In regarding each other as brethren, we recognize the fact of a common brotherhood, and by dealing justly with one another, we exemplify in practical life the force and beauty of the injunction, "As ye would that others should do to you, do ye even so to them."

Someone has well said: "The present generation of Masons are in no wise responsible for the past; they may be largely responsible for the future, but the entire responsibility of the present rests with them." There must be an exact correspondence between our profession and our actions, otherwise we shall be found teaching that which is not supported by our deeds. It is not so much what a Mason professes as what he does that furnishes the standard of measurement applied by the world at large, and the living question which confronts us today is: What are the fruits of Freemasonry in the lives and conduct of those who profess it?

The lives of men and Masons of other days have passed into history. We of the present day are making history which shall be read by those who come after us, and it should be our great concern to give such a character to that history as will bring credit to ourselves and reflect honor on the Order.

The corner stone of Freemasonry is truth. This is not a human but a divine attribute, and being such it can never change. Truth has many phases and can be viewed from a variety of standpoints, yet it is the same truth in all its aspects, no matter from what source we derive our knowledge of it. Resting, therefore, as Freemasonry does, on the bed rock of truth, its principles are as unchangeable as the foundation on which it is built. Truth and the principles of Freemasonry go hand in hand, and we can no more touch the one without disturbing the other than we can remove the foundation of a building and yet expect the superstructure to stand.

King Solomon built on Mount Moriah the most beautiful structure ever reared by human hands. When the bright sun rose over the summit of Mount Olivet to open and rule the day, his glory pales beside the magnificence of the golden roof and onyx pillars of Solomon's temple. When he shed his departing rays before sinking to rest behind Mount Zion, they were reflected back in a thousand dazzling beams from the gold and precious stones which sparkled in the sacred building.

Three thousand years and the ruthless hand of the invader have extinguished all its glory, and today not one stone remains upon another.

But the organization of the workmen has been perpetuated. The Freemasons who built the temple still labor. And at this epoch hour of the ages, the craft is hopefully looking forward to a career of peaceful conquest which shall be limited only by the utmost bounds of the earth.

Venerable as is our Order, it still glows with the fires of unwasted youth. It stretches its hands across the seas, reaches over the walls of prejudice, of language, and of race; penetrates religious creeds and political forms and speaks in all the languages of the earth. It seeks no longer to rear a temple of marble, or onyx, or cedar, or cyprus, but a temple of brotherly love, whose altar is the human heart.

THE FUNCTIONS OF FRATERNALISM.

Man is preëminently a social being. His social nature is the result of the interaction of all his separate and distinct natures. It consists in a balance of faculties. The industrial nature, the political nature, the intellectual nature, the religious nature, are only the bricks and mortar out of which the social nature is constructed.

Man's industrial relation is his relation to the means of physical existence; his political relation is his relation to government and law; his intellectual relation is his relation to truth; his religious relation is his relation to his own actions; but his social or fraternal relation is his relation to his fellowmen. Hence the social relation is the highest one possible.

Manhood is the basic principle and love the binding force of fraternalism. Grounded on such lofty principles, what may we not reasonably expect from the spirit of fraternity? It embodies all that is best, all that is noblest, in the distinct natures of man.

The spirit of fraternalism is the common property of the world. It makes us more useful and more capable of enjoyment, no matter what sphere of life we occupy. Everywhere you turn the voice of cordial greeting sounds in your ear, and the warm hand of brotherly love is extended. Surely the potent power which has brought about this condition is one of Heaven's most priceless gifts to mankind.

You may have heard of the man who was addressed on the street by a stranger, who said to him: "I want to thank you for the great help you have been to me. You have indeed been a friend." The man thus spoken to did not recognize the speaker, and replied: "I don't remember having met you. How, then, is it possible that I can have been of any help to you?" "You are right," replied the other, "we have never met before, but I have passed you on the street many times, and I never saw you without a cheerful and friendly look on your face. When I was depressed your smile was like a ray of sunlight on a cloudy day." Such is the spirit of fraternalism, that like the sun sheds its light and warmth abroad for all mankind.

The primary function of fraternalism is to bring together men with kindred interests, thoughts and ideals, so that they may enjoy each other's society and gain mutual benefit. They are banded together with the object that each individual may lend to the entire group the elements of strength and the talents which he possesses, and may in turn receive the help, inspiration and protection of the whole organization.

Fraternalism is to be valued for what is in it, and not for what may be gotten out of it. When two or more persons unite for purely material benefit, that union is not a fraternity but an association for purposes of business. But the vital and animating principle of true fraternalism is the element of brotherly love, sympathy and coöperation—the ability and willingness to sacrifice to the good of the whole some of the personal interest which may be at variance with the interest of the organization.

Fraternalism owes its enduring power to the fact that it develops friendship. What is a friend? He is a person with whom you dare to be yourself. He asks of you to assume nothing, hide nothing, only to be what you are.

With a friend, you do not have to be on your guard. You can say what you think, express what you feel. With him you breathe freely. You can take off your coat and loosen your collar. You can reveal your little vanities and your absurd hobbies, your likes and dislikes, and in disclosing them to him they are lost, swallowed up in the ocean of his loyalty.

With a friend, you do not have to be careful; he understands. He is like fire, that purifies all you do. He is like water, that cleanses all you say. He is like wine, that warms you to the bone.

In true friendship, there must be both give and take. Patience and forbearance are its essential characteristics. We should not ask too much if we expect to keep a friendship, and most of all, we must be ready to give ourselves at our very best to meet the needs and expectations of our friends.

Again, the power of fraternalism lies in concerted action. Without unity and coöperation there can be no progress. In no previous period of the history of mankind has the power of united action meant so much as now. The tremendous expansion of industrial combination, the great aggregations of capital, the increasing tendency to form clubs, societies and organizations for specific ends, and, most insistent of all, the demand for a federation of nations; all these demonstrate the growing conviction that in concerted action alone lies the power of mankind to effect great and enduring results.

And the basis of unity of action lies in individual self-mastery and self-control. In speaking of self-control, the word is used in its widest sense, meaning control of all the impulses and feelings. There must be discipline of self before there can be discipline of others.

Self-mastery does not consist, as is sometimes thought, entirely of negation. It is at its flood tide when it dominates the faculties and aspirations so that it means initiative, development, enlargement of every faculty and capacity. Discipline and self-repression are but the stepping stones to the higher virtues because life has become attuned to duty and high performance, and not because of regulations or restrictions of position.

As we contemplate the principles which underlie true fraternalism and which govern its functions; as we devote our minds to a consideration of its beautiful teachings, their spirit and sentiment permeate our being, and we unconsciously learn to model our lives more and more in harmony with its truths.

ADDRESS TO KNIGHTS OF COLUMBUS.

It is an honor and a privilege to be permitted to address so splendid and powerful an organization as the Knights of Columbus, which embodies the energy, strength and patriotism of the young manhood of the Roman Catholic Church. To be a consistent member of the Knights of Columbus is to be a true American, proud of the glorious traditions of our great country, and ready to defend her honor and her principles and ideals in the forum, the workshop, and on the field of battle.

Founded in 1882 at New Haven, Connecticut, by a Catholic priest, Michael J. McGivney, with the purpose of promoting social and intellectual intercourse among its members and rendering them and their dependents pecuniary aid when necessary, the order has grown from an original membership of eleven to one of more than eight hundred thousand, with two thousand councils throughout the United States and her dependencies, Canada, Newfoundland, Mexico and Cuba.

The organization has a record of which every member may well be proud. Previous to its entrance into war work, the Knights founded the first chair of American history in this country, at the Catholic University in Washington, and they endowed the same institution with $500,000 for fifty scholarships in perpetuity. State and local councils also supported various educational and social enterprises and aided the sufferers from many catastrophies. The society has accumulated a mortuary reserve fund of about ten million dollars for the protection of its insurance members.

The true patriotism of the Knights of Columbus is shown in their eleven-year campaign against radical Socialism. Lecturers have been sent throughout the country to combat these dangerous tendencies, and this work has met with great success and is being continued.

The Knights first entered war welfare work in the Spanish-American War. When the United States entered the war with Germany, they raised $1,500,000 among their own members and began welfare work in the cantonments in America. Later, at the invitation of General Pershing, they went overseas, and there, as well as at home, carried on a splendid mission of relief and comfort to our soldiers, supported by a fund of $14,000,000 contributed by people of all classes and religious affiliations.

The order received from the liberal hands of the American people a total of approximately $40,000,000 for war relief work. With the balance remaining at the close of the war, they established and financed a nation-wide chain of employment bureaus, finding work for 500,000 ex-service men at a minimum wage of $20 per week; they awarded 500 free scholarships to former service men in universities such as Yale and Georgetown, and established throughout the country free night schools for service men and women, with nominal charges to civilians. These schools graduated 40,000 pupils in 1920, and there are now more than 100 of them in operation, teaching technical, business and citizenship courses. The latest enterprise of the Knights is the project of presenting to the American people through the American Legion a national memorial building to cost $5,000,000 and to be erected at Washington.

The first American soldier killed in the World War, Lieut. William T. Fitzsimmons, of Kansas City, Mo., the last American killed, Chaplain William F. Devitt, of Holyoke, Mass., and the first men to receive the Congressional Medal of Honor and the Distinguished Service Cross were members of the Knights of Columbus. In 1920 the Knights went to Europe, visited the Pope, gave the Knights of Columbus statue of Lafayette to France, and a jewelled baton to Marshal Foch.

During the war, the Knights of Columbus buildings were open to all. Each bore the sign, "Knights of Columbus—Everybody Welcome." Men of all religious beliefs were invited to the services, and it was part of an agreement made with the Government that these buildings should not be used for any secret meeting or any gathering not open to all the men in camp. They were built on the same general plan as the Y. M. C. A. huts and provided like facilities for wholesome and many recreation.

There were over half a million Catholic soldiers and sailors in the service of the United States, and the task of bringing the consolations of religion to these men was no small part in the work of keeping up the morale of our fighting forces. On one of our battleships where the crew numbered 1,200 men, 900 were Catholics. In recognition of the work of the Knights of Columbus, Bishop O'Connell, former head of the Catholic University in Washington, declared: "Your noble and useful work must be a motive of joy to the soul of him who first gave this country to the domain of history and whose name you have inscribed in honor on the banner of your organization."

Cardinal Satolli paid a similar tribute to the order when he said: "I declare that henceforth I shall cherish a special regard for the Knights of Columbus, and trust that it may have a field growing wider with years and a future blessed with prosperity."

Such, then, is the organization which has enlisted your services and claimed your allegiance. In the words of Cardinal Gibbons, "The Knights of Columbus have gone about doing good, holding their religion aloft as a torch to attract the wanderers in the dark, and to illumine their pathway toward God. I entertain the hope that the unswerving loyalty to God and country which has distinguished the Knights in the past, will be their crowning glory in the future."

Knights of Columbus! let us preserve our priceless legacy of patriotic and broad-minded service to our country untarnished—yea, more, let us hand it down with added glory to future generations, supporting our nation's institutions, furthering her great and lofty principles, and rearing a monument of good deeds more enduring than brass and marble.

EASTERN STAR WORK.

The Eastern Star, oldest of the branches of the Masonic Order, came into being as the beautiful handmaiden of Masonry, and is founded upon the same sublime principles of morals and conduct. It is supposed to have established its first chapter in the United States in 1780, but no authentic record has come down to prove the fact.

It has an Oriental relationship and all the brilliant and poetic ceremonies of the most imaginative Eastern mind. Here in the Western Hemisphere where we can boast of the highest civilization and culture that the ancient or modern world has ever known, we are indebted to the mysterious East for a system of philosophy and fraternal organization whose origin was in lands whose customs and manner of living present striking differences from our own.

The teaching of our Order has been described in the following words: "The light that emanates from our central star shall lead to virtue and blossom into true manhood. Electa shall teach them loyalty to truth. They shall learn fidelity to convictions of right from Adah, who is the morning of life surrendered to the grave, the brightest of earthly hopes, that she might prove faithful to her convictions of right and preserve her father's honor. The constancy of the humble gleaner, Ruth, shall teach them that there is loveliness among the lowly, and that in every station of life we should be faithful to the demands of honor and justice. When sore bereavement shall cast them into the valley of sorrow, they shall see Martha beside the grave of her brother, inspired with trustful hope and faith of the immortal life."

Whatever may have been the origin of our order, we are willing to accept it just as we find it, and as it is now honored and loved by every member. It is doing a work among American women that is not excelled by any other organization in our country. As the radiance of the eastern sunrise is followed by the glory of the western sky, so slavery has been followed by freedom, and fraternal institutions have gone from the east to the west.

The rules of conduct which are the fundamental principles of our order make it a system of ethics—moral, religious, and philosophical, of which fraternal love is the foundation and cope-stone, and charity the animating principle.

We are taught to practice charity toward all mankind, and especially to those in need. But charity does not consist only in the giving of alms; it is broader, deeper, grander than that. It means charity for the faults of others, charity for human weakness, charity for the sister who has not the fortitude to withstand temptations, and who needs words of loving counsel and encouragement to help her to fight the battle of life.

If we would be true to our Order in thought, word, and action, as well as in name, we must look deeper than the ritual. We must study the true meaning of our beautiful symbols and ceremonies. With a true knowledge of these ever in our minds, that our lives may be controlled and guided by them, we will be bound together in a lasting bond of union, seeking only the highest good for ourselves and for humanity at large.

We are taught never to enter upon any great or important undertaking without first invoking the divine blessing. At the very commencement of our Masonic career, we are shown the religious character of the institution, and taught that only the noblest designs are worthy of a place in its work, such designs as we may submit for the approval of our Supreme Grand Master and ask his aid in carrying out. By a strict adherence to this teaching we will merit the approval of our associates and will be suitably rewarded when our pilgrimage on earth is ended.

We are taught that all are created equal and that the internal and not the external qualifications are the true standard of worth. A lodge of the Eastern Star is a symbol of the world in that it denotes the universality of the principles of our Order. In whatever civilized country we may travel, the hand of friendship and love will be extended to us. If sickness or adversity overtake us, we have the assurance that our sisters of the mystic tie will be there to render aid and assistance.

We do not claim that all our members reach the high ideals contemplated and taught by our Order. Perfection on earth has never yet been attained. We do claim, however, that its teachings exercise a beneficent influence on its members, and that the world is better for its existence.

We are told that at the building of the Temple of Solomon, there was not the sound of axe, hammer, or any tool of iron, and that when the building was completed, its several parts fitted with such precision

4

that it had more the appearance of the handiwork of the Supreme Architect of the Universe than of that of human hands.

It is after this plan that Masonic work is done. There is no noise or bluster; no pomp or show. Quietly and without publicity its charitable acts are performed. It does not seek prominence in public parades and demonstrations; on the other hand, it seeks retirement in its lodges, there teaching the principles of friendship, morality, and charity, and encouraging its members to live lives of usefulness. Thus it adds to its record of good deeds day by day, until finally, when the work is completed, it will form a beautiful and perfect whole, so that it shall seem to have been the product of other than human hands.

HOW CAN AN AUTOMOBILE CLUB BEST SERVE THE STATE?

Less than ten years ago, that is to say in 1915, there were some three million three hundred thousand automobiles in the United States. By 1925 there will be fully fifteen millions. It is difficult to measure the influence of such a development in methods of transportation. It was Macauley who said, "Of all inventions, the alphabet and the printing press alone excepted, those that have shortened distance have done the most for humanity."

Within the last decade, the principal automobile clubs of the five great nations that are foremost in the manufacture and use of automobiles—America, France, England, Germany, and Italy—have grown to a size and acquired an importance that are making their existence felt more and more in the activities of the times; in industrial affairs, in sporting circles, and in the social life of the communities and countries in which they exist.

They not only promote, through their racing or sporting committees, the great national and international races, but they have taken a strong hand, through their law committees, in legal matters, so far as they affect the regulation of automobile driving and street and road construction and repair. They have also encouraged and in many ways assisted touring, and have promoted social intercourse between the manufacturers of automobiles and men of wealth and position, thereby aiding tremendously in the rapid development of an industry that gives employment to an army of workmen, and whose aggregate business mounts into many millions of dollars annually.

Two types of automobile clubs have developed since the industry sprang up—one best described as the wealthy man's club, and the other the utility club. The former came into being in most cases as a weapon to fight adverse motor legislation. In this it frequently did valuable service; but those who at first worked hard to build the club soon lost enthusiasm, the original efforts waned, and the public-spirited aspect practically passed out of being.

The utility club has been of later origin. It is to all intents and purposes the antithesis of the wealthy man's organization. Club quarters are often not thought of otherwise than as those furnished by a convenient hotel. The spirit of the club has been activity— activity in the stimulation of contests, sane legislation, and the promulgation of the improved highway spirit; in fact, activity has been the warp and woof of the entire organization.

The activity club has drawn its membership from the great masses of automobiledom, from the corner grocery man interested in motorcycle delivery to the multimillionaire with his chain of factories. The bond of union in the utility club has been action—that common spur to progress irrespective of wealth, vocation, or social distinction. The activity club is the healthy club today. It is the club that is accomplishing results, the club that the industry needs and cannot do without.

The automobile club is of direct service to the state through its constant and insistent agitation in favor of better roads. An enormous amount of work will have to be done and vast sums of money will have to be spent before our roads are as good as they ought to be, or as good as European roads actually are. There are in this country nearly 2,500,000 miles of public roads. Of this total, only about 250,000 miles consists of improved, surfaced roads—in other words, for every mile of good roads we have eight or nine miles of bad ones. The automobile is rapidly changing this situation, however. In 1921, motor vehicle license revenues and taxes in the United States totalled $340,800,654, a large part of which was used in road construction and improvement.

The automobile club is one of the most powerful factors in curbing automobile lawlessness and outlawry. To assume that the motorcar theft problem is solely one for the police to solve is a mistake, for there are many things that the motorist can do, and which the club helps him to do, to make it difficult for a thief to steal his car, and to do his bit toward checking the operations of bandits who steal more than $100,000,000 worth of cars annually.

It is an unfortunate fact that the automobile has become one of the most important aids to crime. The same machine that hurries the surgeon to the bedside of a suffering child will hurry the yeggman in his getaway from a hold-up. It is one of the objects of the automobile club to offer the services of their organization in behalf of the detection and prevention of crime, and through the strength of union to make itself a terror to the law-breaker.

The automobile club aids in the enforcement of parking and traffic laws, which are becoming increasingly necessary with the rapid multiplication of cars. The parking of vehicles is probably the most pressing problem now before city authorities in connection with street traffic. Some even hazard the prophecy that eventually no vehicles

will be permitted to park except directly in front of property owned by
those occupying the car or with whom they are transacting business,
and then only for short periods.

One cannot close a discussion such as this without noting the
indirect, but none the less valuable, contribution which the automobile
club is making to the happiness of American life by promoting the
social spirit between the owners of automobiles, and fostering the
many educational activities which result therefrom. In this direction
alone, its service is one of the utmost value to the state.

ADDRESS BEFORE UNITED SPANISH WAR VETERANS.

"When I think of the flag," said one of our Presidents, "it seems
to me I see alternate stripes of parchment upon which are written the
rights of liberty and justice, and stripes of blood spilt to vindicate
those rights; and then, in the corner, a prediction of the blue serene
into which every nation may swim which stands for these great
things." And in the same address, referring to Flag Day, he continued: "I am sorry that you do not wear a little flag of the Union
every day instead of some days, and I can only ask you, if you lose
the physical emblem, to be sure that you wear it in your heart, that
the heart of America shall interpret the heart of the world."

When we review the history of America's participation in the
Spanish-American War, it is no difficult matter to realize the fact
that these are not mere empty phrases, and that the heart of America
in that brief but epic struggle did indeed "interest the heart of the
world."

For let every school child be taught, and every school history of
our country proclaim the fact, that after a clean-cut and decisive
victory over Spain upon both land and sea, we liberated one of her
struggling colonies from a reign of bloodshed, and *bought*, not wrested
from Spain by the right universally accorded to victors, the Philippine
Islands, in order that we might protect and educate their weak and
almost savage population until the time should come when we could
safely present them with complete independence.

Was this conduct not in complete accord with the immortal words
of our First President: "Young though you be, you are the elder
brothers of the ignorant: let your conduct be an example to them.
You can help your country more by your moral attitude than by your
opinions. Your opinions will pass away, for 'We know in part and
prophesy in part.' "

And now we have emerged into the full clear light of international
prominence, after the most titanic conflict ever staged upon this planet,
with countenance unabashed and hands unsmirched with the spoils
of war. Out of the shadows of the past, our nation has swept into a

new and better day. The all-prevailing public conscience is awake, and the American Republic is moving forward to the fulfillment of its divinely appointed mission.

It was in the hope for such a future for his country that Abraham Lincoln carried the crushing burdens of those five torturing years of internecine war. It was his sublime faith in the final outcome of this last national experiment of the Anglo-Saxon race that kept him ever steady, amid the gloom of Bull Run and Chancellorsville, and uncertain issues of Antietam, and the wild rejoicings of Gettysburg and Appomatox.

It is fortunate, sometimes, that the American people do not fully realize the dangers that threaten them. In the early weeks in April, 1898, preceding the war, Spain was rushing frantically from one European capital to another, imploring assistance against the United States. About the busiest men in Washington were Von Hengelmuller, the Austrian Ambassador, and Von Hollenben, who represented the German Kaiser. Americans thought then that our real enemy was Spain; our real enemy, however, was a European coalition against us. Had Austria and Germany had their way, the whole of Europe, backed by its fleets and armies, would have forbidden us from going to war with Spain.

The program fell to the ground for one reason—England energetically refused to join the conspiracy. Sir Julian Pauncefote was then English Ambassador and also dean of the diplomatic corps. On April 6th, acting as dean, he received the Ambassadors of France, Austria, Germany, and Italy, presiding over a meeting big with significance for the United States. The full details of that meeting have never been published.

Enough is known, however, to justify the statement that the Ambassadors discussed presenting to President McKinley a note protesting against American interference in the affairs of Cuba as unjustified, and declaring that such intervention would not be regarded with indifference by the great European powers.

But Sir Julian Pauncefote, acting under instructions received from Lord Salisbury, absolutely refused to join in any such protest. With the world's greatest naval Power taking the side of the United States, and with the general impression that such coöperation might take more than a diplomatic form, the carefully laid plans to coerce this country fell to the ground. Instead of this, the diplomats drew up a harmless note for presentation to President McKinley and Spain was left to her well-deserved punishment.

It was for the permanent commemoration of the glorious outcome of that war that the association of United Spanish War Veterans, now numbering 18,000 members, was formed in 1899. The advantages of membership in this organization are manifold. Not only does it inculcate patriotism and provide for mutual protection and advancement, but its social and fraternal features commend it to the attention of every survivor of that struggle for the rights of humanity.

The United Spanish War Veterans is an organization which represents the spirit of American patriotism in all its chivalry and daring, inspired by the indomitable courage of a Roosevelt, who dared do all that might become a man, and feared nothing but dishonor.

PURITY, LOVE, EQUALITY AND FIDELITY.

(Motto of the Pythian Sisters.)

The Pythian Sisters, founded in 1888, is based upon the same beautiful principles as those which animate the Knights of Pythias, and immortalize the qualities which existed in the friendship of Damon and Pythias, two youths of Syracuse before the time of Christ.

Damon, being condemned to death by the tyrant Dionysius, obtained leave from him to go home to arrange his affairs if Pythias would become his hostage. Damon being delayed, Pythias was led to execution, but his friend arrived in time to save him. Dionysius was so impressed by this beautiful friendship that he pardoned both the youths and paid them marks of great honor.

The Pythian Sisters, who are the wives, mothers, widows, sisters, and daughters of the Knights of Pythias, have as their object the good of universal womanhood, and the purpose of building it up to higher ideals of love and service to humanity.

Their first leader was Brother Hill, then Sister Robinson and Sister Weaver. The order was preceded by the organization known as the Pythian Sisterhood. In 1894 the Knights of Pythias changed the name of "Pythian Sisters" to "Rathbone Sisters," but in 1906 the Rathbone Sisters and the Pythian Sisterhood were united in the one organization known at present as the Pythian Sisters. The membership is approximately 60,000, with 144 temples located in the United States, Canada, Great Britain, Ireland, Denmark, Germany, Sweden, Holland, Switzerland, Italy, France, Argentina, New Zealand, New South Wales and Tasmania.

The departments in which the work of the Pythian Sisters is carried on are Home Life, Educational Interests, Church and Missionary Work, Arts, Moral Reform, Politics, Philanthropy, Social Economics, Foreign Relations, and Press Organizations.

The organization embodies the desire to promote the physical, mental, social and moral welfare of its members; advancing the spirit of fraternal love in the relations of daily life; ministering to the needs of the sick, poor or distressed; watching at the bedside of the dying; performing the offices of love and respect for the dead; comforting and providing for the material wants of the widow; and emulating the principle of the Golden Rule. Its mission is ever to guide the feet of its members onward and upward in the pathway of loving service and devotion to the cause of humanity.

The spirit which animates the order is exemplified in its opening ode:

"Dear Lord to Thee we bring
Our grateful hearts to sing
Thy boundless praise;
Let now Thy grace imbue
Our hearts with friendship true
All discord eschew
Forevermore.

"May Purity and Love
Descending from above
Inspire us all.
Then shall Equality
Our watchword ever be
And strict Fidelity
Reign evermore."

The work of such an order is as vast as human life itself. We are on the threshold of a newer and better age when men will be less selfish and more interested in the welfare of their fellowmen; when they will realize that the individual is a part of the great social fabric, and what unfavorably affects one hurts all.

The right of the strong and ruthless to deny others an equal opportunity in the struggle for subsistence and for happiness, remorselessly trampling and crushing the weak, and appropriating their savings and property, is being challenged and denied as never before.

We are beginning to realize also that to aid in ushering in a new and better era, it is not necessary to be wealthy or powerful, but that the humble workers in the home and in the community are a potent factor in whose united efforts lies a vast potentiality.

And so the Pythian Sisters move forward to the New Century ideals; to weigh the material in the scales of the personal, and measure life by the standard of love; to prize health as a contagious happiness, wealth as potential service, reputation as latent influence, learning for the light it can shed, power for the help it can give, station for the good it can do; to choose in each case what is best for the whole, and to accept cheerfully the individual evils involved; to put one's best into all one does; to crowd out fear by devotion to duty, and see present and future as one; to treat others as one wishes to be treated; to make no gain by another's loss, and buy no pleasure by another's pain; to harbor no unkind thoughts of others; to say nothing unkind for the sake of amusement, and nothing false to please others; to take no satisfaction in the failings of the weak, and bear no malice toward those who do wrong; to pity the selfish no less than the poor, the

proud as much as the outcast, and the cruel even more than the oppressed; to worship God in all that is true and pure and beautiful;
to serve Christ wherever a sad heart can be made happy or a wrong
set right; and to recognize God's coming kingdom in every institution and person that helps men to love one another.

ADDRESS BEFORE THE UNITED ORDER OF AMERICANS.

Dr. Johnson, in his dictionary, tells us that a patriot is "one whose
ruling passion is the love of his country," and that patriotism is
"love and zeal for one's country." It is this principle, translated
into active service, that forms the animating spirit of the United
Order of Americans.

The word "patriot" was taken from the French, where it was in
use as early as the fifteenth century in the sense of "citizen," "fellow-
citizen," or "compatriot." It occurs occasionally in the literature
of the sixteenth century, at the end of which it was accompanied by
such adjectives as "good," "true," or "worthy," until finally a
"patriot" necessarily implied a good citizen, and a true lover of his
country.

This gradual evolution of meaning suggests the probability that
the sentiment itself has undergone transformations; and we find,
accordingly, that although love of country is as old as the history of
nations, the particular form of this universal feeling which we now
associate with the term "patriotism" is really one of the manifestations of comparatively recent times.

Patriotism presupposes a "patria" or country, but the justification of the sentiment must be found in something more than an
attachment to one's native soil; and depends on the pursuit of
common interests, the defense of a common independence, and the
love of common liberties. It is strengthened by a common history
and common traditions, and it is part of a national character formed
under these conditions. It implies undoubtedly an exclusive preference, and this is sometimes made an accusation against it; but in this
respect it is only the natural development of that sentiment of filial
and domestic affection which has characterized the relations of kindred
since men first dwelt together in families.

The Greeks were animated by an intense patriotism, which was,
however, almost universally narrowed to the city. Once or twice in
their history the cities of Greece united in a true sentiment of national
devotion against a foreign enemy; but the union was only for the
moment of danger, and the patriotism of Athens or Sparta or Corinth,
nourished on the rivalries of small communities, was a municipal
rather than a national sentiment.

The Romans with their subject provinces tributary to the mother city, never secured or even attempted to create that community of interest and equality of privilege throughout their empire which might have gained for it the patriotic support of all its population. The feeling may have been more intense among the actual citizens of Rome in proportion as it was more restricted; but it was certainly confined to a very small proportion of those who lived under the Roman Eagles, and it differed in degree and character from the sentiment which has since exercised so great an influence on civilized states.

It is evident that the primary object of patriotism is to defend the freedom and independence of its native land, and to make such preparations as are necessary for its security. The Order of Independent Americans has written prominently into its constitution this idea of national protection and defense, and no one can be a member of the order without first being a loyal and patriotic American.

Every Independent American realizes that patriotism involves duties as well as privileges, and these duties arise in connection with the domestic relations of the citizen to his country, as well as in all that concerns the attitude of the country toward foreign nations. In both cases the idea of patriotism involves that of personal sacrifice. Our obligations do not end with obedience to the laws and the payment of taxes. These things are compulsory and involuntary evidences of our love of country, since the police insist on the one and the tax collector takes good care of the other. But we give a free and additional proof of patriotism in taking our full share of public work and responsibility, including the performance of those municipal obligations on the due fulfilment of which the comfort, the health, and the lives of the community so largely depend.

Today the sentiment of patriotism is more powerful than ever before, and it is strongest in the most democratic of all nations—our own America. Its influence has everywhere tended to secure toleration in religious controversies, and to moderate the bitterness of party contest. It has lessened the frequency of war among foreign nations by encouraging the union of smaller states and nationalities, thereby decreasing occasions of strife. So long as it was restricted to limited interests, the sentiment of patriotism was restless, jealous and aggressive; but with enlarging scope and responsibility, it has shown itself more inclined to respect the rights of others while still claiming the exclusive devotion of its own citizens.

It has encouraged orginality and stimulated every nation to find and pursue its own vocation, and to develop to the fullest degree its national genius and character. And meanwhile it has promoted among the citizens of every land in which it has taken root, a sense of public duty and the growth of a spirit of self-sacrifice and devotion to country.

Members of the Order of Independent Americans, the fact that you have pledged your allegiance to this worthy and noble organization proves that you have faith in our race and our nation. You believe with all the force and enthusiasm of which the citizens of a democracy alone are capable that we will maintain and complete that splendid national edifice, which, commenced under trying and difficult circumstances, has received in these later times its greatest extension; and you likewise believe that the fixity of purpose and strength of will which are necessary to this end will be supplied by that national patriotism which sustains the most strenuous efforts and makes possible the most brilliant and worthy achievement.

MAYOR'S ADDRESS OF WELCOME TO CONVENTION OF KNIGHTS TEMPLAR.

Today our city has donned her brightest robes and extends a hand of cordial greeting and welcome to her honored guests, the Knights Templar. As Mayor, it gives me sincere pleasure to extend to you the freedom of the city, and I hope that your stay among us will be an event to be recalled with pleasant memories.

In the fraternalism and the worthy motives which are so strikingly exemplified in your noble order is seen the coming trend of our modern civilization. The dark night of narrowness, sectarianism and bigotry is rapidly passing away before the beams of the resplendent sun of enlightenment and brotherly love.

Out of the shadows of the past the world has swept into a new and a better day. Forms of oppression and industrial slavery which threatened at times to destroy our social fabric are rapidly being broken up. The all-prevailing public conscience is awake, and the American Republic is moving forward to the fulfillment of its divinely appointed mission and destiny. Never in the history of the world has there been a time when it was such a glorious privilege to live.

The present is supremely an age of expectancy, of anticipation and of prophecy. The opinions and beliefs of the greatest and the wisest have passed away. But their enthusiasm and their courage remain— the enthusiasm and courage that were not daunted by the cold and starvation of Valley Forge and the desperate misery and suffering of the survivors of the Wyoming Massacre as they dragged their bleeding forms through the valley called "The Shades of Death."

The progress of humanity is not marked by the resting places of inaction and self-satisfied contentment, but by the titanic struggles by which the mind of man asserts its God-given heritage of supremacy over the blind forces of nature and the barriers reared by human prejudice, ignorance, hatred, and greed. "Better twenty years of Europe than a cycle of Cathay."

To you, Christian knights of the modern world, is entrusted in no small measure the task of preserving the ideals of humanity, of spreading abroad the principles of sympathy, forebearance and brotherly love, and of disseminating the truths and ideals that have guided the race to every notable attainment through the ages of history.

All men have their ideas of life, some have their ideals. It is when we reach out toward a fuller realization of the latter that we become to some extent what we were intended to be, and the higher and truer the ideal and the more perfect its realization, the grander and nobler will be the life attained.

A few years ago, the novel-reading world was eagerly devouring the pages of that curious romance to which its author, Rider Haggard, gave the strange title of ''She.''

Those of you who may have read this story will remember the impressive description of the ruins of the City of Kor, but you will recall especially the pen picture of the deserted and crumbling Temple of Truth.

Within its inner court stood a statue of the goddess whose worshippers had once filled that waste with their hurrying footsteps; whose voices had filled that silence with the sounds of devotion. Upon a pedestal stood a magnificent marble globe, and upon this globe was poised a sculptor's dream of womanly beauty. There it stood, divine amid that desolation, its hands extended in supplication, for a veil was over the face, hiding the features from view. And thus it had stood for ages—Truth beseeching the world to lift her veil.

In this symbol there is a profound meaning. The desolate city may lie about her, and the very courts once peopled by her votaries may give place to brambles, but Truth herself is imperishable, surviving all wreck and change; and if her prayer be slighted and her veil never lifted, the people perish while she survives.

If I were asked to sum up in one sentence the highest purpose which man can have in this life, I would say it was ''To seek the Truth and live it.''

Not only is this purpose a noble one, but it is one which is absolutely necessary to the true and permanent success of the individual or the masses, the citizen or the government. Creeds have lived and died, laws have been decreed or trampled under foot in exact proportion to the elements of truth they contained. Apparent exceptions prevail, but they do so only in appearance, and the success of falsehood is, in the nature of things, bound to be partial and temporary. The constant tendency of the universe and all that it contains is to conform more and more to truth.

Boundless is the gratitude which society owes to organizations such as that of the Knights Templar. In all ages they have been the repositories of the wisdom of mankind, the guardians of truth and justice, and as a body of true believers amid the shadows of skepticism, the preservers of religion and priests to God.

"Priests to God! In distant ages
    Did we tend the altar fire,
Where the pyramid of sages
    Rose to say, 'Lo! we aspire.'

"Priests to God! The vaulted arches
    Of the heavens' lofty dome
Form the temple-close where marches
    Man to his eternal home.

"Let us bear our tapers, lighted
    At the altars of the East;
Keep the faith that once we plighted,
    Clad in spotless robes of priest.

"Brothers, let us humbly labor
    As God's earthly temple throws
Light divine on friend and brother
    Till each looks aloft and knows,—

"Knows the sanctity of living,
    Knows the Holy Place within,
Knows the incense born of giving
    Life itself to save from sin.

"Priests and Brothers, death may sever
    Ties that bind us to this sod,
But the temple stands forever,
    And we serve as priests to God."

ADDRESS BY AN HONORED GUEST AT A LADIES' LITERARY SOCIETY.

Madame President and Members:

I esteem it a high privilege to address the members of this society, for as I look in your faces I see there the ineffaceable symbols of the seeker after truth.

It is a law of nature that what we seek, we shall, in some measure, find. And so, like a rainbow, life glitters in all its brilliant colors; and like the rainbow, it carries a different impression and meaning to every beholder.

To the butterflies of fashion, life is a fleeting summer day to the seeker after performance, it strikes its roots into eternity. To the vain, it is a yawning chasm; to the thoughtful it is a source of boundless interest. To the indolent, it is a call to despairing resignation; to the strenuous, it is a stimulus to dauntless energy. To the serious, it is fraught with infinite significance; to the flippant, it is all a sorry jest. To the optimist, life is joy ineffable; to the pessimist, it is an atrocious and unending struggle. To those of little faith, the heavens are dumb; to the believer, they disclose the splendors of beautific vision.

Blessed indeed is he who has traversed the realm of nature with a seeing eye and an understanding heart. For him there are no shadows; in his ear no discords sound. He sees the roots of things; he hears the grasses growing in the darkness of the earth; he marks the rising and falling of the tide of life in all the visible channels in which it ebbs and flows; in his mind all things are revealed. And because all these things are revealed to him and the order of creation moves about him in unbroken unity, he becomes the interpreter of this hidden harmony to men, the inspirer of song, the maker of poetry, the solver of the mysteries of the world.

What to him is the cycle of the year? It is the emblem of man and his progress from age to age.

The tenderest green is on the foliage, the whitest clouds are in the sky, and the showers are so sudden that the birds are hardly dry from one wetting before there comes another. These swift dashes of rain seem to fall out of the clear blue, so mysteriously do the light clouds dissolve into the depths of heaven after every rush of pattering drops. Thus in the spring do the petals of life open and expand.

Through the soft splendor of the summer day, overflowing with the gladness of things that are to be, we run without thought or care; and as every sense is flooded with the beauty and joy of the season, our imagination is aflame with a thousand intonations of pleasure. As spring imperceptibly glides into summer, it touches us through every sense, and we feel the depth of the union between our spirit and the great heart of nature.

The first of June! All day great clouds float about the sky, and near evening it rains. Immediately before the night the gloom in the west is swept away by some invisible power and the sunset crimsons the hills until it seems that a halo of golden glory lingers like a benediction. The road, lying between rows of dripping maples, glistens with tiny rivulets; while everywhere, from the green pastures and the foliage-laden trees to the wet church spires reflecting the rays of the setting sun, the world seems to be smiling through tears like a broken-hearted woman made happy, with the marks of her sorrow lingering in her eyes.

So over the undiscovered country of our souls the mists are melting, the clouds rolling up into the blue and dissolving in infinite depths of tender sky; mountain ranges are defining their outlines against the horizon; and the meaning of the world grows clearer, for we begin to understand our own spirit, and in this knowledge confusion vanishes while mystery deepens.

The season ages. In the great expanse of far-spreading fields there is a sense of repose. The tide which had quickened all things that grow and bloom and bear fruit is beginning to ebb, though there is as yet no sign of vanishing beauty on the face of the landscape. Nature has ceased to work, and sits listening to the harvest song of her children. The two revelations of budding and ripening make life one long, orderly, quiet unfolding; but the hour of revelation is not yet ended.

A hush falls upon the world at sunset, so akin to that which fills the dim arches and deep aisles of cathedrals that we pause and look thoughtfully out over the landscape. The air is warm, and moves so gently that it seems the caress of an unseen hand; the western sky turns to gold, and the world becomes a temple. All things are silent, for it is the vesper hour. In the silence which enfolds the world, the watcher is aware of the harmony between his life and the life of nature. The two have moved so long in unison that they have become as one, set to the same music, each fulfilling itself in obedience to that law of order, of beauty, of fruitfulness, under which the world has bloomed through countless centuries. Nature is the emblem of the life of man.

As the grain ripens for the gleaning and the fruit for the plucking, so the spirit of man ripens in the quietness of age. And then passes before him the vision of the life within and the life without, mounting together season after season to perfect fruition.

> "Look Nature through! 'tis revolution all;
> All change, no death; day follows night, and night
> The dying day; -stars rise and set, and set and rise;
> As in a wheel, all sinks to reascend:
> Emblems of man, who passes, not expires."

SHRINE ADDRESS AT DEDICATION OF NEW MASONIC TEMPLE.

The story is told of a farmer who had decided to sell his property, and had it listed by a real estate agent, who wrote a glowing description of the farm. When the agent read it over to the farmer for his approval, the old man said, "Read that again."

After a second reading, the farmer sat for several minutes in deep thought, and finally said: "I don't believe I want to sell. I have been looking for that kind of a place all my life, and it never occurred to me that I had it until you described it to me. I don't want to sell out."

Today as we Masons view this magnificent new Masonic temple, I believe each one is saying to himself, "This is the kind of a place we have been looking for, and we are here to stay."

The subscribers who have contributed so generously to this beautiful structure, and the representatives of the various Masonic bodies who have labored so tirelessly and earnestly toward the project, now see the result of their efforts in the finest Masonic temple in the State of Iowa. It is eminently fitting that such a result should crown the devoted and self-sacrificing work of the many who have given freely of their time, energy and means in its behalf.

The dedication of a great building such as this represents a consecration and a sacrifice—an offering on the altar of the noblest aims of civilized mankind.

Freemasonry, the speculative architect, always laying up perfect ashlars and spreading cement on the ever ascending temple of moral perfection, has acquired and maintained a formula, expressive at once of the objects for which great temples and edifices are erected, and of the human hopes and aspirations which cling around such undertakings.

The operative workman squares, tries and lays the corner stone; the speculative Mason touches it with moral maxims and reads into it the symbolism that the true foundation of the structure lies in the heart of man, and rises on the pillars of his ideals and aspirations. The building reared upon these foundations is but a means—the end is a hope, a profound, suggestive hope, nourished by toil, exalted by virtue, and consecrated to charity and love.

The beautiful temple in which we stand will witness to our people and to future generations that the humanity of Freemasonry is a vital, living force in our hearts, and pleads in visible results for what is great and good.

Freemasons of Davenport, I congratulate you on the completion of this splendid work, and on a success which is commensurate with your devotion and zeal.

The purpose and destiny of this temple is become sacred to the cultivation of all Masonic virtues, and especially devoted to the diffusion of the great principles of liberty secured by constitutional law, of equality of rights, of fraternity and brotherly love, of the protection of the widow and the fatherless, and of the improvement and progress of humanity.

The walls of this temple are builded true and strong, upon foundations like those of the great Order which it represents, so that they shall stand for generations, defying the assaults of time and storm, and devoted to the noble purposes which have always characterized our order.

Conceived in Hope, strengthened by Faith, and bound in Charity, it will fulfill its mission and spread the light of Freemasonry—brotherly love, relief and truth—that men may become equal, fraternal and free.

In Freemasonry, this idea of equality, fraternity and freedom is no political creed, but a comprehensive, fundamental truth, springing from our conception of the Great Architect of all things.

Civilization moves on toward the realization of this idea, not through the ordeals of fire and blood, wars and revolutions, not through extravagant theories and dark paths, but upon the calm and placid waters of benevolence, charity and forbearance.

Freemasonry contributes a distinct impetus to this movement, for it teaches men that nothing but virtue is Godlike, and nothing but truth is enduring.

Let us live and labor in this faith, and our successors after us, and may the grand work now completed so auspiciously, be to us a bond of unity and strength. Then we shall be prosperous, happy and contented; the tie of brotherly love will be stronger than cement the structure of this temple; the harmony of fraternal feeling more beautiful than the symmetry of its form, and our spiritual design grander than the perfection of the architect's skill.

As the roofs and turrets of this temple rise to the pure vaults of heaven, may our soul's ambitions go along with them, that all the great and good things may come to pass to which Freemasonry here anew dedicates its service and its faith, to labor for the welfare of mankind, and to make the world happier and better. Who can do or promise more?

THE BUSINESS MAN'S ALLEGIANCE TO THE FLAG.

The flag of our country is an inspiration. It kindles in our hearts patriotic feelings; it carries our thoughts forward in the cause of liberty and right. On sea and land, wherever the star spangled banner floats on the breeze, it thrills the heart of every true American with pride.

It recalls the memory of battles bravely fought. It recalls the victories of Trenton and Princeton, of Gettysburg and Appomatox, of Chauteau Thierry and Belleau Wood. We see the flag as first carried by Paul Jones across the sea; we see the flag as carried by Commodore Perry on Lake Erie; we see the flag as carried by Farragut at New Orleans; we see Admiral Dewey through smoke and fire hoisting the flag in Manila Bay; we see its tattered but glorious folds plunging through the awful carnage of the Forest of the Argonne.

The flag symbolizes the principles of human progress and human liberty. The stars represent the unity and harmony of our states. They are the constellation of our country. Their lustre reflects its radiance upon every nation of the earth. The flag of 1776, the old thirteen, has grown to be the greatest flag of the world. Its stars reach from ocean to ocean. General Grant once said, ''No one is great enough to write his name on the flag.''

A century and a half under the Stars and Stripes has been the greatest period of progress in the history of the world. No other nation that has ever existed has carried forward such a banner. Its colors were taken from various sources and brought into one harmonious combination, and it waves over a country which unites all nationalities and all races, and in the end brings about a homogeneous population, representing the highest type of civilization.

It is not strange that this flag of Washington, of Hamilton, of Adams, of Jefferson; this flag of Jackson, of Webster, of Clay; this flag of Lincoln, of Grant and of McKinley, should exert such worldwide influence. It has spread knowledge and faith and hope among all classes. It means liberty with justice. Its international influence places it is in the first rank. It twines itself among the flag of other nations, not for destruction and war, but for friendship and progress in the cause of humanity.

In the councils of peace, in the triumphs of war; in everything that pertains to government, in everything that pertains to the advancement of humanity, it calls forth the admiration of mankind. Under its influence the arts and sciences have been fostered, commerce has expanded, and education has been made universal.

To the business man it signifies protection for legitimate industry, the rewards of honest labor, an open market for the products of his toil, freedom from arbitrary seizure of property or the imposition of crushing burdens of taxation to support a reckless and extravagant ruling class, and free schools, libraries and museums for the education of his children.

The business man knows that in whatever quarter of the globe he may take up his residence for purposes of trade, the American flag will secure for him protection and respect. The harbors of the globe salute this banner as the herald of progress and peace.

The Stars and Stripes is the symbol of invincible but unaggressive power. Our sway is undisputed from the Atlantic to the Pacific and from the Great Lakes to the Gulf. In our whole history no nation has declared a war of invasion against us, nor is such an event likely ever to happen. The maxim that ''in time of peace we should prepare for war'' should never be incorporated into our national creed. It was a maxim formulated by monarchs to ensure the stability of their thrones and to enable the ambitious ruler to become a despot. It has been made the excuse and justification for the imposition of the tremendous burdens imposed upon society in all ages for the support of standing armies and navies.

The flag is the emblem of our unity, our power, our thought and purpose as a nation. It has no other character than that which we

5

give it from generation to generation. Though silent, it speaks to
us—speaks to us of the past, of the men and women who went before
us, and of the records they wrote upon it. From its birth until now
it has witnessed a great history, has floated on high the symbol of
great events, of a great plan of government worked out by a great
people. For the principles which it represents, men have been content to die on many a hard-fought battlefield, knowing as they turned
their pale faces upward to the stars that they were martyrs for the
right.

Such is the Spirit of the Flag:

"Long ago I built my watch-tower on the stern New England coast,
    And my altar fires were kindled high above the sounding shore;
I flung my fearless banner to the winds that sweep the world,
    There to wave in storm and sunlight, there to wave forevermore.

"From my watch-tower, looking Eastward, I have seen a million sail
    Sweep on from the horizon line with all their canvas spread,
And, lighted by my living flame that flashed across the sea,
    Make bravely for the port where Law and Liberty are wed.

"From my watch-tower, gazing Westward, I have seen the march of
        men,
    O'er hill and glen and mountain, and through woodlands gray
        and dim.
I have seen them building cities; I have seen them cross the plains,
    And only halt at last upon the far Pacific's rim.

"I have seen my fleets and armies at the rising of the sun
    Spread my colors in the dawning and sail on in proud estate.
I have sent my troops and warships to the islands of the sea,
    And have heard my cannon thunder at the Orient's ancient gate.

"Are my battles waged for conquest or the glory of the sword?
    Have my heroes fought and fallen to oppress and to enslave?
Know you not that Freedom follows where my stern battalion tread,
    And that Liberty is crowned where my triumphant banners wave?

"Liberty to live and labor; freedom, justice and the law;
    Neither tyranny nor license while my beacon fires still flame;
For my vengeance shall be swifter than the lightning's awful stroke,
    Whether demagogue or tyrant plant oppression in my name!

"Peace shall raise aloft her standard where my loyal troops have
        marched,
    And shall brood upon the waters where my pennant is unfurled;
And the deep tones of my canon shall be hushed forevermore
    When my banner sheds its glory through the confines of the
        world!"

A SHORT TALK BY A NEW MEMBER ON ADMISSION TO LADIES' ROTARY CLUB.

Madame President and Fellow Members:

Back of every human action is a definite motive, and to become a member of the Rotary Club is to express a motive which may be defined as the reaching out of the soul toward the ideal. It was this aspiration toward the ideal that inspired the Thracian youth Antisthenes, upon hearing the fame of the teachings of Socrates, to leave a house of ill repute, where he was employed as a slave, and travel two hundred Grecian stadia by night, in order that he might sit down at the feet of the master and partake of the banquets of pure reason. The ideal of better things had existed in his soul, and the impediments of distance and environment crumbled to earth before the invincible strength of his awakened purpose.

An ideal is that which is conceived as the highest type of excellence or the ultimate object of attainment, and idealism may be defined as the habit of forming ideals and striving after their realization. It is the endeavor to obtain perfection by improving and uniting in one form all the best qualities to be found in individual forms.

Rotary has such a collective ideal, and has crystallized it in that clarion call of its motto: "Not Self but Service." That motive is truly eclectic—it borrows some of the courage of the soldier, the devotion of the missionary, and the clear-headed initiative of the modern leader of business and industry. Above all it is progressive, forceful, and original.

The former British Premier, Lloyd George, once said: "Think out new ways to deal with old problems. Don't always be thinking of getting back to where you were before the war. Get a real new world." On another occasion he said: "The less we talk about the theories of the past, and the more we deal with realities and the needs of the future, the better national progress we shall make."

One of the difficulties which confronts all enterprise today is in having things imperfectly done; the lack in individuals of appreciating the necessity of doing things correctly, of analyzing situations accurately, and of giving clear expression in statements regarding them.

Conscientious effort and education will do more than anything else to overcome these shortcomings. By education I mean the systematic development and cultivation of the normal powers of the intellect, so as to render them more efficient in some particular form of endeavor. Efficiency in modern business requires character, idealism and education, as well as experience and effort. I believe that there is as much opportunity for idealism in our commercial activities as there is in literature, art, and music.

Since the European War, there has been a serious recasting of values. Stocks, bonds, money—all things material—have shrunken to more nearly their absolute value, while character, integrity, honor, love, sympathy, and unselfishness, are taking first place in the hearts and minds of thoughtful people.

Evidences are manifold of the tightening of the bonds of brotherhood, and with the more general application of the Golden Rule we see less of social unrest, suspicion, greed of gain, and unlawful exploitation. With the broader views taken by business men, and the new spirit of fraternalism fostered by organizations such as the Rotary and Kiwanis Clubs, industry and commerce will no longer be channels down which a few favored individuals may float without effort in a life of luxury and ease, but will be recognized as mediums providing opportunity for useful service.

Money has its more or less fixed value, but the important thing after all is the character of the service we are rendering, and its adequacy for the needs of the community which we serve. This is high ground; but there are many evidences of the operation of natural laws which will compel us to still greater effort.

Never has there been a greater need for the exceptional, the resourceful, the one who can think and plan, who can advise new and original ways of doing things, who can handle situations and solve problems through the exercise of resourcefulness. And never before was the necessity more apparent for unity of purpose in business, social, religious, and community life—yes, even in our domestic life— to find relief from the stress and strain and uncertainty of our national problems.

As a nation we need most men who put character above wealth; men who possess opinions and a will; men who will not lose their individuality in a crowd; men who will not think anything profitable that is dishonest; men who will make no compromise with questionable things; men whose ambitions are not confined to their own selfish desires; men who do not have one brand of honesty for business purposes and another for private life.

I often wonder whether in our daily life we do not become somewhat narrow in our view of duty, instead of taking a broader outlook and taking such part in national, municipal and community work as our general training and experience give us special fitness for. The time required for such service would be well spent, and our other interests would be benefitted by a closer personal relationship with our fellow citizens. It is exactly this field of endeavor to which the Rotary Club has committed its efforts.

If we are sincerely desirous of being useful in the community, ample opportunity will be found for the exercise of all our qualities, in connection with the various public activities that claim our attention, enabling us, at the same time, to merit and secure a due share of public confidence.

Plato said this: "The punishment suffered by the wise, who refuse to take part in the government, is to live under the government of bad men." Making a living merely, or accumulating money for an independence, is not an ideal objective.

There is honor in business that is the fine gold of it; that reckons with every man justly; that loves light; that regards kindness and fairness more highly than prices or profits. This is the standard which is governed and upheld by the ideals of Rotary, and which is expressed in its laconic but meaningful motto—"Not Self but Service."

CHILD WELFARE.

In years to come when the history of this age is written by the impartial thinker, who at that distance of time may be able to gain a right perspective and may then be able to say which were the most striking features in social development, it may well turn out that he will point to the birth of the interest in Child Welfare as being among the events of first importance.

So let us take first things first. The world needs better men and women—good as those of the present generation may be. Let us begin with the young, the boys and the girls, keeping them in health, sobriety, integrity, virtuous manhood and womanhood of the noblest stamp.

We know it is the boys and girls of today who make the men and women of tomorrow. The influence of unhealthy environment in childhood indeed, drags at life's larger impulses, hampers and stifles the desire for higher things.

Socrates has said, "Only by learning to think aright we learn to do well." I do believe that every Woman's Club should give their deepest thought to this subject of Child Welfare, so that they may be able to do the very best for the children, some who have been placed in the world under woefully unsatisfactory conditions.

Once it was recognized that the high rate of mortality among children was largely due to the ignorance of what was necessary for the health of the child. True; it is no new thought that "of all good gifts the best is health," but that the whole question should be viewed from the medical aspect and from that aspect alone, is a mistake; for the prevention of disease is more dependant on good environment than on aught else.

So let us view the situation from its different standpoints. The child must develop physically, it must develop mentally, it must develop morally.

The physical effects of a wrongly developed childhood are: arrest of growth, puny stunted stature, anæmia, thin emaciated limbs, sunken cheeks and hollow eyes; and diseases of all kinds—of the lungs, of the joints, of the spine—for the arrest of development does not mean mere arrest, but means malformation.

The mental effects are likewise arrest of mental development; and this, too, means not only a stopping short but a development in the wrong direction. The brilliant but short lived intelligence of news-boys, their sinister anticipations of world knowledge, their seeming ability to play the game of life on a par with adults—we laugh at and applaud; we do not look beyond the moment, nor count the cost they pay.

And the moral effects, as is to be expected, are of the same char-acter—loosening of family ties, roving the streets, familiarity with vice and the haunts of vice, a starting independence before the moral nature is fit to maintain independence, a process of selection so trying that while sometimes it leads those subjected to it to distinguished achievement, more often it leads to ruin.

To combat the first of these errors (the physical) we have the Child Labor movement. The emancipation of the child from economic servi-tude is a social reform of the first magnitude. I feel that here is a reform upon which we can agree, which must appeal to every right thinking person, and which is urgent.

If any Woman's Club displays a real interest in the Child Labor movement I rest assured that that club will be attuned to a favor-able reception of sound and sane social reforms generally.

Oh, let us try to understand that a certain sacredness ''doth hedge around'' a child, that a child is industrially tatoo, that to violate its rights is to touch profanely a holy thing!

To annul the effects of the second drawback in the life of a child (the mental) we have our educational institutions. The school has for its object to win from the human beings confided to its care, the human qualities latent in them: imagination, taste, skill, apprecia-tion, vigorous reasoning, will power, character. A more convincing appeal then comes to us from these two movements jointly, the child labor and the educational movements, in my judgment, cannot be conceived of. And without the former the latter cannot succeed.

Then the last of these, and probably the greatest of all, the moral effects, must be dealt with principally within the guarded precincts of the home. Science has not yet discovered what it is that the child loses by being bereft of a home, but science agrees that a very inferior home and a mother's care is infinitely better than a perfect institution without that care.

We are thus brought sharply up against the questions—What causes a child to be such as we find it? Is a child effected more by environment than by heredity?

In answer I would say that in the question of the child and its development the examination must always be carried on from two aspects, approached that is from the hereditary standpoint as also from the environmental.

An effort to obtain for the child a better chance of a full life must take into consideration the type of the child's parents and the influence for good or evil that such parents are likely to bring to bear upon the child. While doing so, however, it has always to be borne in mind that these very characteristics are in a large measure the result of external causes. So we come to the point where we know that certain moral failings are likely to remain in the world partly through inherited influence but largely through an environment that is favorable to their growth. The numbers of those who possess such failings should be largely reduced by an alteration, if alteration be possible, or at least by a modification of this same environment.

In truth we must say that much has been done for the children. So far back as 1803, through the efforts of one Dr. Percival, was passed an act which has taken position as leader of a series of acts dealing with the welfare of children.

An act so passed as was that of 1803 with little provision for its practical administration, only too often remains a dead letter—the public little troubling to ascertain its success or failure. But not so in this case. Though to a large extent a practical failure, this act had results. It was an expression of public feeling and the thin edge of a potent wedge which has been entered deeper and deeper.

While we know that "men's hearts are not changed by acts of parliament or legislation," yet do we not all agree, while so much remains to be done, the little child of today—our own progressive 1923—is being given much more of a chance than that little child back in 1803.

RECREATION AND THE CHILD.

It has been only within the last few decades that educators concluded that in classifying the instinctive traits of children, the most important had received but meager attention. I mean the instinct to play. We are now beginning to realize that all children inherit this instinct, and that this innate tendency towards recreation and amusement needs both cultivation and development.

Even in small children, the play instinct is paramount. The need of mother play in infancy has been demonstrated by the mortality figures in infant asylums. Perhaps nothing is lacking from a scientific standpoint, yet the death rate is appalling. This has been explained by the fact that the child in such institutions lacks his natural playmate. Charity workers recognize this and will never separate mother and child, if possible.

During the first period of child life, that is from birth up to six years, play is imaginative or imitative. Any one who has ever had opportunity to observe children of Kindergarten age, knows that at that period play is chiefly imitative. The reason is obvious. They wish to carry on the activities which they have observed in older persons. They play house, or store, or fireman or policeman, or anything else that may have come to their notice. Even the stories which they have been told, often find realization in their plays. If they have heard of fairies, they make these the center of their amusements and often actually dramatize; however crude their first efforts may be, the whole story, thereby often amusing not only themselves but the adults in whose charge they find themselves. It is this instinctive tendency to dramatize which is often made use of by the primary teacher in teaching reading and the first important facts of history. In fact, play finds a place in almost all drills and lessons of the first few years of school. It is amusement through which the child develops himself physically, mentally, morally, and socially.

In the second period, from six to twelve years, play is chiefly competitive. In this period the child learns lessons of fairness, honesty, democracy, and formation of social habits, for when children play together they learn how to adjust themselves to others. Without the advantages of play with other children the child is likely to grow up puny in body, selfish, overbearing, and self-centered. A boy who is a bully at home soon learns his place when he goes to school.

While we thus see that the early years of life are devoted to play, we should grossly err were we to think of it as an antithesis to work. It is self-activity, pursued for its own sake and as the expression of inner impulses. Or as Prof. L. C. Parker says: "The children's activities are called play because they are doing them for the fun of the thing, for the pleasure which comes from the activity itself."

Although, as has already been indicated all children inherit the instinct for play and the necessity of development has generally been conceded, yet there are still a few persons who think lightly of play. They tell us that practically every school has its daily calisthenics, which, in their opinion, make play well nigh useless. But these exercises are crowded into the curriculum by the regular teacher, who can not be expected to do it as well as a specialist. We are all agreed that calisthenics are beneficial. They correct bad posture and special defects; they exercise unused muscles, encourage deep breathing, teach quick response to signals, etc. But formal exercises are not play. To be sure they will develop a kind of physical efficiency. But calisthenics alone will not awaken little minds or arouse latent energies or banish that apathetic expression all too common in the school room. If we cannot put the spirit of joy into physical training, we may as well give it up. Do you study faces in the streets? If you do you know how many people there are for whom, apparently, "youth is finished without ever having been begun."

The plain truth is that we have too long ignored the fact that the child has a body—a beautiful intricate tool which if well cared for will give service for many years. Or, if we have not wholly ignored it, we have at least dealt with the question very superficially. We have failed to put sufficient emphasis on the instinct for play.

Energetic play leads to the development on body and mind. It encourages the shy child to assert himself and teaches the forward child to await his turn.

Sometimes it may be difficult to decide just what kinds of games children should be encouraged to play. The problem is, of course, to get something that will be interesting enough to capture the attention of the child, and which will bring into play the characteristics peculiar to the period of life in which he is.

It is to be hoped that play will be put into the curriculum of every school in the land. Efficiency studies now being made in the cities are showing that the child approximately makes the same progress in 15 minutes a day that he does in 45 minutes in arithmetic, and a number of other subjects. For the smaller children, at least data would show us to be entirely justified in taking the time out of our present school day.

Let us therefore bear in mind the necessity of developing and cultivating the instinct for play. Amusement is an important socializing factor; it is an education; it is a health preserve. But socially and individually it is a proper and wholesome use of much of the child's time. Let us cultivate the spirit of play, of unhampered self-expression. In other words, "Come let us play with our children!"

HOW TO KEEP HEALTHY AND ITS VALUE TO SUCCESS.

Only one life to live! We all want to make the most of it, to make it last as long as possible, and while it lasts, to fill it full of happiness, contentment, joy. These blessings can only come from the possession of good health, and health can only come from right thinking. Therefore, learning how to think well is learning how to build well.

Health and long life are largely dependent upon scientific choice and use of foods, healthy habits, and temperance in all things, and yet most of us each day violate some or all of these laws and yet expect to retain our vigor and do our part of the world's work.

We meet people everywhere who do not advance or grow in usefulness. Though they walk the streets, stand on the corner, and loaf around cigar stores and pool rooms, they are merely existing, not living. They are like the drones in the busy hive that serve no useful purpose and retard the activities of the workers. They have missed the true meaning of life, which is to live intensely, not extensively.

Pupils of the schools of Jones County, as I look into your bright young faces I see written there the possibilities of lives of usefulness, power and purpose. You have no bad habits that may not be eradicated, no good habits that may not be strengthened and made more noble. You are like the plastic clay in the hands of the sculptor, that may, according to the influence brought to bear upon it, be moulded into a form of strength and beauty or into one of unsightly deformity. You are free to make that choice for your selves: which shall it be?

Nature has endowed you with control of the most perfect machine in existence—the human body. Other machines wear out and must be renewed by an expert mechanic: your body renews itself and asks only your observance of the simplest and most elementary rules of health in order that it may perform all its delicate and intricate functions with ease, and promote your efficiency and happiness.

The one thing which is its first and principle requirement fortunately exists in unlimited quantity. Pure air is everywhere—barrels and oceans of it—it tries to penetrate every crack and crevice, and would if it were not for our blind and mistaken efforts to shut it out with tightly fitting doors and windows. Do you know that out of every seven who die, one dies from lack of pure air? Fresh air is the most valuable thing to the human body, and no trust will ever be organized to control it and parcel it out to human beings at monopoly prices. Sometimes I think that if some one made an effort to do just that thing, it might be a blessing in disguise, for then we should learn to appreciate its value. Consumption is nothing but air starvation, which robs the body of its necessary supply of oxygen. You would not think of drinking foul, impure water; then why should you draw into your lungs air that is loaded with poisonous gases?

The second requirement of a healthy and efficient body is good food and correct habits of eating. Ninety per cent of our ailments come from eating the wrong kind of food or from eating too fast or too much. Whatever we eat must be like the material of our bodies, or it will do us harm and not good. The tissues will absorb only such material as they can make use of; the remainder becomes poison, and though nature has provided us with special organs whose function is to eliminate poisons, if we continually overtax these organs, they will break down, and the impurities they were meant to remove will pour into the blood stream.

Nature has again befriended us in making the best food for the human body the cheapest and most plentiful. Fresh vegetables and fruits contain an abundance of substances called vitamines, which are an essential constituent of plant life and are destroyed by cooking. Vitamines are necessary for the health of the human body, and are furnished in abundance from such foods as celery, turnips, lettuce and other vegetables which are eaten in the raw state, and by all kinds of fruits.

Meat, which is the most expensive part of human diet, is at the same time the most injurious. Most of the symptoms of age, such as high blood pressure or hardening of the arteries, come from the poison in the meat we eat, and result in paralysis or apoplexy. Meat readily ferments and breaks down into harmful products of putrefaction in the digestive tract, forming poisons and ptomaines which attack every vital function and organ, especially the nervous system.

The third requirement of the healthy human body is exercise. Exercise in its best form builds up and develops the bodily powers, and should always stop short of fatigue, which reverses the process, and loads up the blood with waste products. This is the secret of the healthfulness of plays and games for children; they fill the lungs with fresh air, stimulate the muscles, quicken the organs of sense, such as the sight and hearing, and promote restful and invigorating sleep.

Pure air, wholesome food, and abundant exercise are the bricks and mortar with which we build a perfect structure—the healthy human body. The gift of a sound and healthy body is an alert and efficient mind, and the combination of the two means success and happiness.

If you would keep young and happy and reach the highest success in life, observe the simple laws of health; live a clean, moral life; send out good thoughts to all and think evil of none. This is obedience to the great natural law; to live otherwise is to break this great divine law. Every thought and emotion vibrates through the body for health or disease, and leaves an influence like itself. Learning how to think well is learning how to build well. You can build a palace or a hovel out of the same material: build thou a palace.

THE CHRISTIAN MISSION.

What is the Christian mission? We do not have to go beyond the first sentence in the Bible to realize that Christianity believed in work and disbelieves in idleness: "In the beginning God created the heavens and the earth." Paul taught that if a man will not work, neither should he eat—a plan of getting rid of the lazy by starving them, but unfortunately they are parasites who draw their sustenance from the industrious and will not be destroyed.

The Bible is preëminently the day-laborer's book. It is the book of work. Everybody in the Bible is working—prophets, kings, holy women, high priests, apostles, angels ("are they not ministering spirits?") A devotion to strenuous toil has seized on everyone engaged in the mission of holiness.

God is at work in the opening utterance of the Scriptures. How good that is! How elevating to toil! No Brahm sunk in eternal slumber; for even God's work rest is toil continuous and productive; as Jesus says, "My Father worketh hitherto and I work," meaning that what God was doing incessantly by the processes of nature, Jesus was doing by the emergency processes of miracle.

God the Father and God the Son at work—that is the sublime spectacle presented to toiling humanity. Then as if to lift us to a heaven of holy activity, Paul tells us that we are laborers together with God. What a privilege and joy; God and ourselves are at the same tasks— we are partners with Him.

According to the opening chapters of the Book of Revelation, the first man, into whose nostrils God breathed the breath of life with the result that he became a living soul—this man was put at work, and we are certain that the second Adam was a toiler, for, wondering, the people asked: "Is not this the carpenter?" Christ came from a working household, and was sympathetic with and obedient to its traditions. He was a working man his life through; there was no time for rest in the clouded sky of his uninterrupted toil. "Himself bore our griefs," and in simple grandeur it is observed, "He bearing His cross, went forth."

And He chose His disciples from men of toil. He called fishermen and changed the scene of their labor, saying, "I will make you fishers of men," a task more exacting, as they themselves found, than toil all night with their nets at sea. Paul was a tent-maker, and worked at his trade while he preached "Christ and Him crucified."

Christ insisted, "Go work in My vineyard," and bade His followers make haste, for with sadness He added, "For the night cometh, when no man can work." Everybody is at work in the New Testament order, and in the Old Testament order as well. The Jew taught every son a trade, whereby he at once showed the high esteem in which he held labor and his attention to the details of life which might wisely be imitated by parents today. The honor and necessity of toil is the gospel of the Old Testament and the New.

Paul defines the Christian mission in the description of his own life of toil: "To the weak became I as weak, that I might gain the weak; I am made all things to all men, that I might by all means save some. And this I do for the gospel's sake, that I might be partaker thereof with you. Know ye not that they which run in a race run all, but one receiveth the prize? So run that ye may obtain. And every man that striveth for the mastery is temperate in all things. Now they do it to obtain a corruptible crown; but we are incorruptible. I therefore so run, not as uncertainly; so fight I, not as one that beateth the air; but I keep under my body, and bring it into subjection; lest that by any means, when I have preached to others, I myself should be a castaway."

The word deacon means a man of work, a servant. And Paul, at the height of his career, wished only to be known as "a servant of the Lord Jesus Christ." Jesus girded himself with a towel and washed His disciples' feet, and from this act drew the inspiring lesson of the

Christian mission: "Ye call me Master and Lord; and ye say well, for so I am. If I, then, your Lord and Master, have washed your feet; ye also ought to wash one another's feet. For I have given you an example, that ye should do as I have done to you. Verily, verily, I say unto you, The servant is not greater than his Lord; neither he that is sent greater than he that sent him. If ye know these things, happy are ye if ye do them."

The mission of the Christian is to be interested, not simply in his own church, his own race, his own country, but in all work of God's kingdom, in all nationalities and lands. Humanity is his concern. All are "bought with a price, even the precious blood of Christ." Mankind is His specialty. He is interested in the illiterate as well as the learned, in the poor as well as the rich. He leaves nothing out of His reckoning. All are God's and all are His neighbors and friends.

He will not ask where men were born, or how they were reared, but will be eager to know whether they are born of God, to the end that their "citizenship may be in heaven," which is the only credential of genuine citizenship on earth. Or, if they be not born of God, His sleepless efforts will be to the end that they may "walk in the light as God is in the light," and so may "have fellowship one with another, and the blood of Jesus Christ, the Son of God, may cleanse them from all sin."

The mission of the Christian is to be interested in education, civilization, sociology, politics, in the church, and in the individual. These are all provinces in his bailiwick. He must not say, "I am a Christian, and can not meddle with these matters," but must, with comprehension of his high destiny as a Christian, say, "I am a Christian; therefore I am interested in all these matters and all others touching the welfare of the race."

A Christian is God's knight—errant on earth, sworn to fealty to society and to the common welfare of all the world.

ADDRESS TO A BIBLE CLASS.

It has been my pleasant privilege for a year past to be associated as president with this Bible class in the study of God's Word. In that time I have seen it grow from a membership of sixteen members to that of one hundred and seventy-five,—a splendid testimonial to the potency and influence of the Old Book in this modern age.

We have seen the value and beauty of the Bible, and we honor and revere it as the best of all books, because it alone is the inspired Word of God. Men have written great books. Homer wrote the story of the Greeks in his "Iliad" and "Odyssey" and his books come down to us with all the beauty and charm of a great poet, but at best they embody only the thoughts of Homer; but the Bible is beyond the best and purest and most soul-inspiring of all other books, because it is not the thought of man but the thought of God.

What a treasure the Bible is and how men should reverence it! In the quiet hush of their temple the Jews listened to it with uncovered heads. The early Christians in the catacombs and in mountain caves whither they were driven by persecution kissed its sacred pages and on bended knees read its story. As of old the ark of the covenant was sacred because it contained the tablets of stone on which were written the laws of God, so the Bible is sacred because it contains the words of divine inspiration.

What is inspiration? The word is derived from two Latin words meaning "to breathe into." As applied to the Scriptures, it means that God breathed into the minds of the writers and assisted them to write the truth. This was the grace of God bestowed upon the authors of the sacred books and was their special gift for that express purpose.

Why should you study the Bible? Because it is God's Word. In it He has revealed His will on all things pertaining to your welfare in this life and that which is to come.

It is a perfect guide. Whatever God does He does perfectly. You need look no further than the structure of the human eye to prove this assertion, for there you will behold its perfect adaption to the needs of man.

It is written by inspiration for your instruction, edification and encouragement, and designed to promote your present happiness and lead you to a home in eternal bliss.

Its constant tendency is to strengthen the intellectual powers. No other subjects are so far-reaching as those treated in the Bible—creation, Providence, redemption, sin, salvation,—all engage the highest powers of the intellect.

Its study enlarges the emotions, ennobles the hopes and aspirations, and purifies the affections of humanity. It helps to discipline the mind not only on the sublime subjects connected with religion, but on matters of every-day life. If you wish to express your thoughts clearly, you will be better able to do so after an hour's study of the Scriptures.

It cultivates the spiritual nature, and arouses in the mind a desire for a higher, purer and holier life. It meets the demands of every age. To love the Bible is to love its Author. Great and good men have been made wise by the study of God's Word.

Such are some of the reasons why we have met here Sabbath after Sabbath for the purpose of learning more of God through the guide He has given for our instruction.

Our class has been fortunate indeed in having as its teacher the Rev. Walter E. Gunby, who unites with depth of knowledge, clearness and charm of expression. Under his instruction, the sacred page has glowed with life and taken on new beauty. He has visualized for us the scenes of those early days when Christ walked with men on earth. We have tarried with Him at the well of Samaria, at the marriage supper of Cana, and heard the sacred truths that fell from His lips in the Sermon on the Mount.

We have walked with Him beside the stormy waters of the Sea of Galilee and ascended with Him to the Mount of Transfiguration. We have seen Him in the peace and quiet of the home of Martha and Mary, and in the agony of the Garden of Gethsemane.

It is with sincere gratitude and appreciation that we acknowledge Rev. Gunby's splendid service for our class as he has thus broken for us the bread of life and revealed the hidden meanings of the sacred page.

Grateful acknowledgment is due also to the other officers and to the devoted band of ladies and gentlemen who have given their aid from Sunday to Sunday in helping the work by entertaining the class. Their enthusiasm has added much to the success which has crowned our efforts.

The class orchestra has furnished delightful music which has contributed greatly to the enjoyment of our meetings. They have lent a grace and charm to these occasions which would otherwise have been lacking. These meetings have been occasions to be looked forward to with real pleasure, and have established friendships and associations which will be treasured in the years to come.

We have gained from them a familiarity with the Scriptures which will illuminate our study of sacred history for the remainder of our lives. The advantage of the knowledge here acquired cannot be overestimated.

In taking leave of the class as its president, I do so with the pleasant consciousness that our work has been a success in every respect. I congratulate every member upon the splendid devotion and interest which have carried our organization to its present state of efficiency. My best wishes and prayers will follow you.

THE CATHOLIC IN AMERICAN HISTORY.

Few people are aware of the tremendous influence that Catholicism exerted on the development of our country, without stressing the fact that Columbus, Vespucius, and most, if not all, of the first explorers were Catholics, it may be well to emphasize that the Pilgrim Fathers were not the only settlers that assisted in moulding the character of our people.

Fourteen years after the Mayflower reached our shores, Cecil Calvert, Lord Baltimore, planted a colony on the north of Virginia, which he called Maryland. Being a man who hated tyranny of all kinds and who had carefully observed the effects of tolerance and arbitrary rule upon the efforts that had already been made to establish successful colonies in America, he designed his colony as an asylum in which men of all creeds could meet on a common basis of faith in Jesus Christ. Lord Baltimore was firmly convinced of the necessity of religious freedom to the success of a state, and therefore closely adhered to the principles of civil liberty. Maryland's Toleration Act is "the first important landmark in the history of the development in America of that religious freedom which is the pride of the United States today."

While perhaps many of the first French colonists did not adhere to the Catholic faith, but were Protestants or Huguenots, the influence of Catholicism was greatly strengthened through the subsequent arrival of other settlers. In fact, "New France" represented the best spirit of the Roman Catholic Church. It is being estimated that from 1611-1800 three hundred and twenty members of the Society of Jesus labored as missionaries in the wilds of America. These men faced torture, hardship and death, and almost every one of them died in active service. Prof. E. D. Fite, though himself a Protestant, frankly admits that "finer devotion to Christian ideals was never exhibited, greater dangers and sufferings in the name of religion never encountered."

Catholicism was again brought to the foreground during one of the most distracted periods of our history. When the cause of the revolutionists seemed almost hopelessly lost, the timely arrival of a young French Catholic, Marquis de Lafayette, did much to encourage the struggling patriots. Though heir of a noble name, the possessor of wealth and a high social position, and the husband of a beautiful and accomplished wife, yet he left all of these to give comfort and aid to the colonists.

We could thus go on adducing examples of Catholic interest in the development of our country. But we must forebear, for there is still another phase of our subject worthy of mentioning.

A study of the reform movements in our country reveals the fact that Catholics have always been strong supporters of prohibition. As far back as 1838 we find Rev. Theobald Mathew giving a great impetus to the cause of temperance. It is true that Father Mathew lived in Ireland, but the influence of his work was strongly felt among Catholics even on this side of the ocean. Many of our older residents could corroborate this statement. In 1883, Cardinal Ireland began a vigorous temperance movement among the Roman Catholics in the northwest. No adverse argument can be adduced from the fact that some Catholics belong to the "wets." Some Protestants, too, cast their lots with the liquor element. But no sane man will suppose that Catholicism and Protestantism, as a whole, are opposed to prohibition. If they were, how did prohibition come into existence? Surely not among those outside the churches.

Educational history, likewise, shows Catholics to be actively engaged in the intellectual and moral development of a large part of our population. Some of our largest colleges and universities are controlled by Catholics. The Catholic University of America, located in Washington, D. C., has an enrollment of 1,835 students; St. Louis University of 2,618; in fact, there are few states in the Union that have no Catholic school of higher learning.

Again; there is a vast number of hospitals, orphanages, asylums, and similar institutions supported by Catholic philanthrophy, demonstrating that Catholics occupy no inferior position, but have connected themselves with all worth while movements. Statistics will corroborate this statement. According to the Official Directory, the Roman Catholic Church has in this country a membership of 17,885,646 communicants, presided over by 21,643 clergymen. There are 113 seminaries with 8,291 students, 215 colleges for boys, 710 academies for girls, 6,048 parish schools, 295 orphanages with 46,777 orphans, and 118 homes for the aged.

We should, however, be guilty of neglect were we to close this address without reference to the willingness of Catholics to help their country in times of distress. During the Civil War a large number fought on the side of the Union; some of them joined the Confederate ranks. If we should visit any of our National Military Homes for Disabled Veterans, we should be surprised at the comparatively large percentage of Catholic inmates. This fact shows that when the life of the Union was threatened, the Catholics did not lack patriotic zeal and ardor. It is well to remember that not all of them were natives of America. They were living in an adopted country, which they considered worthy of any sacrifice.

Similar truths apply to the Great War. Catholics were no slackers. They did not shirk their duties, but performed them to the best of their knowledge. Perhaps a few of them tried to evade their responsibilities just as some non-Catholics did. But the great majority took active part in the preservation of American ideals and in the defense of American rights and privileges.

THE NEEDS AND BENEFITS OF MISSIONS.

The nineteenth century has been the century of foreign missions. In the history of the Christian church it will be known as peculiarly the period of the Christian crusade in pagan lands. Its distinguishing religious characteristic is the large number of men and women who have gone forth from Christian lands to carry the gospel to the peoples of all nations.

In the experience of the past century, many valuable lessons have been learned in mission work, which should and will shape the methods of labor for the Redeemer's kingdom in the twentieth century. Chief

6

among these lessons established by the experience of the past century are:

1. The evangelization of every nation must be done chiefly by its own people. Noble as has been the work of foreign missionaries, it has been as founders and directors of missionary movements that they have been most largely useful. The words of Christian people, spoken to their own countrymen in all lands, are the most efficient preaching of the gospel, and their lives are everywhere the most conspicuous and conclusive evidence of its truth.

2. The need for self-support and self-reliance of the native churches has become increasingly apparent. Only by insisting on these features can Christianity be permanently established in any nation on an independent basis.

3. Christian missions will increasingly take the form of sympathy and aid to the native churches in foreign lands. While the preaching of the gospel, both pastoral and evangelistic, will be more and more left to native labor and support, those features of Christian work which call for prolonged and thorough training, and for large pecuniary investment, should be continued and increased. These features include medical missions in some countries; the work of translation, preparation, and publishing of sufficient Christian literature; and higher education—especially the thorough training of a native ministry and of Christian laborers along useful lines.

4. Missionaries will be more and more selected for educational and administrative rather than for preaching abilities. The experience of the past points to this as the proper course. Mission fields afford many instances of superior and even eloquent ministers who would have been exceedingly useful in Christian lands, but who have been comparative failures as missionaries because of their lack of ability for executive leadership, while every conspicuous success in missions has been associated with some leader of eminent administrative qualities.

5. There will be a proportionate decrease in the number of missionaries sent out from Christian lands in comparison with the amount of missionary work accomplished. This does not mean that the absolute number of missionaries will be less, but the assignment of their spheres of labor will be gradually readjusted in accordance with twentieth-century methods of mission work, and ultimately the number of foreign missionaries will be reduced without injury to the advance of Christianity. This will effect not only more rational methods, but a great economy, as the support of one missionary, if saved, would employ a dozen native workers, each one of whom might be as effective in evangelistic work as a missionary from other lands.

6. Evangelistic tours in pagan lands by preachers and lecturers from Christian countries will increase in number and frequency. Already such tours have had a profound influence, especially on the people of India and Japan. The resident missionary is often regarded as one

who, receiving a salary, is engaged in missionary work for a livelihood. The lecturer or evangelist visiting foreign lands comes as a witness to the worth and standing of the faithful resident missionary; and beyond what he may be able to say, gives power to the labors of the missionary. With the growing world-wide knowledge of the languages of Christian lands, these evangelistic journeys by eminent pastors and preachers from Europe and America will become more feasible and more widely effective.

It is easy to recall the time when the work of foreign missions was commonly regarded by Christian people as the sending of a small forlorn hope into the midst of great masses of darkness and superstition, from which very little could be looked for in return. The missionaries' work was conceived to be a continued struggle with heathenism, and at the best the converts gained were thought of as little groups of unimportant people, whose conversion was gratifying for the sake of the individuals gained, but who had no important share in the missionary enterprise as a whole.

Now, happily, the Church at home sees further into the true state of the matter, and the most important general conclusion we can draw is that the Church on the mission field is not a mere by-product of mission work, but is itself by far the most efficient element in the Christian propaganda.

In many of the greater mission fields, the Christian people are now recognized as a definite community, whose social life and ideals, as well as their personal faith and character, are already becoming a powerful element in the reshaping of national life. They are everywhere subjected to watchful scrutiny on the part of the non-Christian communities, and there seems to be a general acknowledgment that the life thus jealously watched affords a real vindication of the spiritual power of the religion which they profess.

In this state of things it is necessary to realize that the problems of the future differ in kind, as well as in scope and dimensions, from the problems of the past. We have no longer to think only of teaching a few humble people the elements of Christian truth. Attention must be concentrated rather upon carrying them on to higher levels both of knowledge and of Christian practice; and this must be done on a scale more commensurate than heretofore with the conspicuous and responsible place into which they have come, as influential guides in great social and moral movements, which are stirring the whole mass of their fellow countrymen.

REVERENCE TOWARD GOD AND THE CHURCH.

Some travellers were once in Venice on a high festival. On such days the shutters of the shops are closed, and the people are supposed to be keeping the day holy. On going into the square at San Marco, however, where most of the shops are located, they found the shutters closed, but on looking closely discovered signs of buying and selling going on inside. They stepped in and found trade in full swing. Outwardly these tradespeople were reverential, inwardly they were not.

Is it not the same with many church members today! The mere observance of religious forms cannot compensate for the lack of that true reverence for God and His Church which springs from the heart. Boyle, it is said, never mentioned the name of God without a visible and reverent pause in his discourse. Reverence is the very first element in religion; it cannot but be felt by every one who has right views of divine greatness and holiness, and of his own character in the sight of God.

Go and stand upon Mar's Hill at Athens where Saint Paul stood so long ago. In thoughtful silence, look around upon the site of all that ancient greatness; look upward to those still, glorious skies of Greece, and what conceptions of wisdom and power will all those memorable scenes of nature and art convey to your mind, now, more than they did to an ancient worshipper of Jupiter or Apollo? They will tell of Him who made the worlds, "by whom, and through whom, and for whom, are all things."

To you, that landscape of exceeding beauty, so rich in the monuments of departed genius, with its distant classic mountains, its deep blue sea, and its bright bending skies, will tell a tale of glory no Grecian ever learned; for it will speak to you no more of a thousand contending deities, but of the one living and everlasting God.

Go stand upon the heights of Niagara, and listen in awe-struck silence to that boldest, most earnest, and most eloquent of all nature's orators. And what is Niagara, with its mighty roar of plunging waters, but the oracle of God, the whisper of His voice? Who can stand amid scenes like these and not feel as he bows in reverence that in their sublimity is the expression of the thought of God?

If the consciousness of God is possible to all healthful souls, why are so many men and women without this consciousness? There are men and women, not a few, who do not want God. They would be very glad to have God if He were always on their side; glad to have God if He would always do what they wanted Him to do. They do not like to retain God in their knowledge, says Paul; they put God far from them, says the Psalmist.

The same spirit of anarchism which leads some men to desire to be rid of human law leads other men to desire to be rid of divine law. Not long ago a body of anarchists in Chicago passed a resolution saying in effect, "We have no use for God. We want no laws, either human or divine." The first question of the soul must be, Do I really want God to rule over me? Do I want a supreme will in the universe, to which my own will must in every respect be conformed?

There are men, who, though they do not wish to be rid of God, do not very much care to have Him. They are not opposed to God; but neither are they anxious about knowing Him. The Psalmist speaks of these when he says, "God is not in all their thoughts." There are thousands of men and women of whom that is true. They live their lives without thought of God. Sometimes God is forced into their thoughts by His providence; sometimes He is flashed before their minds by a sermon or a book; but, for the most part, they are living with their thoughts fixed on other things. The kingdom they are working for is not the kingdom of God; the name they are hallowing is not the name of God; the will they are trying to do is not the will of God.

They are busy about other things. One man is busy after his wealth —he is a money gatherer; another after his pleasure, another after his fame. But neither is taken up with God. They do not know what is the meaning of the expression, "As the heart panteth after the water brooks, so panteth my soul after thee, O God." They are not eager to know God; they are not anxious to be friends with Him. They lie awake at night over business anxieties, over earthly disappointments; but they never lie awake at night over the absence of God. We treat God with irreverence by banishing Him from our thoughts. Reverence is one of the surest signs of strength of character, irreverence one of the surest indications of weakness.

A perusal of current literature in reference to the church reveals how prevalent has become the spirit of irreverent criticism, expressed in such titles as "The Failure of the Church," "The Conflict of Religion with the Church," "Is Modern Organized Christianity a Failure?" and "The Ebb of Ecclesiasticism." But let it be remembered that this critical and contemptuous spirit is no novelty: it was a statesman of the eighteenth century who said, "We used to hate and then we despised the church; now we ignore it." Behind a vast amount of this current criticism is the strangely mistaken belief that the ecclesiastical situation used to be better than it is.

In every realm where a popular indictment is found against the church, the fault is still the human folly from which no organization ever yet escaped. Even in that most bitter and monstrous charge against the movement founded by Christ, that preachers fawn and policies are pliant before the subsidizing power of wealth, who without sin shall cast the first stone?

Today the new church within the churches is speaking. The spirit there evinced is more full of hope than all the failures are of discouragement. The last twenty years have seen a reformation in American Protestantism greater than the most sanguine could ever have dreamed. Like the Jews rebuilding the walls of their sacred city, multiplying hands are at work upon the unescapable task of organized religion. It must be half-breed Samaritans who now, as then, heckling the builders with gibes and missles, compel them to work with a trowel in one hand and a sword in the other.

ADDRESS OF WELCOME TO PATRIOTIC ORDER SONS
OF AMERICA.

Members of the Patriotic Order Sons of America:

The occasion is one that stirs the blood and quickens the pulses. As I look into your faces I read the symbols that explain the existence of this great and free nation, and the prophecy of its existence when others have fallen from power and influence through the decay of national ideals.

National eminence is founded upon lofty principles and praise-worthy deeds, and the people who reverence heroic ancestry may be trusted to rear an upright posterity. The best educational system is not enough for the protection of the people until it is joined to patriotism; then you have a national fiber that will resist every strain.

If yonder flag which hangs in graceful folds might find a voice, it would tell a story woven of the fabric of noble deeds and heroic acts that have made it everywhere a symbol of the best elements of national life and the synonym of national honor.

It would say, "I had my birth in Philadelphia; my stripes of red and white, my azure field with its thirteen stars were first caressed by Pennsylvania sunlight. I was the first to reach the top of Independence Hall; I was first to mark the source from whence pealed the music of your Liberty Bell. I led the vanguard of the Continental Army from Valley Forge to Yorktown. I first blushed in protest against slavery in my native Keystone State. The lilies of France that floated to the breeze over Fort Duquesne were lowered to the lion of St. George floating over Fort Pitt, but both yielded place to me when the winds from the lofty Alleghenies unfurled my colors above the waters of the Ohio. I led your victorious armies from Vera Cruz to the city of Mexico; I felt the loyal grasp of Lincoln and Grant, and gave inspiration to the millions who loved the cause for which I stood. I floated from the masthead of Admiral Dewey's flagship at Manila Bay when the pride of Spain was humbled in the dust. I plunged through the battle storm of Chateau Thierry and Belleau Wood, and the awful carnage of the Argonne Forest, and came back with my folds untarnished with defeat. I stand for liberty, for the noblest ambitions of humanity, for peace throughout the world, and for the dignity and honor and protection of all who love liberty and equality, and who claim the sheltering protection I have always given."

Patriotism is love of country and loyalty to its life and welfare; love tender and strong, tender as the affection of a son for his mother, strong as the pillars of death; loyalty generous and disinterested, counting no sacrifice too great, seeking no reward save the approving eye of history.

In the dark days of the early 60's, men were wont to say, "The war is a failure," "The Union is a rope of sand," "It can never be restored." These men, strange to say, had a hearing, a following, had it after Vicksburg, after Gettysburg, even after Appomatox. But the storm of war passed, and the nation addressed itself to the task of restoring the divided Union. How different the spirit, the words of the immortal man who, standing above the new made graves of eight thousand men killed in a single great battle of the war, declared:

"Rather is it for us to be here dedicated to the great task remaining before us,—that from these honored dead we take increased devotion to the cause for which they gave the last full measure of devotion,—that we here highly resolve that these dead shall not have died in vain; that the nation, under God, shall have a new birth of freedom, and that government of the people, by the people, for the people, shall not perish from the earth."

Under God, the nation did have a new birth of freedom, slavery fell, never again to lift its abhorrent front. A few years, and North and South were again united, standing side by side under a common flag, symbolical of an undivided, imperishable Union. Honor to Lincoln, the savior of an imperilled nation. Honor to Grant, to whose military genius we owe a debt never to be repaid. Honor to all who sleeping in thousands of lowly graves rendered possible by valor and sacrifice the Union in which North and South alike rejoice.

And what of the heroes of our late titanic conflict? Surely the mantle of the fathers has fallen upon the sons. To the world that war will stand as the most gigantic and remarkable of all history. Some will study it from the standpoint of military strategy, some from the vast results upon the national life and destiny of the participating powers, but great as were these elements, the one from which that war will derive its most lasting renown is the simple devotion of the American citizen soldiery.

America, rising into the family of nations in these latter times, is the highest billow in humanity's evolution, the crowning effort of ages in the progress of mankind. Unless we view her in this altitude, we do not comprehend her; we belittle her towering stature, and hide from ourselves the singular design of Providence in creating her.

Members of the Patriotic Order Sons of America, we are the heirs of priceless legacies in the unbroken record of brave and glorious deeds transmitted to us from our ancestors. Let us hand on that record to our posterity, not only undiminished, but adorned with new and brighter glory.

CATHOLIC EDUCATION.

We sometimes hear the statement that the Catholic Church is anxious to train her children in the knowledge and practices of the Faith, neglects the other branches of human knowledge. It is true that religion in the Catholic School is the main subject of the curriculum, but it is also true that it is by no means the only subject. To accuse the Church of one-sidedness in her educational policy and to thereby insinuate that her children are purposely kept in ignorance in order to make them all the more susceptible to her teachings, betrays lack of information as to essential facts. Statistics amply proves that among all institutions in the United States none excels the Catholic Church in the promotion of both elementary and higher education. The Census for the year 1920 shows that Catholics in this country were that year maintaining 8,738 schools of all kinds, with 2,106,027 students. In the maintenance of these schools the Catholic Church in the United States spends one-third of her entire income. How absurd, therefore, to impute to the Church hostility towards education and kindred movements.

But it is being said that the Catholic Church as such never encouraged education but was compelled to adopt some sort of educational system in order to compare favorably with secular or protestant organizations. The truth of the matter is that Catholic schools existed in this country long before any one thought of inaugurating the so-called system of public schools. The first school in our country was a Catholic school, opened in St .Augustine, Florida, in 1603, while the first non-Catholic school, the Dutch Reformed School, was opened in New York in 1633. When six years later, the first so-called common school was opened in Massachusetts, the Catholics already had 3 universities, 15 colleges, 30 academies, 7 normal schools, and more than 300 elementary schools in this country.

We know that those hostile to the Catholic faith maintain that the early Catholic schools were founded not by the Church, but by individuals, and that the former would never have consented to their establishment if she could have found ways and means to suppress them without exposing herself to the attacks of her enemies. But the truth of the matter is that practically all of these schools were founded by missionaries and priests, sent to this country with the approval of the Church, and, moreover, with the sanction of the pope himself. Furthermore, a number of religious orders were founded in this country that made it their business to extend educational facilities whenever and wherever possible. One example will suffice. The Sisters of Charity of Emmetsburg, Maryland, had 33 schools in operation before our public system made its first appearance.

The accusation that Catholic schools stress only religion and neglect to train their students in the secular branches, can best be refuted by actual facts. In "The George Washington Essay Contest" conducted in 1922 by *The Daily News* of New York, the first prize of $1,000.00 and the second of $500.00 were won by Catholic school pupils. Moreover, more than half of the twenty-five $50.00 prizes went to pupils of Catholic schools.

Again; in the Montana State Oratorical Contest in 1922, the first prize was bestowed on a student of St. Charles College, Helena, who, as the representative of his alma mater, thus successfully competed against every other college and university of the entire State.

Furthermore, in the Music Memory Contest in Cleveland in 1922, a student of Loudres Academy carried off the first prize. In fact, the pupils of Catholic schools have made such a good showing in the various contests held in this country that to enumerate all of them is well nigh an impossibility. Instead of referring to any more of the prize-winners, let me quote the opinion of a man who, even in the eyes of non-Catholics must be considered, a most impartial judge. I mean Mr. James Clancy, School Inspector of New York City. In a discussion of various school systems now extant in the United States, he made the following statements in the *New York Sun*, November 11, 1904: "For more than twenty years I have been familiar with the public schools and, as school inspector have paid particular attention to methods and results. Until recently, I never set a foot in a Catholic parochial school. When I did enter one,—it was with a feeling that it would be impossible to find anything to commend. But these schools are organized as systematically as are the public schools, with a Board of Directors, a Board of Examiners, teachers and superintendents. Each school has a supervisor or principal and a corps of class teachers, all holding certificates. "The president of George Washington University, in an article published in *The Chicago Examiner*, August 15, 1909, said: "The Catholic system of schools has been a great factor in the development and advancement of the Nation."

This is no idle boast, but a fact well-founded on experience. Secular education has achieved little. The Federal Council of (Protestant) Churches admitted that the public school system "is raising up the youth of America in spiritual illiteracy." Woodrow Wilson, while President of Princeton University, remarked: "We all know that the children of the last two decades in our schools have not been educated. With all our training, we have trained nobody. With all our instructing, we have instructed nobody."

What would our forefathers think if they were to hear such statements! They were a religious people. It was the Catholic Church that made the first efforts to preserve the religious atmosphere of those early days. She foresaw what would be the final result if religion were to be permanently separated from education. She therefore founded institutions that would fill both the religious and intellectual needs of her children. Even the Protestant churches seem now to awake to the correctness of the Church's position. They have started what is termed the Week-Day Religious School, though rather late, almost at a time when conditions got beyond their control.

It is therefore obvious that Catholics, instead of being attacked on account of their school system, should receive thanks. They should receive credit for what they have done, for it is their system of schools that has been a great factor in the development and advancement of the Nation.

THE POETIC BIBLE.

Jesse Lyman Hurlbut, a very devout and learned man, speaks of only five books as being strictly poetical. Job, Psalms, Proverbs, Ecclesiastes, and the Song of Solomon.

The book of Job, whose design is to enlarge men's views of the providence of God, contains some of the most magnificent poetry of the Old Testament.

The Psalms are a collection of sacred poetry gradually compiled between the time of Moses and the close of the Old Testament Canon. In this collection of songs the Holy Spirit surely witnesses to His own work. Each Psalm is full *of* sublime and pathetic utterances. No one can produce from the whole range of the world's literature prior to Christ, a second poem which makes the faintest approach to such Psalms as the 23d, the 25th, or the 103d, either in the mingled grandeur and tenderness of their conception of God, or the loving trustful fellowship with Him to which those writers attained.

In their own sphere, the Proverbs are as superior as the Psalms to anything of like character in the literature of other nations. By their truth and pungency many of them have become as "familiar as household words," even in circles where their source is utterly forgotten.

Ecclesiastes, commonly called "The Preacher" in the English version, appears to have been written with a view of showing the unsatisfactory nature of all earthly sources of delight, and the certainty of judgment. The practical conclusion is: "Fear God and keep His commandments."

Solomon's Song, called also the Song of Songs, or Canticles, is written in the nature of a dialogue between two lovers, and there is a chorus of the "Daughters of Jerusalem," who from time to time join in it. Quite a number of Bible students see in the book a mystical allusion to Christ and His bride, the Church.

These books do not, however, contain all the poetry that is in the Bible. Sometimes poems are introduced in the middle of historical books, as in the Patriarch's blessing (Gen. Chap. 49); the Song of Moses (Exodus Chap. 15); the Song of "the Bow" (2 Sam. 1, 19-27), etc. But whenever we find poetry, whether in the Old or in the New Testament, we find what is usually termed parallelism, that is the thought of one line is made to correspond with the thought of another, or several others. The Book of Job, with the exception of the first two and the last chapters, the Psalms, the Proverbs are written in this style.

We thus see that the Bible is not a single book, but, as Edmund Burke said, "an infinite variety of the most venerable and most multifarious literature," whose poetry is manifold in its designs and purposes. Some of its poetry varies from the wailing cry of the experiences of mundane wisdom and the eager speculations of philosophy.

Don't think that I am giving you merely the opinions of theologians. There are many men, and women, too, who, though no wise connected with the ministry, hold similar beliefs. Albert J. Beveridge, formerly U. S. Senator from Indiana and a lawyer of no mean repute, is the author of a book: "The Bible as Good Reading." Of Solomon he says: "Job is the great dramatic poem of the Bible and abounds in noble passages, lofty conceptions and overwhelming presentations of the majesty of the Creator. It is classed among the "Wisdom Books" on account of its lesson: that man is a creature too fleeting and too finite to question the justice of God of infinite wisdom and limitless power."

But the poetry of the Bible does not merely charm or delight; its real purpose is deeper. In it and through it the Spirit of God speaks to mortal man. The poetry of the Bible speaks to the ear and to the heart as no other poetry will. "Though I walk through the valley of the shadow of death I will fear no evil, for Thou art with me, Thy rod and Thy staff, they comfort me;" those words were repeated by his physician to Daniel Webster on his death-bed; and the great man faltered out, "That is what I want; Thy rod—Thy rod, Thy staff—Thy staff." They were the last words Daniel Webster spoke.

Immanuel Kant, the great German philosopher, a man of great learning and the originator of a philosophical system, which, though in many respects now rejected, at one time attracted the widest attention, said to his numerous students: "I have read and studied many books. But among all the books which I have read or studied, none have given me the consolation as the words of the 23d Psalm: "And though I walk through the valley of the shadow of death, I will fear no evil, for Thou art with me, Thy rod and Thy staff, they comfort me." Thousands of others have rendered similar testimonies. And in the face of such experiences could anyone say that the poetry of the Bible was written in vain?

In view of these facts how lamentable that vast numbers of people have neither eye nor ear for the grandeur and sublimity of the poetry of Holy Scripture. Yes,—some persons are even totally unacquainted with the poetical books and their contents, and, if they were made familiar with them, they would probably answer in the language of Albert J. Beveridge: "Why I never knew these things were in the Bible."

Of course we may occasionally come across passages we do not seem to understand, or words the exact meaning of which appears doubtful. But such facts should not deter us from becoming thoroughly familiar with the poetry of the Bible, always remembering that the Holy Spirit who inspired the several writers, will also guide and direct us in the interpretation of His messages if we had faith enough to invoke His assistance.

BREAKING AWAY FROM THE CHURCH.

Although the public school sentiment did not make its first appearance before 1820, yet it would be erroneous to assume that from that time on the Church lost its control over the education of American youth. Even when the battle for free State schools was at its heighth, the Lutheran parish school system, the Catholic parochial school, and many other educational institutions under the direct control of some church or belief, exerted still considerable influence. It is noteworthy, however, that already during the earlier periods of our history voices were raised in favor of separating school from church, and, thereby, as, for example, in New England, the church from the state. Still, the schools remained under church control until after the founding of our national government.

Up to the time of the outbreak of the Revolutionary War schools had been maintained chiefly for the purpose of disseminating religious knowledge. It is true that a few other subjects were also taught, but merely incidentally, and only then when the time needed for instructions in secular branches did not interfere with the chief purpose,—the promulgation of religious knowledge. When, however, the Declaration of Independence informed people that they had been "created equal" and that they had been "endowed by the Creator with certain inalienable rights, a new motive for education exerted itself.

As early as 1787, Thomas Jefferson stressed this new political motive for education. Col. Yancey, George Washington, John Hay, James Madison, John Adams, and many others of that early period, declared the religious motive for education to be no longer sufficient. It was obvious that, after the colonists had received a new political status and a new country had been created, education had to comprise more than merely an acquaintance with the Catechism and the Bible. To teach young America nothing else but "the principles of Christian Religion necessary to salvation," as had been in practice in the colony of Connecticut, would have made the young Nation short-lived, and eventually led to its downfall.

That, after the establishment of the Republic, a change in existing conditions, was imperative, is shown by the textbooks used in the schools. As long as the religious motive was predominant, American secular textbooks were not in use. If children had learned to read the Catechism and the Bible, they had, in the opinion of those religious "educators" covered the whole field of worthwhile knowledge. When, in 1690, the famous New England Primer made its first appearance, the school under the control of the Church of England were prohibited from its adoption.

As to the qualifications of teachers, really only one was required. In New England, the candidate had to be "sound in the faith." For teaching in one of the schools under the control of the Church of England the applicant had to give satisfactory proof that he had "received the Sacrament in some Anglican church within a year." If, after being installed as a teacher he should attend any other form of worship, he was disbarred and quite often imprisoned.

We thus see that as long as the religious motive prevailed, schools were maintained, not for the purpose of training children in the rudiments of practical knowledge, but to prepare them for membership in the Church. Had there been no churches, schools would have been superfluous.

Gradually, however, the old religious zeal died, especially when secular interests, for example such as preceded the Revolutionary War, became the chief topics of thought and conversation. And when, after the successful close of the conflict, a new era dawned upon the Western continent, new conditions brought into existence a new kind of education.

We should, however, err were we to think that the Declaration of Independence, ended the conflict between school and church. After the establishment of the free school system, a new battle ensued, the Church again raised its head in defense of her alleged right to dictate the educational policy of the State. Finally, though gradually, the Church was compelled to relinquish at least some of its power. A number of legislative acts were passed which still further hastened the break. Massachusetts, for example, in 1827, enacted a statute, which declared that school committees should "never direct to be used or purchased in any of the town schools any school books which were calculated to favor the tenets of any particular sect of Christians."

One of the most notable men championing the new conception of schools, was Horace Mann, who most ably defended them against the cry that "the public schools are godless schools." Notwithstanding all sorts of onslaughts by both the pulpit and the religious press, he continued his warfares nobly and courageously.

But even now the fight was not ended. It broke out anew in 1853, when the representatives of the Roman Catholic Church made a demand on the Massachusetts Legislature for a share of the school funds of that State. An amendment providing for the distribution of school funds among religious sects, was adopted in 1855. New Hampshire had settled the same question in 1792, and Connecticut in 1818. Other States were deluged with similar demands, but in 1840, the break, at least in this respect, was complete. Churches were barred in practically all States from sharing in the funds set aside for public education.

Of course, there is still some opposition against our system of public schools, chiefly on the part of the Church of Rome, but since the question of the public school funds has been settled, and our present system of free schools has developed beyond the keenest expectations of its earliest sponsors, and has thus shown its ability to maintain itself, notwithstanding the attacks of individual adherents to the religious motive or the Church in general, it stands to reason that the separation of Church and public education has been made complete for all time to come.

ADDRESS AT COUNTY FEDERATION BANKERS' MEETING.

There is no need for me to tell you how glad I am to be here tonight. These group meetings of our Association have come to be bright spots amid the routine of business, red-letter days to be looked forward to with pleasant anticipation. They are delightful for their social features and valuable as a means of forming new friendships and exchanging ideas.

The call of our president has brought together representatives from ten different counties of our State, and in these many localities a variety of conditions must exist which will illustrate almost every phase of the banking profession. While we certainly do not expect to spend all of our time in "talking shop," the opportunities for comparing experiences and views can by no means be neglected.

The banking world has its humors as well as its serious problems. It is said that the first banking transaction ever recorded was when Pharaoh received a check on the bank of the Red Sea. Since that time the children of Israel have figured largely in the banking world— in fact I hardly know how we would get along without them.

A Jewish clothing merchant whose business had not advanced

beyond the push-cart stage (he had but lately arrived in New York), went with a friend to a bank and with open-eyed wonder saw him sign a slip of paper and receive in exchange a large roll of bills from the cashier.

"How did you get that money, Ikey?" he asked.

"I borrowed it and gave my note for it."

"Can I do that, too?"

"Yes, certainly."

The peddler stepped up to the window and said to the cashier, "I want to borrow some money."

"How much do you want?" asked the cashier.

"How much have you got?" came the characteristic reply.

That Jewish emigrant's knowledge of banking was similar to that of a colored resident of Detroit, who occasionally lends a few dollars on good security, and who was asked to lend a neighboring cobbler thirty dollars on a note of hand running thirty days.

"S'pose dat note came due an' yo' hasn't de cash?" inquired the capitalist.

"But I will have."

"But s'posen yo' hasn't?"

The cobbler couldn't get around that, and was looking very serious, when the capitalist got a bright idea, and said:

"We can fix dat. Yo' make de note, yo' see. Yo' mought be good er yo' moghtn't. I's good, anyhow, an' we bofe knows it, 'kase here's de cash right here. Yo' make de note an' I'll back it. I knows mahself, yo' see, an' de cap'list dat won't lend money on his own 'dorsement hain't no business haid on him." And they fixed it that way.

There are few bankers who could not contribute a chapter to a volume of "Humors of the Inexperienced." A young wife who had just started a bank account and was enjoying the exhiliration of writing checks for her purchases came running into her bank one morning and indignantly announced that she had received a notice that her account was overdrawn.

"How much is it?" she asked.

"Twenty dollars."

"Then I'll just write you a check for the amount," she replied.

A man engaged in banking took his son into the bank, intending that this should be his business also. The young man got on very well until it came to the time when the annual examination of the books was to be made, when it turned out that there was a slight difference between the debit and the credit accounts. It did not amount to more than a fraction of a dollar, but the boy's father said to the clerks, "You must go over the books again. You know that we cannot have an error whatever in the accounts."

The son overheard the remark, and said, "Why, father, are you going to put them to all that trouble for a trifle? I will pay the money myself and let them off."

Upon which the father looked at the boy and said, "My son, you may leave the bank. It is not the kind of business you are fitted for. I will see that you are put into the ministry."

It is a wise father who knows his son, and a wise son who knows his father. A teacher asked a boy at school, "Johnnie, if your father borrowed from you one hundred dollars and should agree to pay you at the rate of ten dollars per week, how much would he owe you at the end of seven weeks?"

"One hundred dollars," said the boy.

"Johnnie, I'm afraid you don't know your arithmetic," said the teacher.

"Well," said the boy, "I may not know my arithmetic, but I know my father."

That boy had the last word, like the one in the following story, which shall also be my last word.

A minister was called to deliver a funeral sermon, but before beginning, the thought occurred to him that it might be advisable to learn what the last words of the departed had been. So he turned to one of the sons and asked:

"My boy, can you tell me what were your father's last words?"

"He didn't have none," the boy replied. "Ma was with him to the end."

THE HANDICAP OF POVERTY AND THE VALUE OF THRIFT AND CASH IN HAND.

Poverty is the great blight upon humanity through the ages; hand in hand with ignorance, disease and crime, it goads its victims through an existence barren of the refining influences of education, culture, and travel.

Such phrases as "Poor but honest," and "Poverty is no disgrace," have sometimes created an assumption that poverty is actually a virtue. Because a few men like Abraham Lincoln have risen to eminence, not *because of,* but *in spite of* poverty, proves no case for poverty as a requisite for greatness. Lincoln studied his half dozen books by the light of the burning logs, but how much better that masterly mind would have been prepared for the great problems of the future had he been blessed with the educational opportunities possessed by every one of the boys before me today.

Theorists in every generation have tried to cure poverty by legislation, to isolate the specific germ and apply a governmental cure-all in the form of socialistic schemes for the equal division of property. We are having an object lesson in the value of such theories in Bolshevist Russia at the present time. The trouble is that these experimenters begin at the wrong end—they deal with *distribution* instead of *production*, and the consequence is that Russia is on the verge of starvation, and is practically in a state of anarchy.

When a man has a family housed under a roof which he owns, he then becomes a citizen anxious for the maintenance of law and order; he does not wish anarchy to reign, which will be likely to destroy his property. If he has such a home partly paid for, and other payments ahead, he will be slow to vote for a strike, which must throw him out of work and endanger his ability to continue his payments. This shows us that thrift is the foundation of law and order, and of happiness as well.

And how is thrift to be cultivated? Not by reading books on political economy or by envying your neighbor the good things he possesses as the result of his labor, but only by *systematic saving* and *wise investment.*

Before you spend that dime, take a look at it and say to yourself: "This coin represents the interest for one day at 4 per cent (a good savings bank rate) on the sum of $912.50. If I can save one dime every day for seventeen and one-half years, and deposit it in a savings bank that pays 4 per cent interest, I will then have to my credit $912.50—enough to earn a dime a day for me."

This is the secret of wealth—the reproducing power of money put out at compound interest. If you save ten cents a day and get 4 per cent per year, compounded semi-annually, you will have:

In six months	$18 25
In one year	36 86
In five years	199 79
In ten years	443 31
In twenty years	1,102 03
In twenty-five years	1,543 15

Ten cents a day dropped into the bank when you are twenty, will enable you to interpose between yourself and the wolf more than $1,500 when you are fifty. Figure out for yourselves what fifteen cents a day, and twenty-five cents a day will amount to, compounding the interest semi-annually. Suppose your father had put away $100 in your name at your birth, with instructions that the interest be compounded twice a year,—how much would that amount to by now?

When Mary E. Sissons, of Harrington Township, New Jersey, was adjudged insane in 1896, she had $56,000 in the bank. When her guardian filed his report several years ago, it showed that the original $56,000 had grown in the twenty-two years to $396,221.01.

A thousand dollars invested at 6 per cent, with reinvestment of the interest, grows in a hundred years to $339,000. Invested at 8 per cent, in a hundred years it reaches the startling sum of $2,200,000.

As a people, we are wasteful and extravagant. Up to the present time, our land has abounded with nearly every comfort, and we have been led by the very abundance into lavish waste and foolish expenditure. The present high cost of living may teach us some very important economic lessons.

At every turn today you hear the remark, "A dollar is only worth fifty cents; I am only getting fifty cents' worth for every dollar I spend."

Why spend all your dollars, then? Especially when there are excellent indications that in a few years your dollar will again purchase 100 cents worth of goods?

Let us say that you have saved a hundred dollars. You undoubtedly have in mind the immediate spending of it on something you would like to have. But *don't do it*. You will only be getting fifty cents' worth for every dollar you spend, whereas perhaps in five years your dollar will bring you a full dollar's worth of value—you will have twice as much for your money, as well as the interest upon it in the meantime.

But in addition you will have the feeling of security which a substantial bank account gives to its possessor. Once you have had the experience of being a bank depositor you will never care to go back to careless and wasteful habits with your money. Your ambition will receive a new stimulus in the knowledge that you are laying the foundation for a successful career. If opportunities come to you, they can be accepted immediately.

Your experience in thrift will increase your happiness by removing the fear of want. This fear lies at the very heart of prosperity; it is the cloud that darkens good times. As long as the poor suffer from this worst evil of poverty, the country is sick with a disorder which sooner or later must declare itself.

The cure of poverty rests with the individual and not with the State or the nation. And in applying that cure you will not only be adding to your own store of happiness but indirectly helping everyone about you.

THE RELATIONSHIP OF MONEY TO THE EVANGELIZATION OF THE WHOLE WORLD.

Money is one of the cardinal facts of our civilization. It is the great object of endeavor, the great spring of power, the great occasion of discontent, and, improperly used, one of the great sources of danger. For Christians to apprehend their true relations to money, and the relations of money to the kingdom of Christ and its progress in the world, is to find the key to the problem of world evangelization.

Money is power in the concrete. It commands learning, skill, experience, wisdom, talent, influence. It represents the school, the college, the church, the printing press, and all evangelizing machinery. By means of it a man may at the same moment be founding a missionary church in South Dakota, translating the Scriptures in Africa, preaching the gospel in China, and distributing ten thousand Bibles in India.

Money is the modern miracle worker; it has a marvellous multiplying and transforming power. Sarah Hosmer of Lowell, Mass., though a poor woman, supported a student in the Nestorian Seminary, who became a preacher of Christ. Five times she gave fifty dollars, earning the money in a factory, and sent out five native pastors to Christian work. When more than sixty years old, she longed to furnish Nestoria with one more preacher of Christ; and, living in an attic, she took in sewing until she had accomplished her noble purpose. In the hands of this consecrated woman, money transformed the factory girl and seamstress into a missionary of the cross and then multiplied her power six-fold. The results of her consecrated devotion are written large in the history of missionary progress.

The wealth of the United States is stupendous, estimated on February 1, 1921, at $300,000,000,000, or $2,800 for every individual in the nation. Our position as the richest nation on the face of the earth lays on us a commensurate obligation. If our power is without a precedent, our responsibility is likewise without a parallel. Is not the lesson which God would have us learn so plain that he who runs may read? Has not God given us this matchless power in order that it may be applied in furthering his kingdom on the earth?

The kingdoms of this world will not become the kingdoms of our Lord until the money power has been Christianized. Talent has already been Christianized on a large scale. Architecture, arts, constitutions, schools, and learning have been largely Christianized. But the money power, which is the most effective and potent of all, is only beginning to be; though with promising tokens of a final complete reduction to Christ and the uses of his kingdom. That day, when it comes, will be the morning of the new creation.

Is it not time for that day to dawn? If we would Christianize our Anglo-Saxon civilization, which is to spread itself over the earth, has not the hour come for the Church to teach and live the doctrines of God's word touching possessions? Their general acceptance on the part of the Church would involve a reformation scarcely less important in its results than the great Reformation of the sixteenth century.

What is needed is not simply an increased scale of giving, an enlarged estimate of "the Lord's share," but a radically different conception of our relations to our possessions. Most Christians need to discover that they are not proprietors, apportioning their own, but simply trustees or managers, stewards of the manifold bounty of God.

Christians generally hold that God has a thoroughly real claim on some portion of their income, possibly a tenth, more likely no definite proportion; but some small part, they acknowledge, belongs to Him and they hold themselves in duty bound to use it for Him. This meager and un-Christian view has sprung apparently from a misconception of the Old Testament doctrine of tithes.

God did not, for the surrender of a part, renounce all claim to the remainder. The Jew was taught, in language most explicit and oft-repeated, that he and all he had belonged absolutely to God. "Behold, the heaven and the heaven of heavens is the Lord's, thy God, and the earth also, with all that therein is." (Deut. 10:14.) "The earth is the Lord's, and the fullness thereof; the world, and they that dwell therein." (Ps. 24:1.) "The silver is mine, and the gold is mine, saith the Lord." (Hag. 2:8.)

God's claim to the whole rests on exactly the same ground as his claim to a part. As the Creator, he must have an absolute ownership in all his creatures. Manifestly, if God has absolute ownership in us, we can have absolute ownership in nothing whatever. Does one-tenth belong to God? Then ten-tenths are his. He did not one-tenth create us and we nine-tenths create ourselves. He did not one-tenth redeem us and we nine-tenths redeem ourselves. His ownership in us is no joint affair. We are in partnership with Him. All that we are and have is utterly His, and His only.

The Christian has given himself to God, and is under obligations to apply every power, whether of mind, body, or possessions, to God's service. He is bound to make that service as effective as possible. Certain expenditures upon himself are necessary to his highest growth and greatest usefulness, and are, therefore, not only permissible, but obligatory. All the money which will yield a larger return of usefulness in the world, and greater good to God's kingdom, by being spent on ourselves and our families than being applied otherwise, is used for the glory of God, and is better spent than if it had been given to missions. And whatever money is spent on self that would have yielded larger returns of usefulness, if applied otherwise, is misapplied; and, if it has been done consciously, is a case of embezzlement.

The general acceptance, by the Church, of the Christian principle that every penny is to be used in the way that will best honor God, would cause every channel of benevolence to overflow its bank, and occasion a blessed freshet of salvation throughout the world. "But," says some one, "that principle demands daily self-denial." Undoubtedly; and that fact is the Master's seal to its truth. "If any man will come after me, let him deny himself, and take up his cross and follow me." (Luke 60:23.)

TOASTMASTER'S ADDRESS AT BANKERS' ASSOCIATION.

When Andrew Jackson overthrew the Second Bank of the United States, the American banking system was broken up into many small institutions possessing little desire or power of helpful coöperation. Large banks with numerous branches, such as exist in Canada and Scotland, have been practically unknown in the United States.

A central institution, enjoying Federal patronage and serving to unify banking interests, has been a virtual impossibility since Nicholas Biddle rashly ventured upon a trial of strength with the masterful statesman from Tennessee.

National banks, State banks, private banks, trust companies, competing vigorously for public favor, have met tolerably well the needs of the country in fair weather; but in times of stress and storm these various institutions have been unable to oppose a united front to the forces of financial disruption.

For twenty years following the Civil War, the national banks, which stood at the head of the banking system and possessed the exclusive power to issue circulating notes, found this privilege sufficiently remunerative to gain for them a decided predominance over the banks of deposit and discount incorporated by the several States, but after the early eighties, various causes reduced the profit derived from the issue of notes and decreased the attractiveness of a Federal charter.

The State banks of discount multiplied rapidly in the Mississippi Valley, and especially in the South and West. In general, the laws under which they are formed are more liberal in their provisions concerning loans on real estate, and permit the establishment of banks with smaller capitals than are required under the Federal statutes. This last circumstance accounts for the rapid growth of State associations in communities where a capital of 25,000, the minimum fixed for national banks, is too large to be employed with the greater profit.

Private banks are very numerous in most parts of the United States. In most sections their resources are small, and their average capital in many States does not exceed ten or fifteen thousand dollars. Our large cities, however, have many private bankers who are conducting enterprises of great extent and importance. Besides receiving deposits and making discounts, these firms frequently do a brokerage business and deal in foreign exchange. Many of them have gained their greatest reputation and profits from promoting, consolidating, or reorganizing large corporations.

In recent years, a new class of institutions has forced its way into the field of American banking. Trust companies have existed in the United States for nearly a century, but up to thirty or forty years ago their number was small and the scope of their operations was restricted. Originally they were formed to act as trustees of estates and to execute other trusts, while they often conducted a safe-deposit business.

With the growth of corporations, trust companies began to act as transfer agents, or as trustees under mortgage deeds executed to secure corporation bonds. Today, besides receiving time deposits, they accept deposits that are subject to instant withdrawal by check; and they make extensive loans, generally upon collateral security.

To their original business, therefore, they have added the ordinary banking functions, and the result has been that trust companies have multiplied rapidly, especially in the financial centers.

In the ordinary discount and deposit business, the national banks still predominate, but their supremacy is challenged by the competition of other institutions. State banks appeal to the needs of certain sections of the country; private bankers maintain an important position, especially in financing corporate enterprises; and trust companies are constantly increasing the scope of their enterprises.

The enactment of the Federal Reserve Law completely revolutionized our money system, and came just in time to prevent a financial panic and preserve the credit of the nation at the outbreak of a worldwide war which suddenly destroyed the existing system of financial and commercial exchanges all over the world. This law, which places the currency under control of the Government, renders financial panics impossible, for the necessary amount of money to tide over any stringency flows into circulation automatically from the Reserve Banks and the public does not know that anything unusual has happened.

The marvellous development of American industry in recent years has increased very decidedly the demands upon our banking system. To no small extent this demand for additional capital has been met by the establishment of new institutions, particularly by the formation of trust companies; but in a much larger measure it has occasioned an increase in the resources of existing banks.

The increased capital of the larger banks has been secured in many instances by subscriptions from the existing stockholders, but in other cases it has come from the consolidation of two or more institutions.

In addition to these centralizing tendencies, every effort has been made to secure coöperation on the widest possible scale, through arrangements designed to unify the world of finance. The larger life insurance companies have become interested in various banks of trust companies; and their officers, in a purely private capacity, are influential in many other institutions.

Private banking houses are represented among the owners and managers of national and State associations, while the good offices of influential capitalists have been enlisted as far as practicable. As a prominent banker has stated, ''We now have skill and resources combined, with a strength never before seen in the United States, and perhaps never in the markets of Europe."

EXECUTIVE ABILITY.

The call of the business world is for the man who knows. If also he is a man who thinks and works, a thousand doors of opportunity swing wide before him. He has but to choose, to enter, to command.

Everyone was born to achieve something worth while. Science and experience both declare that the average man can train himself to do finer, bigger things than the man of genius ordinarily accomplishes. More than half the men who have gone beyond you in your line of work are probably less gifted than you are. They have merely learned where their greatest power lay, then learned how to develop, train and use it,—in other words, to acquire executive ability.

Scientists tell us that the brain of a Shakespeare, a Napoleon, or a Lincoln does not differ in chemical substance from ours. These men simply worked their brains beyond the average. Not the cells of a man's brain, but the sinews of his ambition put him high on the world's honor roll of fame.

Although some men are born with greater executive ability than others, it is a fact of observation that great skill in getting things done comes more from constant practice and earnest study than from inherited ability. Some men make more out of the odds and ends of opportunities, which many carelessly throw away, than others get out of the big chances of a lifetime. The thing we build depends on the way we handle the material as well as upon the material itself.

A celebrated executive attributed much of his success to strict adherence to a few simple methods. Early in life he had formed the habit of making careful notes covering all ideas of an important nature occurring to him both during and after business hours. These notes were later dictated to his secretary, who classified them and prepared the way for the development and execution of the plans suggested. Much mental effort was thus saved by this plan of capturing stray ideas. Each day's work was scheduled as nearly as possible, and an effort was made to adhere to the program thus arranged.

One of the first things this official learned was that manufacturing and other costs may sometimes be materially reduced by increasing the rate of wages paid the employees. In one of his plants, output had been increased seventy per cent largely as a result of a thirty per cent advance in wages. In all branches of the business, it was his policy to keep a careful record of each employee, making frequent and accurate notes of the worker's gains, losses, virtues and faults.

Another plan which he adopted was that of offering rewards to his workmen for useful ideas for improving the quality and quantity of the goods manufactured. This scheme brought to light a number of valuable methods that later were worked into practical inventions, saving time and money for the company and bringing a reward to the ingenious workman.

Most so-called managers do only the work of a foreman. The latter is employed chiefly to do routine work in directing others, while the manager is employed to be more than a boss,—he is expected to turn out original ideas and plans. Too many managers are paid for merely holding down a job, whereas the amount of their salary should be determined by the quantity of the work they turn out.

It is unfortunate that up to the present time we have not been able to standardize mental processes in the same way as we have physical processes; however, it is now an accepted fact that a person is efficient only in proportion to how much and how fast he can think.

Time can be saved by reserving the best hours of each business day for the hardest tasks. Efficiency experts state that a man's mind is at its best between eight and eleven o'clock in the morning. That is then the time to do the difficult work of organizing, creating and planning. It is also a good idea for an executive to arrange his duties so as to alternate different kinds of tasks.

Perhaps nothing causes greater waste of time and effort on the part of executives than the practice of doing many pieces of detail work that can be done just as well by one of the employees. Many a man with a splendid mind works at half efficiency because he has not learned to dismiss worry and discontent from his thoughts, even during the hours when he is engaged on the most important duties.

The men who accomplish the greatest amount of work each day have become proficient in the art of allotting the minimum amount of time for each operation in the day's work and then striving to reduce this minimum in actual practice. The best kind of schedule is the one that assigns a certain time each day for the performance of a special task.

An effort should be made to train each employee to become a critic of his own work. One way to cause a worker to take pride in his accomplishments is to entrust him on certain occasions with special tasks requiring a sense of personal responsibility. Special talent in employees should be watched for and recognized. Whenever it is possible the worker should be given some kind of daily task in addition to his regular duties so that he will have an opportunity to spend a part of his time in working along the line in which he is most adept.

The wise executive makes ample provision for the comfort and health of his employees by providing abundant light, pure air and water, healthful and nourishing lunches and efficient medical attendance. The modern tendency is toward making a manufacturing establishment a great coöperative concern where the success of the company is a vital interest of each employee. In such an organization, the executive ability of the manager has the most ample field for expression.

THE GOLDEN RULE.

Although the Golden Rule is almost as old as the race itself, for, rightly considered, it is the primitive command of God in the hearts of all nations, yet it was through the instrumentality of the Great Teacher that it was rediscovered and brought to light, in a more positive form and with new authority.

Unfortunately, Americans as well as other peoples, have not always striven to obey the commands of the Master as laid down by Him in the Sermon on the Mount. It is noteworthy, however, that since the close of the Great War, and especially during the various industrial upheavals that have come to us within the last few years, frequent reference has been made to the Golden Rule as the only effective remedy to do away with strife, discord, and enmity both among nations and among individuals. The strange thing, however, is that many of those who talk about the Golden Rule, do so without really knowing what they are advocating.

What is the Golden Rule? It is easier to see by examples than by tedious deductions what the rule really means. Suppose a tramp wants you to give him your house or a lazy man wants you to turn all your property over to him. Are you really supposed to grant these wishes? Or how about the criminal who wishes the judge to let him go free or the boy who asks his father to cease restraining him? Or, to be still more definite, we will suppose that someone, while passing the jail, is hailed by a burly fellow behind the bars, who asks the passer-by to come back during the night and bring him a good file or saw so that he can break out and again mingle with his fellows. Should the man behind the bars have his wish granted? Could it not be said that if the passer-by were in the prisoner's place, he would surely like to be free, and that, since we are to do unto others as we would like them to do unto us, the jail-bird has a moral right to expect the man to bring him the tools wherewith he could gain his freedom? The answer is simple. The Golden Rule does not demand fulfillment of wishes of this kind. These things are not to be given. But the rule does command us to do what would be fair, wise, and best to have done to us in the same circumstances.

We hear much of the Golden Rule in business. President Harding, in his last address in his home town before leaving for Washington, said: "If you blend in your lives the consciousness of service, you have wrought the greatest thing in the world," and service is carrying out the Golden Rule in our everyday lives and in business. Hence our obligation to assist in establishing justice, in promoting domestic tranquility, and in securing for ourselves and our posterity all the blessings of liberty.

We hear much about "drives." Whatever we may think of them, we can scarcely get away from the fact that they point to some lessons, which when applied in one other direction might fill one of the needs of this whole business world of ours.

I wish that we might have a day or a week set aside when the thoughts of business and working people throughout this great country could for one day or for one week be riveted upon the Golden Rule. I would call such a day or such a week "Golden Rule Day" or "Golden Rule Week." I would hang in the window of every home and in the window of every store and factory a motto something like this: "This is Golden Rule Week; we propose to conduct the affairs of this house during this week upon the basis of the Golden Rule."

There is a certain psychology in centering our thoughts for a given day or week upon a great principle, which will come nearer to solving our great economic problems than any other.

You might say: "Why not do this for 365 days, during the year?" It is absolutely sound in theory, but we know the psychology of the drive for riveting our attention for a given period upon a specific thing, which slips by us if it is before us all the time.

Just think what would happen in America, if for one whole week of seven complete days a great majority of the people should, in every transaction, stop a moment before they entered into it and think of conducting that particular piece of effort to its finish on the basis of treating everybody involved exactly as they themselves would like to be treated? What a revolution it would bring about in this country!

Don't consider me a visionary, or a mere theorist formulating plans without practical value. That the Golden Rule can be applied, and is being applied, by some industrial concerns, is a fact known to all who have given the matter both thought and study. Let me give you one concrete example. More could be adduced, but one will suffice to show that the application of the Golden Rule is no impossibility. In the National Cash Register Company, of Dayton, Ohio, as well as in many other large progressive industries, there is no spirit but that "big family" spirit which all right-minded employers strive to cultivate. It is in an equal degree assuring to those who pin their faith and hope to the principles upon which American institutions were founded, to know that in these great organizations the flowers of loyalty and coöperation are ever blooming more abundantly. These outstanding examples show that it is not impossible under the present industrial system for capital and labor to work harmoniously together for common good. They point the way for all industry to the happy solution of the capital-labor problem, which is possible through wise and unselfish management.

I know someone may say: "But it is so hard." Why should it be hard to do that which it pays big dividends to do? I am not speaking of cost dividends alone. It is the only way to get and keep a maximum of friends and a clear conscience. But it does not exclude material profits. On the contrary it vastly enhances them. It follows that it is expensive to hate; in fact, no one can afford to hate. Love is so much better than hate. For it pays to love and to live to love.

WHY PEACE IS BETTER THAN WAR.

There is a celebrated painting entitled "They Shall Beat Their Swords Into Ploughshares" that gives a vision of that coming time in the history of the world which was predicted by the poet Tennyson:
"When the war-drums throb no longer, and the battle-flags are furled,
In the Parliament of Man, the Federation of the World."
Is such a time possible in the evolution of nations, and is it more desirable than the present state of armed watchfulness, when the god of war seems continually ready to shake his iron dice and plunge the peoples of earth into another frightful struggle such as the one from which we have just emerged?

Let us look at the question first from the standpoint of expense— the most practical phase of the subject. The latest estimates of the total cost of the World War to all nations involved place the cost at approximately two hundred and thirty-five billion dollars, which is considerably more than the entire estimated wealth of the United States.

The United States was in the war eighteen months, during which brief period, according to official data made public on July 1, 1921, the cost to us was $50,168,625,707. The Civil War debt on July 1, 1865, was in round numbers $2,500,000. From July 1, 1865, to July 1, 1922, is fifty-seven years—more than half a century—and $600,000 of the original war debt still remains unpaid. If it has taken the country more than half a century to pay only two billions of dollars of its Civil War debt of two and one-half billions of dollars, how long will it take us to pay the present war debt of fifty billions of dollars—at the same rate of progress, one thousand, six hundred and seventy-five years! Quite a burden this for eighteen months of participation in a European war. It is quite certain that the great-grandchildren of the men who participated in the World War will still be paying heavy taxes in the effort to reduce its crushing costs.

We have come out of the war with victorious arms, but now in common with the other nations of the world we realize that the cost was staggering. When Pyrrhus, king of Epirus, was congratulated on his victory over the Romans at Asculum, he replied, "Another such victory and we are ruined." The doom of war is written in the frightful burdens which it imposes upon the present and future generations. It is now admitted that the bulk of the ten billion dollars which the American Government loaned to the Allied nations during the war is practically lost.

The railroads of our country are staggering under the effect of the strain of war time and neglect of upkeep. Increased freight rates have paralyzed the building trades and imposed high prices upon every consumer of the commodities of life. What is the teaching of these sobering facts and figures—in what direction lies the path of safety if we are to avoid a general collapse of the social and economic structure of our civilization, which even now seems threatening to engulf all of Europe? Evidently it is a return to the arts of peace, and the enactment of such international agreements as will make war impossible.

The first important move in this direction after the World War was the International Conference on the Limitation of Armament held at Washington on November 12, 1921, to February 6, 1922, which was undoubtedly one of the most momentous deliberative assemblies which ever convened on the face of the earth.

This conference agreed to seven treaties, the first and most important of which was the naval limitation treaty, by which the United States, Great Britain, Japan, France and Italy agree to convert or scrap sixty-eight capital battleships, and so to limit future construction that, after a ten year holiday, their first-line naval strength will remain at 525,000 tons for the United States and Great Britain each, 315,000 tons for Japan, and 175,000 tons each for France and Italy.

This conference of nine great nations of the world accomplished an achievement which will give new hope to humanity and will mark the beginning of a new and better era in history. It will help to lift from the shoulders of hundreds of millions of people the crushing burdens of taxation to support vast military and naval establishments, and will turn the money thus saved into the avenues of production, manufacture, commerce, invention, and educational and social advancement.

As a great object lesson in the possibility of coöperative international relationships, it has set a new standard for the world, a standard from which there can be no retreat. As never before, the world now understands the potential dangers of war lurking in colonial expansion, closed markets, preferential tariffs, spheres of influence, and economic penetration, as well as the perils of secret diplomacy, but having weighed the costs of war against the maximum gains from all of these sources of national aggrandizement, is ready to turn the war god out of doors.

The waste of militarism is awful in its extent. The soldier produces nothing and adds nothing to the wealth of the country, but is only a consumer, and while we have heard the dictum, "The best guarantee of peace is to be prepared for war," if there is to be no war, necessarily there must be peace, and a reign of law binding upon the nations will put an end to war and bring about the era of universal peace.

MEMBERSHIP TALK ON THE SOCIETY OF VETERANS OF FOREIGN WARS OF THE UNITED STATES.

Every American citizen who has served in the defense of his country either on land or sea is entitled to public recognition of his patriotism and to the benefits to be derived from association with his comrades. Such benefits can only be secured to the fullest extent by membership in an organization designed for the advancement and protection of America's soldiers and sailors.

Such an organization is the Society of Veterans of Foreign Wars of the United States, which is the only national society composed exclusively of veterans of the wars and campaigns conducted by the United States of foreign soil and in foreign waters.

The Veterans of Foreign Wars had its beginnings in five cities, Columbus, Denver, Pittsburgh, Altoona, and Philadelphia. The American Veterans of Foreign Service, the parent organization, was formed at Columbus on September 23, 1899, and on October 10th of the same year was chartered by the State of Ohio. This society was active until 1905, when it amalgamated with a society of similar name formed in Pennsylvania several years before.

The Colorado Society, Army of the Philippines, was formed in Denver on December 12, 1899, and in the following year became national. Early in 1901 a group of Foreign Service men in Altoona, Pa., formed a society, and on October 13th of the same year another group formed a similar society in Pittsburgh. This was called the Society of Philippine War Veterans, but the name was later changed to Foreign Service Veterans. In the summer of 1902 there was formed in Philadelphia the Society of American Veterans of the Philippine, Cuban and China Wars. The following year the three Pennsylvania groups met at Altoona and formed a United Society which took the name of American Veterans of Foreign Service and, in 1905, amalgamated with the Ohio society of the same name.

The Army of the Philippines and the American Veterans of Foreign Service gained in strength and prominence until 1913, when at Denver they amalgamated and became the present organization of

Veterans of Foreign Wars of the United States, which thus became the first, and has remained the only society composed exclusively of veterans of more than one war or campaign.

The objects of the Society are fraternal, patriotic, historical and educational; to preserve and strengthen comradeship among its members; to assist worthy comrades; to perpetuate the memory and history of our dead, and to assist their widows and orphans; to maintain true allegiance to the government of the United States of America, and fidelity to its Constitution and laws; to foster true patriotism; to maintain and extend the institution of American freedom; and to preserve and defend the United States from all her enemies, whomsoever.

This is a creed to which any patriotic American can subscribe; it is broad enough to give full play to the aspirations and ideals of the most energetic and philanthropic. Its sheltering arms stretch out to protect the weak and destitute, and it believes that the best is none too good for those who have offered their best in the service of the Republic.

The Veterans of Foreign Wars is the coming Grand Army of America. The Grand Army of 1861-5 soon will gather around its last camp fires, and its flags and trophies will hang in empty halls. But the mantle of the fathers has fallen upon the sons, and the glories of Gettysburg and Appomatox have found their parallel in San Juan Hill, Manila Bay, Chateau-Thierry, Belleau Wood, and the Forest of the Argonne.

Today the South and North know each other as never before. On many battlefields we learned to respect the courage, patriotism, devotion and tenacity, of which both sections have given so many examples. We have all been taught the inestimable value of our Union. We have seen that America united commands the deference of the world. We now understand how much each section of the Republic contributes to the prosperity of the other. We comprehend at last that it is the destiny of this union of States to establish a commonwealth of freemen in which the principles announced by the Declaration of Independence and embodied in our Constitution have provided a government for a great nation, stronger than empires upheld by a million bayonets, and contributing more to the welfare of its people than any fabric ever before constructed by human hands.

Because of the principles and ideals for which its members have fought, the diversity of the service represented, and the fact that the soldiers and sailors who compose its membership are those of the world's greatest republic, the Veterans of Foreign Wars of the United States is destined to become the greatest veteran organization of all time.

Affiliation with such a Society not only reflects honor upon the individual member, but helps to advance and perpetuate the principles for which he offered his services to his country. The Veterans of Foreign Wars of the United States represents true Americanism, the doctrine of Roosevelt—one flag, one country, one language,—and is tolerant, non-partisan, and non-sectarian.

In connecting yourself with this organization, you can be assured that it will do all in its power to aid the service and ex-service man. The organization is controlled by its membership and its elective officers, there being no stockholders, and no part of its revenue accrues to any private individual, all funds being devoted to the purposes for which it was formed, which are especially those of educating its members in the principles of true Americanism and rendering aid and relief to service and ex-service men and their dependents.

There is no other rank and file organization like the Veterans of Foreign Wars of the United States, and if you have seen foreign service beneath the American flag, you should be a member, because your comrades need you, and because you need the organization.

FUTURE DEMANDS OF AMERICAN MANHOOD.

While it may be true that the American manhood of the future will be characterized by some entirely new traits, it is also true that it will have to place a still greater emphasis upon its present traits.

If American institutions are to survive, our manhood must be characterized by a greater regard for the day set apart by God Himself. Hon. William H. Seward said, "The ordinances which require the observance of one day in seven, and the Christian faith which hallows it, are our chief security for all civil and religious liberty."

Don't think that I expect the men of the future to display a zeal for Puritan simplicity, or that I urge a revival of the "Blue Laws." Far be it from me to advocate any such measures! Still, it will be well for us not to forget the admonitions of Daniel Webster: "Sunday is nature's law as well as God's. No individual or nation, habitually disregarding it, has failed to fall upon disaster and grief."

Economy will be another characteristic of the men of the future. The war has made most of us spendthrifts, to whom it seems nigh impossible to return to the road of long ago. Yet, no matter how many self-denials it will cost us, we shall have to live differently, that is, more economically. Extravagance has turned the heads of many; of young and old, of men and women, of rich and poor. No wonder, the number of divorces granted is out of proportion to that of marriages contracted.

Again; the Americans of the future will be loyal men. True; we already have in our midst people who are firm believers in loyalty. They talk about it; they preach it; they advocate, but, at the same time, are not aware that real loyalty is impossible without the coöperation of every citizen. It is true, some sort of loyalty has always had a place in practically every community; every city, town, or village has been so fortunate as to have at least a few citizens that stood for American ideals; that did their country's bidding even if severely hampered in its execution. But the new loyalty which I am advocating, is more exacting and more universal. It calls on every man, young and old, rich and poor, to put the hand to the plow and to keep it there, and brands every slacker as a derelict and deserter. During the war, we heard much about universal liability to service. Every community that wishes to prosper must adopt a similar principle. It must enlist every man in its campaigns. Let me illustrate what I have in mind. We read of the world's decisive battles, in which great questions were settled, questions that had agitated men for centuries. How were these battles won? Was it by allowing each soldier to march when he pleased, to fight when he felt like fighting, to undergo privations when it suited him? Was it by armies marching scattered or perhaps in the wrong direction, by soldiers disregarding the commands of their superiors? No battle could be won in such a way. Different conditions must prevail in order to obtain a victory. Read history and you will find shoulder to shoulder against the enemy. They had only one aim, and that aim was supreme. Their eyes were fixed upon their commander, anxious to hear his voice and do his bidding. They flew to their country's rescue with filial zeal and affection, resolved to partake its sufferings, and to die in its defense. This is loyalty in action, fidelity to a noble cause. It rests upon the same principle as patriotism. The men of the future will be both loyal and patriotic.

The future American manhood must be dependable. The business of the future will entail so many complex responsibilities that an employer will not be able to have around him a single employee whom he could not trust to perform duties assigned to him. There will be enough to worry about without having to worry as to whether this employee or the next employee could be depended upon to do his part. It will be much more important to be dependable than to be smart. Smartness or cleverness without dependability will be an asset no employer will any longer buy; in fact, it is not an asset, but a liability.

The American manhood of the future will do its share towards the rejuvenation of the world. Since the war, and beginning with the wild rush for economic and political advantage as the fruits of victory, the nations have been bent more upon getting all they could, than upon making necessary concessions in the interest of world prosperity. Their efforts have not been without military gestures and the rattling of swords. Doubt, distrust and jealousy and a selfish wish to perpetuate old institutions and to consolidate new gains, have moved the leaders of many peoples. Each has sought to live within itself, and whenever possible to throw up obstacles against its neighbor's attempt to heal up old wounds and to enjoy the fruits of rights and privileges.

If there is to be progress and prosperity, it must come through our men, through their future associations and coöperation. Barriers must be stricken down. The arteries of commerce must be freely opened. It rests upon us and those that come after us to see to it that unjust trading restrictions are abolished. In a word, the future American manhood will be asked to correct financial systems, and to enlarge and extend the commercial processes which facilitate the exchange of goods.

The greatest danger to many Americans always has been that they, instead of being the molders, have become molded. God has crowned us with the kingship of our own lives. Will American manhood surrender the crown, the robes, the scepter? Will they become mere crocksmere potsherds?

WOMEN IN THE MODERN BUSINESS WORLD.

There are a great many qualifications that are necessary to a successful business woman. But first among these qualifications I would place ambition. This may seem a curious statement at first, but have you ever paused to consider how few business women are really ambitious? Unless a woman is willing to devote the very best part of her mind and energy to her business, she can never rise to great success.

Ambition helps her first of all to overcome her natural timidity. A young woman in entering employment in an office is apt to discount her own ability and to magnify that of her employer. With a lump in her throat, of which her manner is too likely to give evidence, she knocks at the door of enterprises that seem to her to present real opportunities, and from many of these she is turned away disheartened.

Life is a harsh fact for the average woman who enters the business world. Only the woman who realizes this truth at the very beginning of her career can go on gallantly and lose none of her charm and loveliness that is woman's birthright, if not her real reason for being.

The price we women pay for business success is not a slight one. The easy acceptance of the good things of life that the non-working woman possesses we lose very early in the game. And it is quite as hard to maintain enthusiasm over business and the people with whom one is thrown in intimate contact as it is to be enthusiastic over the daily round of household duties which once seemed the be-all and end-all of woman's existence.

What one must retain is a passion for work, and for the accom-

8

plishment of real things, and for making oneself constantly a more useful, a more intelligent, a more idealistic human being.

You remember Christian Rosetti's wistful poem which begins:

"Does the road wind uphill, all the way?
Yes, to the very top."

But the top, however small and unimportant one may feel there, is worth a life of toil to reach.

It is ambition, coupled with a deep-seated pride and determination, that makes a woman seize and cultivate every opportunity for self-development. She must study the minutest details of the business in which she is engaged, and be willing to begin at the bottom in order to learn these details, and through mastery to rise above them. Honesty and common sense, which are her natural attributes, are two of the rarest and most valuable things in the business world.

That popular and time-worn phrase, "a woman's place is in the home," has a pleasant sound to any woman's ears. But women cannot see the justice of the phrase when offered as an excuse for their not working when they know that they must work.

Nothing is more irritating to women than the placid and reiterated assurances of the world that women are a highly specialized sex, the sex that must be sheltered and protected, the while the world makes no economic recognition of this specialization.

To be told that she must stay in the house because she is a woman; to know that she must work for a living because she is a human being; and to be told that she can't have a position because she is a woman—how many women have had this experience! A woman's place *is* in the home, but unfortunately there aren't enough homes provided for her, and so eleven million women in the United States engage themselves in gainful occupations.

I know of one girl who began work as a stenographer in a manufacturing firm at the age of sixteen. For some time her only task seemed to be to take dictation and transcribe notes. This she did for a while until the slipshod methods all around her began to get on her nerves. Even to her untrained mind, things were not going as they should. Gradually she realized that the cause of the chaos was that the goods that were being made were apparently sold at prices fixed without any regard to cost.

At this point she began to use the brains God has given her and to use her time when not taking dictations in talking to the foreman and superintendent of the plant. She investigated the stockroom, talked to the salesmen, and finally worked out a system by which the cost of production could be figured out quickly and accurately.

She was fond of figures, and devised slips for the various departments through which the goods would go during the process of manufacture, that recorded the amount and kind of materials, and the time spent on all orders in each department. It was not an easy task. Not only did it require hard work and originality, but at every step she had to fight tradition and the fact that she was a woman.

But somehow she plodded on, and by the time she had been with the firm a year, she had accomplished a revolution in its business. The house was actually on a business basis. In fixing its prices it no longer guessed. It had the detailed and aggregate cost of manufacture for each pound and for every one of the many varieties of its products. The overhead charges were figured to a nicety, and it could arrange its sales prices to produce any percentage of profit it deemed justifiable and desirable.

I quote this case as an instance of the value of ambition and initiative to women in the business world. It is the difference between success and mediocrity. The firm by which the girl was employed woke up and offered her an attractive salary. But she realized her capabilities and was launched on a successful career. If her story has been an inspiration to anyone present, my point has been made— ambition is the key to success for the woman in the business world.

ADDRESS AT LAYING OF CORNER STONE OF WORLD WAR MEMORIAL.

Ladies and Gentlemen:

It is with considerable emotion, as well as with great appreciation, that I have accepted the invitation to address you on this occasion.

The hour is one dedicated to memories and informed with the spirit of patriotic devotion. Our loyal citizens have gathered here to dedicate a shrine that shall speak to future generations of the loyalty to their nation of this State's heroic sons.

For many who are here today, interest in these ceremonies is tinged with a profound sadness that yet is a proud sorrow and borders on the realms of joy. For since all must die, how noble and beautiful a thing it is to die for an undying cause and under the approving eye of history. So fell those for whom our hearts mourn today, and history has no fairer or more inspiring page than that which records the splendor of their devotion and the completeness of their sacrifice.

They thus are the subjects not only of our pride and love, but even of our envy. For it may not be given to us so to close the volume of our years and to write our names high upon the imperishable scroll of fame. Chateau Thierry, Belleau Wood and the Forest of the Argonne—these are names that will forever stand as synonyms for the splendid courage and irresistible energy of the American soldier —for a courage that stormed up to the very gates of death and snatched the fruits of victory from the jaws of defeat.

The autocratic central powers of Europe had perfected the greatest and most terrible fighting machine that ever existed on the face of the earth, to which the Macedonian phalanx and the bronzed legions of Julius Cæsar were but as pygmies, but in the grim determination written in the pale, set faces of the American soldier was written the doom of autocratic government and military tyranny.

Millions had bridged the watery gap of three thousand miles, and the tramp, tramp, tramp of their march echoed throughout the length and breadth of the old world. Millions more were on the way, an endless stream as irresistible as the thunderous waves that break on some rock bound coast. A series of memorable and blood-bought victories astonished and electrified the world at the fighting qualities of the American soldier. The German salient was wiped out, the German line of communications cut, and the towering armed colossus of military domination tottered and crashed to the ground.

In ancient Greece, there was a band of three hundred cavalry in the Theban army which proved a terror to any enemy with whom they were called to fight. They were companions, who had bound themselves together with a vow of perpetual friendship, determined to stand together until the last drop of their blood was spilled. They were called "The Sacred Battalion," and united by affection for the state and fidelity to one another, they accomplished marvels that seem incredible. Such was the spirit which animated the American soldier.

The American soldier went forth to battle for the cause of human justice and freedom with no hatred in his heart for any people, but hating war and the things that lead to war. He held in reverence the blood-bought rights of our free nation and defied the threat of armed domination.

He died for his country without question or complaint, with faith in his heart and hope on his lips, that his country should triumph and its civilization survive. As a representative soldier of the world's greatest democracy, he offered his life as a sacrifice for the victory of her principles of right and justice over the armed forces of autocratic and military rule.

This ceremony today is a symbol and a tribute to the patriotism and sterling qualities of the American soldier. In a sense it is the enthronement of Duty and Honor. These our fathers, sons and brothers, who died for their country, symbolize these qualities. No historian of future years shall rise to modify or disparage their fame. The have an immunity for which kings might pray. The years may bring erosion to the granite of this memorial, but they can never obliterate the memory of the principles and deeds which it commemorates.

Sanctified by the tears of mothers, sisters and daughters, this is a sacred and religious ceremony which we observe today. The exaltation of the occasion would not be possible except for Belief. Where are Duty and Honor, the wellsprings of Victory, if mankind fears that death draws a black curtain beyond which lies nothing but the dark?

So all in whom the spark of hope has not died can well believe that we, to whom the death of these our fallen heroes, may still be a mystery, is no mystery to them. They can well believe that these survivors today as they gather to do honor to the departed, are not merely a few thousands of the living, but that with them gather the countless battalions of the fallen brave.

The impressive ceremony of today would be a mockery if we did not believe this, if we did not believe that out in infinity which astronomers cannot chart or mathematicians bound, the glorioius dead whom we honor are looking down upon this spinning ball of dust, conscious of our reverence.

For us who remain in this world of opportunity, with our characters still plastic as clay in the hands of the sculptor, the message of these young lives sacrificed to duty and principle is too plain to be disregarded. The golden bars of sunset, though tender in their softness, are impenetrable, impassable. They mark God's record of a day past recall. They are the lower signal lights warning youth of the danger of delay. They are beacon fires, set in the blue of the western heavens as our call to duty. They urge a full statured manhood and womanhood, the product of a noble creed:

THE AMERICAN CREED.

"I believe in the United States of America as a government of the people, by the people, for the people, whose just powers are derived from the consent of the governed; a democracy in a republic; a sovereign nation of many sovereign states; a perfect union, one and inseparable, established upon those principles of freedom, equality, justice and humanity for which patriots sacrificed their lives and fortunes. I therefore believe it my duty to my country to love it, to support its Constitution, to obey its laws, to respect its flag, and to defend it against all enemies."

WHY I AM A REPUBLICAN.

The Republican party was born of the anti-slavery movement, when a need arose for a party which was opposed on principle to slavery, and which at the same time could make its resistance within the limits of the Constitution and embody its principles in practical legislation.

The opportunity came with the break-up of the Whig organization, and in June, 1854, the first formal adoption of the name Republican was made by the Michigan State Convention, due to a suggestion in a letter from Horace Greeley.

The name spread rapidly, and was adopted by State conventions in Maine, Ohio, Indiana, Illinois, Wisconsin and Iowa. The new party principle prevailed in the Northern States, and wherever the Republicans ran a straight ticket, they carried everything before them. In spite of lack of national organization, it elected enough members of Congress to control the House and to choose Nathaniel Banks, speaker.

The first convention met at Pittsburgh on February 22, 1856. A national organization was there formed, and a call issued for another convention to nominate candidates for President and Vice-President. This second convention met at Philadelphia on June 17, 1856. John C. Fremont, of California, was nominated for President, and though his opponent, James Buchanan, was elected, the Republican party carried every northern State except Pennsylvania, New Jersey, Indiana, Illinois, and California. When it is considered that only four years before all effective opposition to the Democratic party had appeared to be extinct, the results achieved by the Republicans in the election of 1856 was most impressive.

In the following election, that of 1860, by the most fortunate choice ever made by a political convention, the name of Abraham Lincoln was placed in nomination for President. The results of that nomination are familiar to everyone present. The party came out squarely for a liberal construction of the Constitution and the policy of protection of home industries.

The interests of slavery were closely linked with free trade. Where slavery ruled, cotton was the only staple grown, and there was no diversification of labor. It was therefore to the advantage of the slave states to be able to buy in the cheapest markets. Protection was the first weapon ready to the hands of the Republicans in their warfare against slavery, and they used it with telling effect.

The South, the stronghold of the Democratic party, lost the election, and immediately began a movement to break up the nation. Secession and civil war followed, and the Republican party was charged with the mighty task of preserving the Union. When this task was successfully accomplished, one almost equal in magnitude awaited it, that of reconstruction.

Under Republican rule, the war was followed by a period of amazing national expansion, and increased in wealth from sixteen billion in 1860 to one hundred and eighty-seven billion in 1910.

In 1912, by an unfortunate division in the Republican party, a Democratic president was elected. A free trade bill was passed, and the industries of the country went into eclipse. Factories closed and industries were paralyzed until the outbreak of the European War, which shut off competition from foreign manufacturers.

When America was finally forced into the war, the preparations which should have been begun a year before were taken up and required another year, during which time the armies of England and France were almost driven to surrender.

The war was conducted with a blind extravagance unparalleled in history. One thousand millions were wasted on airplanes, only a few dozen of which were ever used on the fighting line. The only feature which redeemed the war was the splendid heroism and devotion of the American soldier, which finally proved the deciding factor. The German line of communications was cut and the colossus of militarism crashed to the earth in spectacular collapse.

Fortunately the war was followed by a Republican victory, and the chimerical scheme of a league of nations which would have made America the lackey of European powers was repudiated. America, fast becoming the laughing stock of the world, regained her place of honor and her liberties were protected.

Why am I a Republican? Because the Republican party was founded on a national need, and has measured up to that emergency.

I am a Republican because that party recognizes the fact that labor constitutes the country's greatest asset, and its protective tariff policy has made the wages of the American laborer the highest in the world.

I am a Republican because that party stands for a system of federal taxation which shall not interefere with the industry of the people, but which shall provide the means necessary to pay the expenses of the government, the pensions, interest on the public debt, and a moderate reduction of the principal thereof.

I am a Republican because the Republican party is the friend of the farmer, on whom the burden of taxation rests, and whose interests should be protected.

Finally, I am a Republican because that party has an unbroken record of successful administration of the country's affairs, and under its guidnce it has brought our nation to the front rank in industrial, educational, financial, social and moral advancement.

DEMOCRATIC SPEECH.

For a long time, in one of the cannibal islands, it was believed by the natives that all-powerful and malignant gods dwelt in a certain volcano. But one day an incredulous white man, followed and observed by the trembling islanders, boldly cast his shoe into the crater, whereupon it was seen that no harm resulted, and the superstitious worship of the volcano came to an end.

It seems incredible that so many people could have been deceived by Republican high-tariff arguments and literature, circulated by those who use the taxing power for their own private advantage, but the fat-frying went on campaign after campaign, until actual experience proved to the country that prosperity does not depend upon high tariff rates.

The discussion of the Tariff Bill in the present Congress revealed such a difference of opinion among Republicans themselves as they fought over the various schedules, that the Democrats did not have to do much talking—they could not have framed a more severe indictment than some of the Republicans made against the more outrageous rates.

The extravagance of the demands made by the tariff barons was probably due to the fact that they recognized that this Congress is giving them the last chance they will likely have for many years. The Tariff Bill has brought out and polished up nearly all the old shams and humbugs that have been employed in years past. The home market argument has been used wherever the protectionists could find any voter gullible enough to listen to it, and the attempt is still being made to bring the farmer into the protectionists' camp by vaunting the benefits of a tariff on agricultural products, although farmers ought to know as a whole they will pay ten dollars because of protection on manufactured products where they collect one dollar because of a tariff on agricultural products.

The old and absurd claim that "the foreigner pays the tariff" cannot well be used at this time, because prices have already been advanced on domestic articles in anticipation of the tariff on foreign imports.

The Democratic party this fall comes before the people with an issue of universal interest, which can be easily understood by everyone. When the Ways and Means Committee reported the Revenue Bill, it contained, among other vicious provisions, two that deserve the condemnation of all who favor justice in taxation.

The first provision repealed the tax on excess profits, giving an estimated benefit of $450,000,000 a year, according to the tax reports of last year, to the profiteers, namely those who are collecting excess profits.

The tax on excess profits was for two reasons the most just tax that we had. In the first place, it tended to restrain profiteering by imposing a sort of fine, through taxation, on those guilty of extortioning from the public. In the second place, it was the easiest tax to pay, because it was paid out of money which the profiteers should not have collected.

While the repeal of the tax on excess profits was utterly inexcusable, there was another reduction which was, if possible, more iniquitous, namely the reduction of the tax on great incomes from a maximum of 65 to a maximum, as originally proposed, of 32 per cent.

According to the tax records of last year, less than five thousand persons paid a rate of over 32 per cent, but the reduction conferred a benefit of $90,000,000 on this small group with large incomes. The bill, as presented to the House, contained what was known as the retroactive clause, which made these two items take effect on the first of January of last year, although the bill did not pass until late in the year.

What injustice could be more gross than to select these two groups—the profiteers and the money barons—the least deserving of aid of all the groups affected by the bill, and give them relief nearly a year earlier than any other persons. This retroactive clause was stricken out by a majority of nine—the majority vote coming largely from the West.

If this clause had remained in the bill, it would have kept out of the treasury for last year $450,000,000, the sum which, according to estimates, the profiteers would have paid, and $90,000,000 that the people of large income would have paid. This would have made it necessary to devise new taxes to make up the deficit, and these new taxes would have been collected from poorer people. Nevertheless, through the clauses remaining in the bill, the profiteers and the holders of big incomes are now getting the benefits of the favoritism shown them by the Republican party.

The farmers have a special grievance in the effort of the Administration to defeat the passage of the measure directing that a farmer be appointed on the Federal Reserve Board. That Board is more powerful than any other arm of the government. It can act more quickly and more effectively than the House, the Senate, or the President.

The farmers constitute about 30 per cent of the nation's population. This is the largest group; the laboring men constitute the second largest group. The farmers, the laborers, and the business men who are not bankers constitute more than one-half the population of the nation, and yet neither of these three groups has a representative on the Federal Reserve Board. However, the farmers have had influence enough to protest against this situation, and a farmer will probably be appointed on the Board.

The Federal Reserve Law, the creation of a Democratic administration, has made the greatest contribution to the stability and efficiency of American business credit and financial enterprise, and was one of the most important pieces of legislation ever passed in this country, placing the currency under control of the government, and making financial panics impossible. Yet the Republican members of Congress voted almost solidly against it. Only two Republican senators voted for the measure, and they were progressives.

Anyone who surveys the extraordinary series of legislative and executive act accomplished by the Democratic party during the recent administration will realize that the party accomplished more for the country in this period than the Republican party did in three times as many years. In the face of such a record, can anyone doubt that the Democratic party is a party of progress, and that the periods when it has been in power will be memorable in American history for wise and beneficial legislation?

A SHORT REPUBLICAN SPEECH.

The Republican party was born "under the oaks" at Jackson, Michigan, on July 6th, 1854, in a resolution expressed in the following words:

"*Resolved*, That, postponing and suspending all differences with regard to political economy or administrative policy, in view of the imminent danger that Kansas and Nebraska will be grasped by slavery, and a thousand miles of slave soil be thus interposed between the free States of the Atlantic and those of the Pacific, we will act cordially and faithfully in unison to avert and repeal this gigantic wrong and shame.

"*Resolved*, That in view of the necessity of battling for the first principles of Republican government, and against the schemes of an aristocracy, the most revolting and oppressive with which the earth was ever cursed or man debased, we will coöperate and be known as 'Republicans' until the contest be terminated.''

As when the seed is sown and the blades of grass spring up almost simultaneously, now here, now there, in different parts of the field, so in the spring and summer of 1854, from the seeds of the Abolition and Anti-Slavery movements sprang the Republican party in Wisconsin, Michigan, New York, Maine, Massachusetts, Iowa, Ohio, and other northern states. But because of the fact that, in formal convention assembled, a platform was adopted and a full state ticket nominated on the 6th of July, 1854, at Jackson, Michigan, that day and place must be conceded to be the birthday and the birthplace of the Republican party.

Little did those determined pioneers and patriots of 1854, who so firmly laid the foundation of the Republican party, dream of what it would be called upon to undertake, and how courageously and successfully it would carry out its mission. Those patient, but none the less earnest men, had one great object in view—to check the further extension of slavery. The new party was victorious from the start, for, while not politically successful till 1860, it secured a moral victory at the first elections in which it participated in 1854.

In two years' time, it was able to poll a vote of 1,341,264 while in its last national election in 1920, this vote numbered 16,152,200. A party, no matter how well founded, or how auspiciously inaugurated, could not reach such proportions without well-fixed and meritorious principles and achievements of the highest order.

The Republican party is constructed on the principle laid down by Abraham Lincoln, that this is "a government of the people, by the people, and for the people.'' It has triumphed over other parties since its organization because of its courage to fight for the principles formulated by the judgment and conscience of the people; it has been governed not by hysterical or revolutionary impulse, but by conservatism and common sense.

The record of the party is written in the Amendments to the Constitution and in the Federal statutes of the past sixty years; it is also written in the most remarkable period of development that the United States has ever known. It is written in the exalted position which this government now holds among the great powers of the world. It is a record of sturdy Americanism, good business management, and wise diplomacy. In times of greatest emergency, with the nation's welfare at stake, the strongest men of all other parties have supported its policies.

For the most part the history of the Republican party and its achievements since the first election of Abraham Lincoln has been the political history of the United States, as in but eight years of that time has the Democratic party been in full control of the government and able to carry out unopposed its policies and designs.

Under the administration of the Republican party, the political history of the country, its amazing progress, its accumulation of wealth, the unprecedented advance of its people, materially, socially, and mentally, has been written.

Under the leadership and control of this great party, the United States has been compactly welded into a nation governed by great patriotic and business principles. The nation has marched forward under its control until it stands today in the front rank of the world's powers. It stands first in its record of development in industrial, financial, military and moral achievements. It stands first in the contest for industrial and commercial development, able to hold its own in the markets of the world. It stands first in its military achievements, and in the heroic and successful deeds of the American citizen soldiery.

At no time in its career has the Republican party been on the defensive. It has always been not only aggressive, but progressive. There has been no turning back; there has been no halting, but a steady, continual advance, carrying with it the solution of the greatest questions that have ever faced the nation, and the successful prosecution of every work which it has been called upon to undertake.

It stands now, as it has always stood, as the exponent of honor, of liberty, of enlightment, of progress, and of humanity in all the phases in which the action of a political party can conserve the interests, not only of the American people, but of the people of the entire globe, wherever its influence may be felt.

The Republican party, if continued in power, will in the future as it has in the past, sustain the honor, the credit, and the integrity of the nation by sound financial legislation; it will not only preserve our incomparable home market, which it has built up under the American system of protection, giving to our labor the largest income and the highest standard of living found the world over; it will not only be the champion of liberty and enlightenment in its influence upon foreign powers; but it will see to it that the Constitution and every amendment is enforced in every corner of the land, and that the Stars and Stripes shall have an honored place with the flags of other nations in every port of the world.

SENIOR CLASS ADDRESS OF WELCOME.

To the friends and relatives gathered here, to the teachers who have been our guides, and to our fellow students and classmates it is my privilege to give a hearty welcome. We appreciate your presence on this occasion, the tangible evidence of your interest in our class.

The occasion is both sad and joyful. It would be easy to fall into the melancholy manner of Ophelia, "loaded with sweet flowers," and to murmur, "Here's rosemary, that's for remembrance; and there's pansies, that's for thoughts;" "here's a daisy, the class to follow; I would give you some violets, but they withered all when '23 passed from her school life."

For many months our little fleet has been riding in harbor; today the anchors are weighed and slowly we drop down the tide toward unknown seas. A few hours more and these clustering sails will be scattered and fading specks, each in its own horizon, straining or drifting toward its goal.

But I would not in these few words bring in "the eternal note of sadness." Rather I would speak of the better, brighter part. We cannot but see as we leave these walls that we go out to a broader, fuller life. Above all, it is the real life for which this was but the preparation. To most of us the education we have obtained here will be our only capital in beginning life; and whatever of wealth and honor we may win in the world we shall owe largely to the training we have received in school.

But the great object of the instruction we have received here has been to teach us the value of all education. Training is everything. In the natural world we are always confronted by the fact that nature of herself and unaided never gives us her best. It is only by human coöperation that she is able to approach the higher levels of perfection.

The forces of nature wait for the intelligent aid of man in order to attain their best results. The difference between the wild rose and the cultivated, between the wild cherry and the ox heart, between the wild nectarine of Arabia and the Elberta peach, between the wild grass and the wheat, is the difference between what nature will do when left to herself and what she can be made to do by intelligent cultivation.

Leave your finest flowers to propagate themselves and they will start back toward the weeds from which they have been evolved. Neglect our high-bred animals and they will soon lose their fine qualities and revort to their primitive roughness and wild nature. So it is with human education. Our efforts for the advancement of the race are like those of the swimmer who is fighting his way against a mighty current. To stop, to rest, to be careless, is to lose all we have gained. Even to hold our own we must keep going on.

The life-giving power of education is intended to fit us, not for cultivated leisure, but for earnest work. A liberal culture binds men together by giving each one interests beyond himself. It incorporates the power and nobility of the individual into the strength and grandeur of the larger individual, society. The talents we possess are for the service of all; our activity and progress go into the general social condition; our faults and failures subtract from the public good.

As soldiers in the ranks of humanity, we are under a law of duty that allows us no stopping-place short of the utmost capacity of our nature and the best use of the opportunities God has given us. We must not only learn our powers, but guide and impel them. A vigorous purpose makes much out of little, breathes power into weakness, disarms difficulties, and snatches victory out of defeat.

Wherever there is life there must be growth. A vital principle is an expanding principle—that is the proof of its vitality. The idea of citizenship is larger today than it was yesterday. Beginning with a declaration of rights it has developed into a declaration of obligation. From the principle of independence it has advanced to the principle of coöperation. The right of the individual to life, liberty, and the pursuit of happiness has been merged into the duty of the individual to share his life, liberty, and happiness. This is the new and larger meaning of citizenship, coming to expression in the social struggles of the present.

Phillips Brooks well said: "Sad will be the day for any man when he becomes absolutely contented with the life he is living, with the thoughts he is thinking, and the deeds that he is doing; when there is not forever beating at the doors of his soul some great desire to do something larger, which he knows that he was meant and made to do, because he is a child of God."

Each one of us is placed here for a definite and distinct purpose in life, and the highest, purest and best should be our only standard. Our every-day life is the battle-ground where we have the opportunity of displaying heroism and true nobility of character.

"What is noble? 'Tis the finer portion of our mind and heart,
Linked to something still diviner than mere language can impart;
Ever prompting, ever seeing some improvement yet to plan,
To uplift our fellow being, and like man to feel for man.

"What is noble? That which places truth in its enfranchise will,
Leaving steps like angel traces that mankind can follow still.

E'en though scorn's malignant glances prove him poorest of his clan,
He's the noble who advances freedom and the cause of man.''

ADDRESS BEFORE LEAGUE OF WOMAN VOTERS.

Sheridan once wrote the beautiful sentiment: ''Women govern us: let us render them perfect. The more they are enlightened, so much the more shall we be. On the cultivation of the mind of women depends the wisdom of men. It is by women that nature writes on the hearts of men.''

Over the ashes of Cornelia stood the epitaph, ''The mother of the Gracchi,'' and over the graves of the mothers of Plymouth Colony we may write as proudly, ''The mothers of the Republic.''

There was Mistress Carver, wife of the first governor, who, when her husband fell under the stroke of sudden death, followed him first with heroic grief to the grave, and a fortnight after followed him with heroic joy up to heaven. There was Mistress White, the mother of the first child born to the New England Pilgrims on this continent; and it is worthy of note that this historic babe was brought into the world on board the Mayflower between the time of the casting of her anchor and the landing of her passengers—as though to foretell the fact that this nation was to have supremacy over both land and sea! There, also was Rose Standish, whose name is a perpetual June fragrance; and there, too, was Mrs. Winslow, whose name is more than a fragrance: it is a taste, for as the advertisements say, ''Children cry for it.''

In those early days, and in many succeeding decades, the influence of woman was exerted in the quiet atmosphere of the home circle: the Pilgrim Fathers, like the rulers of Congress, relegated them, so to speak, to the galleries; and it is encouraging to see the sons of those pious sires setting their affections upon ''things above.''

As the years roll on, woman has materially elevated herself in the scale of being. She delves into the most abstruse problems af analytical science, and can figure out the exact hour when her husband ought to be home, either according to the old method or by daylight saving. The first woman learned that it was Cain that raised a club, and though the modern woman sometimes finds that it is a club that raises cain, it is an undeniable fact that to the influence of their clubs women owe much of advanced position in the world today, and likewise that upon women's clubs will rest much of the responsibility of preparing women for the vastly enlarged sphere of influence assigned to them by the Federal Suffrage Amendment.

Today millions of American women feel a sense of uncertainty regarding the exercise of their new privilege of the franchise. They realize that a gigantic task confronts them, and that having the vote imposes upon them a grave responsibility for wise action, but exactly what to do at the moment to achieve their ideals they do not know.

It is just here that such organizations as our league of women voters come to the aid of women, teaching them that citizenship in a democracy is the greatest and most thrilling experience in coöperation that the human race has yet made; that rural government is the countryside's experiment in the art of living together, village government the village's experiment, and so in ever widening circles, until the great experiment embraces the races of the earth and fulfills their immemorial hope of the brotherhood of man.

They also learn why it is important to find out how a ballot should be marked; how a candidate should be nominated; the duties of a county or state committee; and why it is important to insist that every candidate for office should declare himself plainly upon the questions in which his community is vitally interested.

They also learn another thing—that no matter how intelligently and energetically they may work, only failure can result unless the whole of their community is intelligent and energetic with them—unless citizenship—suffrage—is widely, wisely, and universally taught.

As for the formal work of preparing women for suffrage, there has been an enormous increase since the war revealed our menacing shortcoming in civic education. Massachusetts passed a law making a course in American history and civics obligatory for high school pupils. The colleges enlarged their work in political science, history, and allied subjects, and many introduced obligatory courses in government.

The latter course undertakes a systematic study of fundamentals. Consideration is given to the underlying ideals of liberty, equality, fraternity, and justice, as expressed by leaders of American political thought, also of individual and group rights growing out of these ideals as found incorporated in American law.

This embraces the reasons for and against proposals before Congress and State Legislatures and under discussion in the current press; the necessity for the maintenance of law and order; the use and abuse of the constitutional right of free speech, free press, and freedom of assembly; the admission or refusal to admit representatives of socialistic constituencies into the councils of state or nation; the right of collective bargaining; workmen's representation in the management of industry; the right and limitation of right to strike for higher wages and for better working conditions; the reasons of and remedies for the high cost of living, and many similar topics of public concern.

These are the questions upon which the woman voter should seek, through study and public discussion, to become informed, and this is the field in which the league of woman voters exerts its helpful influence upon every woman who casts a ballot.

For the carrying on of its work, the league must depend upon voluntary contributions, and without funds its activities can only be circumscribed and limited in their effectiveness. It is this appeal which I bring to you tonight, and in doing so I feel confident that with a proper estimate of the work being accomplished and projected for the future, you will consider this financial support not only a duty but a privilege and pleasure.

ADDRESS OF CANDIDATE FOR STATE SENATORIAL COMMITTEE.

The American woman of today is finding in politics her great opportunity, her most important field, the supreme test of her capacity, her sincerity and purpose, and her courage.

With the passage of the Federal Suffrage Amendment, the question of woman's participation in community, state and national politics is removed definitely from academic consideration and becomes a matter of intense practical interest.

That the political coming of age of the American woman should come at a time when society especially needs her services is one of the interesting coincidences of history. But in a sense it may be said that the European War which disclosed woman's vital importance to the nation in the time of war's supreme emergency, also pointed the way to the successful employment of her talents and faculties in the arena of politics.

To do her political thinking clearly and originally, a woman should be trained, or should train herself, to be logical, to be accurate, to be practical. To say that a woman cannot deserve any or all of these adjectives, because of some defect of previous training or environment, is absurd. When she begins to take an interest in the political problems which demand logic, accuracy and practicality for their adequate handling, she will find it perfectly possible to cultivate these traits.

Women can bring to politics the contribution of those qualities of mind and heart which are inherent in the feminine nature. She can bring her instinctive hostility to the professional politician. From the days of Andrew Jackson we have left the running of our country largely in the hands of men who go into politics for a living or who have an axe to grind. The disinterested, public-spirited, intelligent and high-minded women voters of the country have the opportunity and the desire to combat this time-worn evil.

She can bring her love of fair play and social justice. The weak and the down-trodden will find her ears open to their cry of distress. She can bring her ideals of a broader educational system, and of civic betterment.

We have here a civic spirit which has made our city a synonym for enlightened progress. With our magnificent schools, museums, libraries, parks and systems of police and fire protection, our city has consistently held her place in the forefront of American municipalities.

Most important, politically speaking, is the representation of women in all bodies—in city councils, state and senatorial committees, in legislatures, in conventions. Women should make an issue of this representation. Women and men should work together on committees. It is not necessary that the number of men and women representatives should be equal, but there should be a fair proportion of women.

The rules of the Republican State Committee provide that its members shall be elected by the Senatorial districts. Each Senatorial district shall elect one male and one female member of the State Committee, except when a Senatorial district is composed of one county or part of a county, in which event there shall be elected in each county or part of a county embraced in said Senatorial district one member of the State Committee, who may be of either sex.

For the first time. in the coming election, women are to be represented on the State Senatorial Committee. The duties of this committee are to aid in the State Senatorial campaign, appoint local committees, distribute literature, handle correspondence, and take charge of the various meetings and other matters that form a part of the State campaign.

In Mr. George Wharton Pepper, we have a Senatorial candidate who deserves the united and enthusiastic support of the women voters of this district. As a scholar, lawyer and author, Mr. Pepper's name is known throughout the United States. He has been a distinguished contributor to legal literature, his "Pleading at Common Law and Under the Codes," "Digest of the Laws of Pennsylvania," and "Digest of Decisions and Encyclopedia of Pennsylvania Law," being used at textbooks in the best schools of law. As a member of the State Committee on Constitutional Amendment and Revision, his services have been of the highest value to the State.

General George E. Alter, Republican candidate for governor, brings to his candidacy for the highest office in the gift of the State the qualities which commend him to every enlightened voter. He has been a colleague of Mr. Pepper in revising and amending the State Constitution. He is a champion of clean politics, and his experience in public affairs is a guarantee of his ability to guide the affairs of our Commonwealth in the most successful manner.

To the women voters of this district I commend these candidates as worthy of their loyal support in the coming campaign.

ADDRESS OF NEWLY-ELECTED CITY OFFICIAL.

Ladies and Gentlemen:

On an occasion as this it behooves me, above all, to express to you my appreciation of the hearty support that you have given my candidacy. I am glad that you have voted the way you did, not only for my sake, but also for your own.

9

When I announced my candidacy, I expressed to you my willingness and my earnest desire to serve you in the best possible manner, that is, to consider your interests first and mine second, and to take charge of the office as a servant of the people and in behalf of the people. From this position I have by no means receded. In fact, since my election the conviction has grown upon me that there is really only one effective way to show you my appreciation, and that is by the most painstaking and conscientious administration of my office. I shall make no distinctions. No matter whether a man is a Republican or a Democrat, he can be certain to find in me a true fellow-citizen to whom he may come for advice or counsel. Whoever may enter the city treasurer's office, let him be sure that I will be there to serve him.

But I have proposed to myself to do still more. Realizing that I am to be a servant of the people, for it is they who have put me into office, I shall endeavor to assist in promoting the best interests of the city wherever and whenever I can. To be a faithful servant shall be my highest ambition.

We often hear much of adherence to party interests. I have no quarrel with the man who believes that the candidate of his party is the man for whom he must vote. Neither do I censure the man who adheres to the belief that, at least in local elections, the candidate best fitted for the office should have his support, no matter what his party affiliations chance to be. I say I am not quarrelling with any one of these. But I do believe that whenever a man has been elected, he should have the full support of all well-meaning citizens. I hope for your coöperation, and I am confident I shall not be disappointed in my expectations. I rely on you to help me wherever you can, to assist me in making the city treasurer's office first-class in every respect, in performing my various duties to your entire satisfaction. So let us not think so much of whether we are Republicans or Democrats, but let us think more of pushing onward and upward, of making our municipality one of the finest in the State.

You know all of us have various duties to perform. We owe duties to our families, to our city, to our State, to the Nation. There is much comprised in these duties, and yet they are not all the obligations that await us. Now while we think of our duties as citizens of a great Commonwealth and of our manifold obligations towards the Nation, let us not forget that commonwealths consist of cities, towns and villages, and, of course, open farming districts. In other words, a commonwealth can only attain the highest scale of success or prosperity, when every part of it, large or small, does its fullest duty. It is for this reason that we, fellow-citizens, should earnestly strive to make our city count for something in total aggregate that constitutes the State.

Of my coöperation you can be sure. For I am entering upon my office, not with the desire to see what I can get out of it, but what I can put into it, that is, with the sincere wish to serve my fellow-citizens in the best possible manner by placing the city treasurer's office on the highest scale of usefulness.

Don't think that I am giving you simply some after-election talk; that I am following merely common usage by elaborating on the fine prospects ahead of us. True, before and after election we hear a lot of talk and comments. Voters talk of the abilities or shortcomings of new incumbents, and new office-holders assure the voters that they are about to launch upon the finest administration ever known to anyone. But such talk usually comes from professional politicians who propose to use the new office as a stepping-stone to something else, or as a means to some personal end. But I am neither a professional politician nor a rank optimist who thinks everything is resplendent with beauty because he happens to be in the lime-light. The best, safest, and perhaps the sanest thing is to let the future speak for itself. In politics, actions speak lounder than words. So I will not make you any more promises, and give you further assurances of my intentions, but instead of it, I will ask you to follow me day after day and see whether my assurances were but empty talk or whether they really stood for something. In other words, I invite you to see for yourself how I conduct my office, and then you may judge.

No doubt, not every citizen voted for me. I am not quarrelling with them. We live in a free country where each can cast his vote as he pleases. But I invite such as opposed my candidacy to postpone their criticisms and see if, after all, they were not too hasty in their pre-election conclusions.

Once more I take this opportunity to thank those that supported me during the last campaign. I am conscious of my obligations toward them. May they feel that the confidence they have centered in me, has never been misplaced. In a word, I am earnestly resolved to do my share, and I sincerely hope that my fellow-citizens will do theirs. If we thus shall work together, success will be certain.

I thank you.

INSTALLATION ADDRESS, ORDER OF ELKS.

Brother Exalted Ruler and Brothers:

It is a well know fact that in the Benevolent and Protective Order of Elks there exists an organization which has been singularly successful in developing and maintaining the principles of fraternalism, good fellowship and coöperation. The consistent and steady growth of the order is sufficient evidence of that fact, but we who are members realize that of all fraternal orders with which we may have connected ourselves, this is the one whose doors we enter with the greatest feeling of at-homeness and relief from the constraints of formality and the cares of our daily life.

The primary object of fraternal organizations is to bring together men with kindred interests, thoughts and ideals so that they may enjoy each other's society and gain mutual benefit. In this order we have banded ourselves together so that each individual may lend to the entire group the elements of strength and talent which he possesses, and may in turn receive the help, inspiration and protection of the whole organization.

Fellowship is to be valued for what is in it, not for what may be gotten out of it. When two or more persons unite for purely material benefit, that union is not a fraternity, but an association for purposes of business. But the vital and vivifying principle of true fraternity is the element of brotherly love, sympathy and coöperation,—the ability and willingness to sacrifice to the good of the whole some of the personal interest which may be at variance with the interest of the organization.

It is impossible that there should not at times be differences of opinion, but no organization can make the progress it should if it countenances mere destructive criticism. Abraham Lincoln once said: "When I am dead, I want it to be said of me that I always plucked the thistle and planted a flower where I thought a flower would grow." This is the spirit of true fraternity.

It was this spirit which caused the Puritan in Massachusetts, the Quaker in Pennsylvania and the landed aristocrat in the South, each to lay aside his individual interests and prejudices and unite in forming the Continental Congress and laying the foundation for the world's greatest republic.

Without unity and coöperation there can be no progress. In no previous period of the history of civilized men has there obtained such wide recognition of the power of concerted action as at the present time. The tremendous expansion of trade unionism, the great combinations of capital, the increasing tendency to form societies for specific ends, and, most insistent of all, the demand for a federation of nations; all these demonstrate the growing conviction of the fact that in concerted action, and there only, lies the power of mankind to achieve great results.

And the basis of unity of action is in individual self-mastery and self-control. In speaking of self-control, I use the word in its widest sense. I mean control of all the impulses and feelings. There must be discipline of self before there can be discipline of others.

Self-mastery does not consist, as we sometimes think, entirely of negation. It is at its flood tide when it dominates the faculties and aspirations so that it means initiative, development, enlargement of every faculty and capacity. Discipline and self-repression are but the stepping stones to the higher virtues of doing one's best because life has become attuned to duty and high performances, and not because of regulations or obligations of position.

As we contemplate the principles which underlie and support the great fraternal organizations such as this, when we devote our minds to a consideration of their beautiful teachings, the spirit and sentiment of them permeate our own being, and we unconsciously learn to model our lives more and more in harmony with their truths.

The spirit of fraternalism is the common property of the world. It gives us the capacity for enjoyment and for becoming more useful, irrespective of what sphere of life we occupy. Everywhere we turn, the voice of cordial greeting sounds in our ears, and the hand of friendship is extended in cordial greeting.

Manhood is the basic principle, and love the binding force of all fraternity. Grounded on such lofty principles, what can we not reasonably expect? It embodies all that is best, all that is noblest, in the nature of man.

Man is preëminently a social being. His social nature is the result of the interaction of all his separate and distinct natures. It consists in a balance of faculties. It is higher than all others, because it includes them all. The industrial nature, the political nature, the intellectual nature and the religious nature, are only the materials out of which the social nature is constructed.

Friendship, fraternity is the watchword of the age. The human race is drifting toward brotherhood. All the forces of history—religious, industrial, political and social,—are drawing and binding men together. Never did the human heart know and feel a broader and deeper fraternal feeling. Touch the chord of sympathy, and it vibrates around the world. Reason may teach the unity of God, faith leaps to a trinity, but faith and reason both declare the fraternity of man.

As Exalted Ruler of this lodge of Elks, it will be my object to foster and cultivate the principles of fraternity which I have tried to set forth. To this end I ask the coöperation of each individual member. I deeply appreciate the honor conferred upon me, and shall try to evidence my interest in the progress and walfare of the lodge throughout my term of office.

AFTER-DINNER ADDRESS AT INSURANCE CONVENTION.

I consider it a great privilege to have an opportunity to address a few remarks to this intelligent assembly of men and women on the subject that has brought us together here in a bond of mutual interest.

A subject of prime importance in any state or nation is social and economic adjustment, which includes the relations and activities of all mankind. Lack of adjustment in these fields is pronounced and destructive. Adhering to the utilitarian principle, which is the extending of the greatest good to the greatest number, we are brought face to face with the necessity of relieving and correcting existing maladjustments in these directions.

Powerful and beneficent agencies are at work for the accomplishment of this purpose, and important results have already been attained. Since the organization of our government, political parties and various social agencies have offered and urged methods and remedies designed to ameliorate the condition of the wage-earning class and advance the interests of humanity in general.

There is one great and beneficial institution that makes all mankind kin, effecting a genuine form of solidarity of social and economic effort. It is the one instrumentality capable of effecting world-wide readjustment of social and economic conditions. This institution is life insurance.

With the extension of insurance, the social and economic balance automatically becomes more stable, and when insurance becomes universal in all its branches, then these conditions will have most nearly reached a state of perfect adjustment.

For the great institution of insurance to accomplish social and economic adjustment, every organization forming a part of that system must be of a substantial character, and conducted upon an equitable and honorable basis, with its affairs ministered by skilled and capable hands. Under such conditions only may the full purpose and efficiency of insurance as an economic equalizer be realized.

Having trustworthy mortality tables and generally accepted legal standards, the progressive influence in life insurance companies must be directed toward the working out of correct systems and the perfection of methods for securing practical efficiency and economy in operation.

We should not assume, at this period in the evolution of the insurance business, which is comparatively new to civilization, that it has reached the stage of ideal perfection. It suffers from some abuses and is burdened with mistakes, for which remedies are being speedily applied. The present agency system demands our attention, as a feature of great importance, in the interest of efficiency and improved conditions.

Having the great institution of insurance available, and embodied in adequate and efficient insurance organizations and systems, the representative who brings the benefits of this institution to the great common people, for whom it was created, must be a disciple of all that it exemplifies. He must be a model of honesty and integrity, a representative of human upbuilding, a faithful employee of the insurance organization, and a true servant of the people. Such a man is the kind of life insurance agent for whom the companies are constantly searching; one who dignifies the profession, and not only enhances the value of his own work, but makes the work of every other representative easier.

To be this kind of a man, he must be fundamentally a good man, and, with this groundwork, other qualifications are easily acquired. An inexperienced and unskilled life insurance salesman exerts ill-balanced and misdirected energy, but these are only incidents of minor importance in his early career. They are defects that are easily corrected, impediments that are easily overcome, experiences that are helpful in the mastery of the business.

The life insurance salesman must have a confidence born of the mastery of his profession. He must be a man imbued with human emotions and warm sympathies, that he may comprehend the high purposes of insurance. He must have broad conception to appreciate the economic need for insurance; and he must have discernment and judgment to fit the kind of insurance to the need of each prospect. He must have business ability and aggressiveness to meet the practical needs of his vocation.

The company employing the salesman must make it worth his while to represent it unselfishly, by due recognition of faithful service and full compensation for efforts expended. Insurance is like the grace of God; it only covers those who accept it, and the insurance salesman is the minister of the economic gospel, deserving rank with the minister of the spiritual gospel. The insuring public should receive him in manner and in keeping with the great institution which he represents, and with full appreciation of the great service he renders. He should be accorded that welcome and that consideration which is given to the minister, the teacher, the physician, and the lawyer.

When the great institution of insurance gives to all mankind that protection that safeguards against poverty, misery and suffering, and elevates all mankind to a point where health, comfort and happiness prevail; when insurance organizations become the unselfish exemplification of the beneficent insurance principle; when the insurance salesman effectuates this great purpose by bringing to the public that protection—then we have found the kind of insurance, the kind of an insurance organization, and the kind of an insurance salesman that will exalt the insurance principle to its destined and deserved position as one of the greatest gifts of human ingenuity ever bestowed upon mankind.

THE SOCIOLOGICAL BASIS OF SCHOOL DISCIPLINE.

Pedagogy in its simplest form is the oldest science practiced by man. The man who mastered the first rude art taught it to his children and his neighbors, and because he knew more than they, assumed a position of authority among men. This authority soon took on a disciplinary character, and it was then, and has ever since been true, that all the training which society gives to its members, and which helps them better to control their powers, may be called disciplinary.

That a teacher stands in the place of the parent is a maxim universally accepted; and the nature and workings of the teacher's authority have shown a decided tendency to imitate the methods of control in vogue in the home. The era of stern discipline and severe corporeal punishment in both was contemporaneous; and when parental severity was relaxed in favor of more gentle means, the school was forced to fall into line.

The mode of control by appeal to absolute authority is the school's oldest, simplest, and most direct means of securing good order. Combined with the type which rests its power on the personal appeal of the teacher to the child, it is the mode which has been consciously employed until very recent times.

Nor is by any means an outworn or discarded type of school government. Not only in theory but in practice it rests upon a justification so sound that it will never become obsolete. Its acknowledged existence and justice give dignity and stability to all other forms of control. As a starting point if possible, as an ultimate appeal if necessary, the teacher's authoritative control of the situation, as society's rightful representative, makes his position tenable and secure. He controls his domain—within the reasonable limits set by custom and public opinion—as rightfully as civil officers execute the statute law.

That this mode is to be abandoned in favor of others when possible, then, is not because it rests upon any untenable principle, nor because it is inherently unjust or harmful. It is because it is not the mode that is best calculated to teach pupils to be self-governing, and so to order their conduct that it gives the best service to society, for we must constantly bear in mind that all disciplinary processes have a sociological basis.

The use of authority is at best society's temporary expedient, when it finds itself confronted with many classes of people whose wishes do not conform to the public good. So the teacher's authority is to be exercised as a concession to actual conditions, keeping always in mind the possibility of attaining an ideal condition in which it will not be needed—"the object of all law is to make law unnecessary."

Following the instinctive obedience to parental authority and its substitutes, and closely allied to that first allegiance, comes the motive for conduct which is allied with personal interest. At first the desire for self-gratification leads usually to defiance of authority. As the power of thinking develops, however, and reasoning gives them an insight into final gains and losses, children learn to deny themselves an immediate gratification in view of an ultimate gain.

When this point in development has been reached it is possible to appeal to the child's sense of self-interest. He begins to do things because he knows it is good for him—either because he reaps some reward that is pleasant, or because he has faith that a given course will bring him pleasure in the future. He learns to balance values, and to choose the one which his training and disposition hold most worth while.

There is one motive which may be used at all ages, although it is probably most active and potent during adolescence. This motive is the hope of reward, the aim of self-improvement or gratification. Provided care is taken to call attention to the fact that rewards are sometimes long delayed, diffused, or subjective in character, the use of the motive of immediate and concrete reward is harmless and commendable. There is nothing in the awarding of a deserved honor that does harm, if the nature of the reward is such as to be unobjectionable. Every time a child receives a recognized reward for doing right, his faith in the paying qualities of goodness is increased.

The story of civilization is the record of the development of man's social consciousness. As successively larger groups have supplanted the individual, in man's long struggle for existence, more economical and beneficial ways of living, finer emotions, and bigger-planned enterprises have grown. Following the history of the race, each child born into the world may pass from a state in which its own wants bound all the stimuli to action, to the highest pinnacle of unselfish effort for all society.

From the standpoint of ethical training and social efficiency, the most important function of the school is the part it plays in making the child's social relations plain to him. This establishing of social consciousness has begun, for the family relation, long before the first day og the first grade; but as there is as yet no abstract conception to aid in carrying it over into a new sphere, the work must be freshly started for the new relation when the kindergarten or primary school begins.

The process is progressive, variable, and unending. It goes on daily at every stage of formal education. All moral effort since schools began has consciously or unconsciously been directed toward its development. Its establishment is the fundamental condition for the mode of self-government under direction—in other words the portal of life in an organized society.

ENVIRONMENT NECESSARY FOR CHARACTER BUILDING.

Human life may be compared to a tree or plant. In order to thrive, it requires certain degrees of moisture, temperature, and a certain kind of soil. Plant a lily or some other delicate flower out on a prairie, and how long will it retain its fragrance and beauty. In a short time it shrivels up and passes into oblivion.

So it is with most members of the human family. In order to rise to our fullest heights, we must have every gale of misfortune arrested and every beam tempered. Instead of imagining that we are creatures of circumstances, it would help us greatly to think that we are creators of our circumstances. Our lives and actions build as an existence and character out of our environment.

From the same bricks and stones one man erects a palace, another a hovel. They both had the same building material, but what a contrast is displayed in the appearance of the two buildings! Many times in the same family and the same circumstances one man erects a colossal structure, while his brother, weak and vacillating, exists eternally amid wreck and ruin. The very stone that was an obstacle and stumbling block in a weak and susceptible man's path proves to be a stepping stone to success and greatness of character to one who is strong and less easily influenced.

Many a youth and maiden gone astray from paths of rectitude can trace their downfall to the lack of parental vigilance; for vigilance is the price of many things besides liberty. It is the duty of parents to acquaint themselves with all that enters into their children's lives and forms their habits; and this watchfulness should begin with their first consciousness. It is far less trouble to begin early to form or to guide the formation of children's habits, than to break them of wrong habits ignorantly formed.

The children must attend the public schools, and it is not possible to exclude them from all undesirable associates; but we can and should make ourselves acquainted with those whom they make their intimate companions in order that we may recognize and promptly take measures to check dangerous tendencies. The aim of our teaching should be to fortify them against the evils they are bound to meet in the world rather than to seclude them or keep them in ignorance.

Teach them that all the habits they acquire in childhood will grow with their growth and strength, until these habits control their whole lives. Insist on truth in all their statements. Never pass over untruthfulness in matters however small. Do not make promises where the ability or intention to perform is doubtful. Train children to accuracy of thought, observation and statement, and you will have given them an equipment that will prove most valuable in all the relations of life.

Every child should be taught to account for every dollar spent. The boy who is permitted to spend all of his first earnings on himself is acquiring habits that may spell ruin to him when he is obliged to make his own way in the world. The girl who has the privilege of ''charging'' her candy at the confectioner's and her hats and gowns at the department store is likely to grow up with a financial irresponsibility that will make her husband a bankrupt or a suicide.

To teach of us individually, our moral ideas come first of all in childhood through the medium of education, from parents and teachers, assisted by the unconscious influence of language. They are impressed upon the mind which at first is like a waxen tablet, adapted to receive them, but they soon become fixed and set. They may be corrected or enlarged by experience; they may be brought home to us by the events of our lives; they may be intensified by imagination, by reflection, or by a course of action likely to confirm them.

Under the influence of religious feeling or by an effort of thought, anyone beginning with the ordinary rules of morality may create out of them for himself ideals of holiness and virtue. They slumber in the minds of most men, yet in all of us there remains some tincture of affection, some desire of good, some sense of truth, some fear of the law.

All of us have entered into an inheritance which we have the power of appropriating and making use of. No great effort of mind is required on our part; we learn morals as we learn to talk, instinctively, from conversing with others, in an enlightened country and in a good home. A well-educated child of ten already knows the essentials of morals—"Thou shalt fear God," "Thou shalt obey thy parents," "Thou shalt not steal," "Thou shalt speak the truth."

The home is the greatest agency of environment in its influence upon the formation of character. When once a home is regarded as only a place to eat, drink and sleep in, the influence is begun that ends in saloons, poolrooms, gambling houses, and moral degradation. Young people must have fun and relaxation somewhere. If they do not find it at their own homes it will be sought at less desirable places.

Therefore let the fire burn brightly at night and make the home delightful and attractive. Don't draw the curtains lest the sun should fade your carpets, or be afraid to see the children play their games lest they injure the furniture.

The child feels and understands the spirit and temper of the home. It knows when it is welcome and when it is not by the home spirit. It rests contentedly in the spirit of a loving home.

We may safely assert that in a hundred men, there are more than ninety who are what they are, good or bad, because of the early instruction they have received. The least and most imperceptible impressions received in childhood have consequences very important and lasting. It is with these first impressions as with a river, whose waters we can easily turn into different channels until, they arrive at destinations far remote from each other. Environment is the great power in the formation of character.

OPENING ADDRESS FOR WOMAN'S LITERARY CLUB.

At the opening of this new club year, with its myriad opportunities for self-improvement and for social service, you must be impressed, as I have been, with the great and increasing significance of the woman's club movement as a whole.

That movement has been so rapid, indeed, that it has been difficult for the public to keep pace with it, and there are good women, themselves members of active clubs, who have failed to catch the full significance of a force in modern society which teems with possibilities and with power.

There have been those outside the membership who have thought that the movement signified a banding together of women who desired power and position or social prestige. But the club movement among women is in reality none of these things. It is a simple phase of the whole scheme of evolution, a natural result of the readjustment necessary to the great economic and moral awakening of the present time.

The germ of its existence may be found as far back as the period of the Renaissance, which placed the first emphasis upon the value of the individual. There were a few women of leisure, even then, who yearned to be of real value to civilization, women who willingly gave up the pursuit of purely personal pleasure for the sake of culture.

The woman's club, as a feature of civilization, is an organization in harmony with the part which seems to have been marked out for women in the great scheme of evolution. If we look backward over the ages, we find that the distinction and differentiation of the sexes is not so much a difference of labor and recreation as a difference of function. The hard and fast lines with which the conservative people of the present day seek to surround what they are pleased to call woman's sphere, seem to melt away when differences of time and place are taken into consideration.

In America today, man ploughs the field and tills the soil, but one need not go far among the peasant people of Europe to find that this masculine occupation in America is a feminine one in many countries abroad. With the generality of people in this country cooking is a distinctly feminine accomplishment, but it becomes a masculine art in the hands of a French chef in one of our great hotels or restaurants.

But there are certain functions of man and of woman which may be relied upon as constant throughout the ages. Women are not creators; they are not discoverers; they are not warriors. The function of man seems to embrace the creative, inventive, exploring and fighting qualities. But whenever man has entered new fields, either of country or of thought, he has brought woman with him to conserve and preserve the good of the new life into which he has entered. In all times and nations, this high calling of conserver and preserver has belonged almost exclusively to woman.

It is upon this fundamentally true basis that the woman's club movement is founded. There was no great scheme of separate or distinct work laid down by the founders of the movement, nor do we find today, after the organization has been in existence sixty years, a desire or effort, on the part of its leaders, to attempt any great work which shall be apart from that of other forces which are striving toward the same end, namely, a higher and better civilization.

The earliest form of the woman's club, was the study club, in which the membership was ordinarily confined to women of similar walks in life, women who had interests in common, and whose tastes were congenial. It was an unusual thing to find in these earlier clubs women who did not meet often at social gatherings elsewhere, or at church, or each others' homes. These bodies of congenial spirits met regularly and discussed questions in the realm of art or literature.

But while this is true of the earlier clubs, and to a greater or less degree of those of today, there has grown up with it a spirit of greater and deeper significance, which may be summed up in the words "public service."

In 1868 we find Sorosis of New York setting forth in its articles of incorporation the fact that the society was formed for the promotion of useful relations among women and the discussion of principles which promised to exert a salutary effect on women and society, making them helpful to each other and actively benevolent to the world.

And in 1869 we find Mrs. Croly introducing a measure which commended to the attention of the club matters connected with public education and reformatory schools, hygienic and sanitary reforms, female labor, the department of domestic economy, dishonesty in public life, and so on. The introduction of this measure shows conclusively that, even at the outset, the woman's club movement had in mind the organization of a body of social workers which should strive to make better conditions on every hand.

Even as the child creeps before he walks, so the pioneer club woman developed slowly but surely her own independence of thought and action; and the resolute, useful club worker of today is the true outgrowth of the club woman of prophetic vision and awakening sympathies of thirty years ago.

To the crucial question: Is it worth while? no one in close touch with the whole great movement can hesitate to answer, Yes. If educational work is worth while; if juvenile courts are worth while; if a more scientific knowledge and practice of domestic science is worth while; if better legislation for women and children; if organized effort for the benefit of the poor, the needy, and those who have faltered by the wayside, is worth while; if a better understanding of the fullness of life, with its responsibilities and privileges, is worth while, then the woman's club movement is a worthy and indispensible feature of modern society, for along all these and many other lines women are working together for the upbuilding of a kingdom on earth in which each shall serve her fellow creatures and all shall work together for the good of humanity.

CLUB IDEALS.

Some years ago, Jane Addams published an essay on the subjective necessity of settlement work. The objective necessity of such work was obvious: the necessity that help be given to the less fortunate members of society. But it seemed to Miss Addams that deeply important as the objective need was, there was a need still deeper— the need for the humanizing transformation of the character of the well-to-do that comes of seeking to understand, to live with and for the less fortunate members of the human family. To Miss Addams the work at Hull House was an experiment, not in philanthropy, but in democracy. And to many a club woman has come the illuminating discovery that only in the yielding of one's life to the understanding and service of others does one gain a life that is truly worth while.

In many communities today the persons who most deeply understand its problems and needs are the public-spirited club women. Such women are becoming increasingly the guardians of public health, education and morality. The determined, difficult fight that has been waged against that most cruel of the iniquities of our civilization— most cruel because it strikes down the weak and defenseless—the fight against child labor, has largely been planned, officered, and carried to execution by the devoted mothers and sisters of little children. The fight for decent housing, for clean air and sunlight, the fight against sweatshop work, the fight to gain the joy of life for children in the crowded streets by providing for their enjoyment parks, playgrounds and recreation piers; the fight against tuberculosis, against overlong hours of woman's work, against insanitary and morally dangerous conditions of labor—in all of these struggles that have counted so deeply for the humanizing of community life, woman's ideals as expressed through women's clubs have led the way in every forward movement.

To have a part in the world's work is not simply or chiefly to discover new applications of natural forces, to promote industry, to develop material resources; it is concerned also with the discovery of intellectual and spiritual forces and their application to daily living, with the promotion of earnest purposes and high ideals, with the development of the resources of the mind and of the heart. These really vital things come within the province of every woman's club. Society can exist without great wealth, enlarged industries, invention and discovery; it cannot long exist without integrity, honor, truth, purity, and idealism.

There can be no question that for practically every advance in the physical and material conditions of life, in the improvement of the conditions under which men and women live and work and play, in the vast changes which have made better homes for all, better food for all, better clothing for all, and in the provision of means for the preservation of health, facilities for fighting disease, and for safe and speedy transportation, we are indebted to the ideals, translated into action, of the vast army of workers, trained to correct thinking and decisive action, of which American club women form a prominent and important part.

The earnest woman of today does not look upon education as a personal acquisition, without bearing upon the common welfare, nor does she consider that schools and colleges exist in order that she may be "highly accomplished," and stamped with the hallmark of culture. She realizes that the century calls for many kinds of service, from women as well as from men. It needs the service of the home-maker; but for the woman of the twentieth century the question of homemaking must broaden into a conception not to be confined within the walls of her own dwelling. The responsibility includes as well the home of the other woman.

In other ways, the "homemaker" of the twentieth century has a much wider responsibility than her grandmother—a responsibility for the industries taken out of the home and entrusted to bakeries and restaurants, laundries and soap factories, canneries and dairies, mills and tailoring establishments; a responsibility for pure food and clean streets, hygienic school rooms and healthful amusements, for the prevention of contagious diseases of the body and contagious diseases of the soul. Above all upon her rests the responsibility for the child life of the nation, that it may not be defrauded of the child's right to play and happiness, education and good influence.

There is a quaint description in the Book of Judges concerning one of the tribes of Israel. "For the divisions of Reuben there will be great searchings of heart." In the twentieth century there are already great searchings of heart, new ethical standards, higher business, political and personal morality, and a purer, more purposeful civic life.

The business and professional woman's club of today meets life at many angles. It realizes that health is an essential factor in every woman's life work, and that one of the benefits that comes from physical vitality is a certain joyousness in living, the ability "to take the old world by the hand and frolic with it," to quote from Stevenson: "To keep the eyes open, the heart warm, and the pulses swift, as we move across the field of life," find that "half the joy of life is in little things taken on the run"—in Dr. Jordan's suggestive words.

On Copley Square in Boston, at the side of Trinity Church, there is the bronze figure of a bishop who was in a peculiar sense the bishop of New England, a personality too great and inspiring to be limited to any church. One of his messages to the men of the nineteenth century may well be taken as a message to the women of the twentieth and as an epitomen of Club Ideals:

"Do not pray for easy lives. Pray to be stronger! Do not pray for tasks equal to your powers. Pray for powers equal to your tasks! Then the doing of your work shall be no miracle. But you shall be a miracle. Every day you shall wonder at yourself, at the richness of life that has come to you by the grace of God."

ARE GOOD ROADS WORTH THE COST?

Men who are not yet old can remember when the United States was a country of bad roads. Thirty or forty years ago, it was only in the vicinity of towns and cities that the roads were good. With the advent of the bicycle, however, our roads, in about 1890, began slowly to improve, and with the coming of the automobile a few years later they began to improve very rapidly. The movement for better roads has gained strength year by year, and the day is not far distant when the United States will be a country of good roads.

But an enormous amount of work will have to be done, and a vast sum of money will have to be spent before our roads will be as good as they ought to be, or as good as the roads of most European countries actually are. There are in this country nearly 2,500,000 miles of public roads. Of this total, about 250,000 miles consists of improved, surfaced roads. So, for every mile of good roads, we have eight or nine miles of bad ones. In some of the States, the proportion of good roads is much greater than this. In Massachusetts more than half, and in Indiana nearly half, of the public roads are surfaced.

Since one mile of good macadam road costs anywhere from $3,000 to $10,000, it can be seen that it will require billions of dollars to put our roads in good condition. Yet costly as good roads are, the people are so thoroughly convinced of their value as an investment that they are meeting the expense in a free-handed manner, and are spending each year more than $250,000,000 on road improvement. This is about half as much as is spent for public schools, but it is money well spent, for good roads are one of the most valuable assets of a nation.

In the work of road improvement the Government is lending a helping hand. For more than twenty years there has been maintained in the Department of Agriculture a Department of Public Roads. In this office there are altogether about three hundred persons, among whom are many engineers and road experts. For the support of the office Congress appropriates about $500,000 annually. The work of the office is almost entirely educational in character. Men are sent out not to build roads, but to show others how to build them. Any community in any State desiring instruction in the art of road-building may, upon request, secure from the Office of Public Roads the services of an expert road engineer.

The expert visits the locality and supervises the construction of a short stretch—a few hundred yards or a few miles—of road built in a manner that best suits the needs of the community. This serves as an object lesson to the local road builders. In the building of these model roads, the Office furnishes the engineer, but the local community furnishes all material, labor and supplies.

It is universal experience that one mile of good roads breeds another mile. Put a State-wide good road down anywhere in the country, and in ten years there will be dozens of good roads reaching it from all parts of the State. Put down a system of national highways, built and maintained by the national Government, and the various State Legislatures and county officials would soon see the advantages of connecting all parts of the States with those national roads.

That good roads are vastly important to farmers and through them to the entire nation has been well demonstrated abroad, for the good roads that are everywhere in Europe are substantial evidence of this fact. They are maintained with the utmost care, the traffic is regulated, and there are restrictions as to the width of tires used in connection with various vehicles and the loads they carry.

In comparing European roads with our own it is interesting to note that it costs a European farmer an average of 9 cents to deliver a ton of produce, while in America the expense averages 23 cents.

The fact that there are 850,000,000 acres of land to cultivate in this country and only 450,000,000 are now under cultivation is perhaps due in great measure to the meagerness of transportation facilities. All of this ultimately has a definite bearing on the cost of living problem that faces the majority of people in the United States. This fact brings the good roads movement home to more people than is evident on the face of it, and makes the plea for better highways one of nation-wide necessity, and not only one of interest to those who actually use the roads, whether for business or pleasure.

10

In a dark corner of one of our Southern States, the sparse population arose a few years ago and said to one another, "People go to places where there are good roads. They avoid places where there are bad roads. We have bad roads. Few people come here. Let us make good roads and see what will happen." They went to work building good roads from Nowhere to Anywhere. County and townships went into debt. Private persons put up money.

By great agitation and much sacrifice, they built road after road through the lonely woods. At first nobody did travel them. A lonely, perfect highway through a thinly-settled corner of the world: it did look foolish to incur a debt for that. But presently people came in motor cars; then more came. Somebody discovered that the land along the highways was good land. It had before been taken for granted that because it was not cultivated it was of little value. Now its price has doubled and in places quadrupled. Prosperous farms already bloom where there was only waste before.

The cost of the Spottsylvania-Fredericksburg road in Virginia was about $28,000 for the twelve miles, and the annual saving in hauling on this road is more than $14,000. With good roads in Spottsylvania County, the school attendance increased 30 per cent.

There is no phase of life in the country, social or economic, that is not affected by good roads. There is a direct relation between improved highways and the value of land, school attendance, the health of the community, and everything that tends to make life in the country healthful, profitable, pleasant and efficient. Good roads always pay for themselves many times over.

ADDRESS AT A FAMILY REUNION.

Artemus Ward was once asked about the nationality of his ancestors, and made the following reply: "I think we came from Jerusalem, for my father's name was Levi, and we had a Moses and a Nathan in the family; but my poor brother's name was Cyrus; so perhaps that makes us Persians."

Artemus was probably so busy writing and delivering his famous lecture on the Mormons and their intricate family relations that he had little time left to determine his own family history. It is true of most of us that in the hurry and turmoil of modern existence we give little thought to the associations that link us with the past:

> "The world is too much with us; late and soon,
> Getting and spending, we lay waste our powers;
> Little we see in nature that is ours:
> We have given our hearts away, a sordid boon."

It is only on occasions such as this, with their sacred joys and crowding memories, that we realize the full meaning of family ties, for blood indeed is thicker than water, and though other associations, religious, social and commercial, may promote our interests and happiness, there is after all no bond like that of blood, no organization that can take the place of the family. So much is this true that the historian Taine has declared that the family is the only remedy man has found for death.

Marriage is the keystone of the family arch. That is why its character is of so much importance in any social system. This contract, the most ancient and most universal of all, was not invented by human legislators. Its origin goes back to God himself. Among all peoples, marriage has beeen a religious act placed under the tutelage of the Divinity.

Marriage is not created by law, like other contracts. The law, finding it already in existence, recognizes it, establishes it, strengthens it. In all the ancient forms of society, this sacred origin of marriage was so clearly understood that it was placed under the protection of religion. Such was its position in the social systems of Egypt, Greece, and Rome. Christianity, which in its turn inherited the institution of marriage, made it a sacrament, so as to put upon it clearly the stamp of religion.

This sacrament the husband and wife administered to each other as they exchanged their eternal promises in the presence of the priest, God's witness and representative. Its sacramental character made it clearly indissoluble. Its chief aim was not the happiness of the contracting parties, but the creation of a new family from which the union of heart and of flesh, of will and of deed, would allow no turning back.

The family is thus considered as the foundation of society and the symbol of government itself. And this is not merely a theory for philosophers to discuss, but a fact proved by experience in the course of the many perilous and glorious centuries which constitute the course of recorded history. "The nation," says Joseph de Maistre, "is an association of the living with the dead and with those still unborn." That is to say, the nation is a collection of families. The family alone honors its dead and sustains life.

In the dark ages, when the barbarian hordes swept down from the north and the Saracens from the south, the family was the only institution already organized and prepared to come to the rescue. To save themselves from extermination, these little societies—the families—sought out one another and united together. The first combination was merely the family enlarged, and this in time became the fief. And from the authority exercised by the father of the family, grew, like a flower blossoming upon its stem, the white lily of royal authority.

"The king," said Hugues de Fleuri in the eleventh century, "represents in the kingdom the idea of the father." And later, in the sixteenth century, when the legal writers wished to define the State, Jean Bodin contented himself with this comparison: "All the households taken together form what we call the people. It is only by the succession of families that the people is rendered immortal. The republic cannot possibly stand fast if the families which are its pillars have weak foundations."

The family is the oldest of all social organizations. As it is the oldest, so it is the most fundamental and the most important. Upon the family are built both the State and the Church. Whatever weakens the family ties and tends to the dissolution of the family weakens both the political and the religious bonds and tends to the dissolution of society. Whatever tends to lower its moral tone tends to corrupt society at its fountain head. Whatever makes for true, pure homes, makes for a pure religion and an honorable State. And neither statesman nor ecclesiastic, however great his fame or high his position, equals in dignity and influence the fathers and the mothers, who are the first of sovereigns and the divinest of priests.

The real bond which holds the family together, and which explains its power and permanence, is love, "the bond of perfectness." There is no spectrum that can analyze the white light of love into its various constituent elements, but we may safely say that family affection has features which distinguish it from other forms of affection; that the love of parents for children is something more than the compassion which the strong feel for the weak, and the love a husband and wife have for each other is something more than the love that either has for friends of the same sex.

Without attempting any difficult analysis, we may say that this kind of love includes a feeling of chivalry on the part of the man for the woman, a feeling of trust and confidence on the part of the woman for the man, a guarding and protecting love in the parents for the children, and a loyal and filial love in the children for the parents.

This mysterious, indefinable, transcendent feeling, which binds the family together, which makes its possible for the family to fulfill its functions, is a love that is more than good nature, that is more than friendship; a love that takes not only for sickness and health, and for richer and poorer, but also for better and for worse; a love that "beareth all things, trusteth all things, hopeth all things, endureth all things." Thus the family in human relationships becomes the closest approximation to the divine.

ADDRESS AT BANQUET OF A VOLUNTEER FIRE DEPARTMENT.

Ladies and Gentlemen:

A fireman occupies somewhat the same position in a community as a doctor—his importance is only fully realized in time of need, but when we do need a fireman or a doctor, how badly we need him! The cry of "Fire"! wakes and thrills the most lethargic. Even if we are insured in a sound company, there is no tumult that is made by civilized mankind that will so fill with terror the breasts of the nervous or so stir the most lymphatic temperament.

The fact that most of the great firemen of today rose from the ranks is proof that the men in the ranks of the volunteer fire departments are, as a rule, efficient, intelligent and ambitious fire fighters. The true fireman is not content with just holding his job, and a number of qualities, amounting almost to special faculties, develop rapidly in the born fireman.

In the career of a fireman, knowing your business is as essential to success as it is in any other walk of life. But the knowledge involved is not confined between the engine house and the sudden fire. For instance, the captain and the lieutenant of a company will, if they are devoted to their duties, make it their business to become acquainted with the district in which they are to operate. To know a district means more than to be sure of the location of buildings, the conditions of streets and alleys, and the situation of the fire hydrants. It means also a thorough and continuous familiarity with the construction of every house, the disposition and character of the contents of every mercantile establishment, the arrangement of fire escapes, and the points of vantage from which a fire may be attacked.

It is not possible to exaggerate the value of this information, for the chief of a fire department has something more than the saving of property on his hands. The lives of his subordinates may, any day or night, depend upon his absolute knowledge of the construction and the contents of some particular building. To master all these details requires time and careful investigation, and the officer or man who expects to be of the greatest and most lasting service to the department will find, if he is industrious, that there is plenty for him to do between fires.

It will not do to depend always upon higher officers for their superior knowledge, for occasions may arise in which the chiefs are absent or off duty, and in such an event the authority over the company reverts to one of the firemen, who thus has an opportunity to display his thoroughness of training and capacity for leadership.

The public is apt to fancy that the fireman's work is over when the "fire out" signal is sounded, but this is far from being the fact. The truth is that every fire engine house is an informal training school for the men whose business is to save from flames the property and often the lives of the citizens.

It is a fact that few men who adopt the career of a fireman do so on account of the pay. Nine out of ten of them are born firemen, and they bring to their work something more than the common ability to work hard. They have a pride in their work which is not apparent in many trades. Their courage, their physical strength, their eternal preparedness, are regarded by themselves as matters of course.

But as a rule they go beyond this. The fireman in the ranks, if he has the proper spirit, if he means to excel, is likely to know all about his district. If he is serious about his work, he will know where the blind alleys are, and either by personal investigation, or by conversation with his comrades, he is likely to know a great deal about the layout of every fire that occurs in his district.

Perhaps no branch of public service requires more time and attention than the fire department. Its members must not only be ready for the call of duty during the day, but their ears must constantly be on the alert for the fire signal at night. There are thousands of firemen who forget their private interests and concerns in the desire to properly fulfill their duties.

Besides the work of fighting fires, there is an endless routine of less interesting but necessary work around the engine houses. They must be kept clean or orderly; the apparatus must be maintained in immaculate order and instant readiness for service. Fire drills, physical training, and the constantly changing conditions of the buildings, streets and alleys of the city, give the energetic, industrious fireman plenty of occupation, and as a rule these less heroic details of their duties are performed with systematic faithfulness.

The practical side of a fireman's life is sure to be a busy one. In this respect it is like any other business. The lazy and careless never become good firemen, and they do not last long. The industrious, thoughtful, observant man, if he is fitted physically, is the one who rises to a position of authority. It is a hard life at the best, and like all hard lives, brings out the best that is in a man. Everybody knows that it requires courage and strength to be only an average fireman. But quick intelligence, continual study of the details of the work, absolute devotion to the service at all hours and under all conditions— these are the least showy features of a fireman's life, but at the same time the most necessary.

ADDRESS AT A SCHOOL OPENING.

Ladies and Gentlemen:

One year ago the cause of education in our city seemed to have suffered a staggering blow in the destruction of our public school building by fire, but today as you admire this new and modern two-story building, with its various appliances for the comfort, health and convenience of teachers and pupils, you cannot but realize the vitality and supreme importance of education as a feature of our community life.

Not only do we rejoice in the architectural beauty of the structure here erected, which will have a potent though silent influence upon every pupil gathered within its walls, but we rejoice also because we have another splendid monument in our community, setting forth to all eyes the great fact that our citizens are alive to the importance of educating the young for the service of their generation.

For service is the supreme test of education: without its genial warmth the choicest fruits of the tree of knowledge become like the apples of Sodom that turned to ashes upon the lips. Phillips Brooks well said: "Sad will be the day for any man when he becomes absolutely contented with the life he is living, with the thoughts he is thinking, and the deeds that he is doing; when there is not forever beating at the doors of his soul some great desire to do something larger, which he knows that he was meant and made to do."

Character-building is a slow process. It must be worked at continually, and we are building even when we are not conscious of it. It is an individual matter. You cannot have another's character. You may try to imitate the character of some great man, but at best the result can only be an imitation. Someone has said that "character is not something that is added to your life, but it is life itself."

In the great work of building character through education for a life of service to humanity, two forces go hand in hand, the home and the school. Neither can accomplish its best results unaided: for though each are continuous forces, as powerful as the sunshine and rain that transform the tiny acorn into the towering oak of the forest, like these elements themselves they are mutually dependent upon each other for their best effects.

The success of an enterprise in which there is a division in the proprietary rights depends largely upon the extent of coöperation between the proprietors. Educational work is a great enterprise in which parents and teachers are partners; parents becoming responsible for about eighty-four per cent of the time element in the child's education, and the teacher sixteen per cent. The tendency of modern education is to crowd all of the work of education into books and class rooms in the sixteen per cent factor and to surrender the child unguided to its environment during the eighty-four per cent factor— which is both a pedagogical and psychological blunder which time is sure to reveal.

The teacher is sometimes of the opinion that she is the senior partner and as such she assumes supreme authority over the child. The parent also frequently maintains that he is the sole proprietor, that the teacher is a paid servant of the public, and, as such, should take orders from the parents. When such feelings on the part of the parent and the teacher prevail, the child, for whom the school exists, becomes the victim of misunderstandings, of friction, and eventually of antagonism between these partners.

There must be some means by which right relations may become established between the home and the school, and by which an under-standing of the great work of education on the part of these two great American institutions become indelibly stamped upon each of them. It is perfectly logical to assume that an association of the two great forces in education will add to the efficiency of their mutual under-taking.

The principal misses his opportunity and fails to utilize at least half of the force for education, if he does not encourage an association of parents and teachers. The success and influence of the home and school association depends largely upon him. He must have clearly in mind the aims, methods, and needs of the school in order that he may have these presented to the parents sympathetically. He must be able to answer inquiries about the school work, accept occasional adverse criticisms, and adopt those that have a constructive tendency.

He must prove that the school is sincere in its aims, and efficient in proportion to its means. The material needs of the school should be presented occasionally. Parents are very willing to help when a material project is clearly presented to them. Tardiness, absence, and the conditions of home study are subjects that may be helpfully dis-cussed by parents and teachers. Sympathetic coöperation on these points should be established and the requirements of the school adjusted with those of the home life.

Parents want to know the latest ideas relative to training their children physically, mentally, and morally. They want to know how to supervise their study, their reading, and their out-of-school hours. They want to know of the opportunities the school presents, the char-acter of the teaching corps, and the efficiency of the school based upon the results of previous years.

The association of home and school is one of the strongest factors for educational uplift in the community. It is a constructive agency which helps in the development of principles of conduct and morality, and establishes the necessary coöperation in the training of children.

SUCCESSFUL MOTHERS AND THEIR RELATIONSHIP TO THE COMMUNITY.

There is a supreme moment in the life of woman—a moment when God shows his face and the divine and human meet and merge. It is the moment when with the miracle of motherhood the depths of human feeling are touching and awakened and the heights of human possibilities are disclosed.

The birth of a child has often meant the birth of a mother—to a higher, better plane of living, with wider understanding, deeper feeling, and more positive aim. It is one thing to idle away one's own life and waste one's own talents. It is quite another to neglect the possibilities of a new life entrusted to one's care. After the first rush of joy and pride and gratitude, which are the initial qualities of mother love, comes a realization of new responsibility which is limitless.

What may have been the purpose of the Infinite in giving life to this tiny atom of flesh and blood? To what magnitude may the soul within this little body expand? To what heights may the raw material of the mind be trained, to what beauties cultured! What part of the work in life's vineyard were those baby hands sent to perform, and will the fruition of their work be wheat or chaff?

What is the end of life? For what purpose are we here in this world? A brief consideration of the course of life answers that vital question. A child is born, grows up to manhood, marries his chosen mate. Children are born to them; they give to these children the' benefit of their knowledge and experience of life, train them to take advantage of its opportunities and fulfill its obligations.

These children in turn marry and have children. The grandparents linger a little while to enjoy the pleasures of the second generation of children without caring for them, and then go out into the unknown world that lies beyond. Generation after generation this process is repeated. We enter the door of life, pass through its educational experiences, and make our exit at the other.

The end of life is the rearing and training of children into efficient and well-balanced manhood and womanhood. It is the building of character. If you believe in personal immortality, then you will believe that this character-building is for some life of unknown splendor beyond the grave. If you believe, with the Positivist, only in a social immortality, still you will believe that this character-building is the end of life, though its issue be a social order in some unknown future of the earth. In either case the object of life is the development of manhood and womanhood.

That this process may be carried on, the fathers and mothers and children must be fed and clothed and sheltered. So material industries are organized—agriculture, manufactures, commerce. They must learn the laws of nature and human nature with which they have to deal; for this purpose the higher institutions of learning are organized. Questions of mutual right and mutual obligation will arise between them which must be peacefully settled by arbitration; hence laws and courts of justice exist. They will be threatened at times by wrong-doers within the community or by other communities foreign to their own; hence domestic government, armies and navies. They must not only be equipped with intelligence but inspired with noble motives;

hence the institutions of religion. But all institutions, religious, military, political, judicial, educational, industrial, are tributary to the work of character-building, to the education and development of children into a complete manhood and womanhood.

In this work of character-building the mother takes first place. The child in this plastic condition is given to her to mold, to fashion, to instruct, and to inspire. The teacher in the primary and secondary schools takes the second place. She is a kind of second mother, supplementing and continuing the mother's work. If in this great complex organization which we call life, in which every function is essential to the completed result, one work can be called more important than another, then the most important work in life is that of the mother in the home.

The mother of a family has her mind and hands full; but her heart is also full of happiness, and her life is filled with all that makes life worth while.

Her task is not easy. The successful mother requires to be so much. She requires not only patience, but poise; not only justice, but judgment; not only energy, but properly applied energy; not only tenderness, but firmness; not only the desire to form character in her children, but the character in herself which shall be a living example.

It is not sufficient for a mother to say to her children, "Be truthful" if she herself is not truthful. She must not discipline her children for misrepresenting facts, while she frightens them into good behavior with the terrors of bugaboos. Else she loses the point, not only by shaking their faith in herself when they learn better, but by conditioning their tendency to goodness upon a wrong and therefore temporary motive. She should rather teach them the advantages of truth according to the law of compensation, setting forth that every good thought or act has its harvest in kind, just as every evil thought or sinister act has a certain return in misery.

The children of a real mother are not incidents in her life. They are her life. Her interest in them does not vary with her moods. They create her moods. The unfolding of their natural tendencies day by day is the textbook from which she studies. Therein she finds the derivatives around which she builds to form their character. She keeps her heart young. Her sympathies are keen for the things that interest youth. She is their friend, their confidante. She is one of them—a superior one—with the knowledge of her years and the spirit of theirs.

These are the mothers we need. If the women who yearn to accomplish something would cease straining their eyes toward the distant horizon for a life-work and look to the field in which they stand, we might have more of them. The economics of home and nation are closely allied. The government of our country depends upon the men who rule it. The character of these men has its genesis in the home.

The character of the home is made and enlarged or limited by the woman who is the mother of that home.   The national capital is founded on the national hearth.

THE COUNTRY DOCTOR.

The country doctor—I see him still with memory's eye, as I saw him often on the country roads, a ruddy old gentleman, somewhat stern of countenance, somewhat shabby of attire, his loose and wrinkled garb time-worn by trips of mercy over the Pennsylvania hills, sitting erect in his buggy, one muscular hand resting on his knee, the other holding the reins of his familiar old white mare.

The doctor who in my mind's eye typifies all country doctors, had a Websterian head set on a gladiator's frame, the massive face edged by luxuriant side-whiskers. While shaving carefully the rest of his face, the doctor left his "sides" quite untrimmed, so that the effect was that of a shaggy forest flanked by a new-mown field.

On his head, save during the summer heats, he wore the familiar "coon" cap given him years before by a patient weak in purse but strong at the trigger, and owner of the best "coon-dog" in the country. The cap was one of the doctor's most cherished treasures. As the years flew by and the linings wore out, he renewed them, preserving ever the cap's form and the whalebone vizor, on whose upper and central edge the coon's striped head had been sewed, nose outward. It was a whimsical medley—the doctor's strong human face below, the coon's sharp vulpine features above, and both symbolizing the keen wit and sterling character which blended in the doctor's personality.

He was in no outward way an extraordinary man, nor was his life eventful. There among the Pennsylvania hills he grew up, and there he lived in the same sunny old farm homestead where he first saw the light of day. In old neighborhoods, and especially farm neighborhoods, people come to know one another—not clothes-knowledge, nor money-knowledge—but that sort of knowledge that reaches down into the hidden springs of human character. A country community may be deceived by a stranger, but not by one of its own people. For it is not a studied knowledge; it resembles that slow geologic uncovering before which not even the deep buried bones of the prehistoric saurin remain finally hidden.

He was a bachelor, whose household goods were guarded by a spinster sister. Folks hinted at an old love affair, as a sequel to which the doctor had given up a promising city practice for the arduous toil of the way-back country town. But the tale rested on the vaugest of tradition, and the old doctor had long before lived down, alike, his neighbors' serious matrimonial advice and homespun jokes on the same theme.

In the sick-room, the doctor was a healer even without medicine, joining in one flesh skilled physician and trained nurse. Quiet foot, tender hand, features which by the bedside seemed like sunshine on rock, were allied with wondrous skill in diagnosis and in treatment—a sort of healing instinct inherited from an ancestory of doctors.

His brothers of the profession marvelled that so bright a flame could hide itself under the bushel of a country practice. Summer and winter he drove the country roads, where he had seen most of the population into the world and had held the hands of many who went out. It was the plain, hard life of a country doctor, and yet it seemed to rise in the community like some great tree, its roots buried deep in the soil of our common life, its branches close to the sky.

To those accustomed to the excitements of city life, it would have seemed barren and uneventful. And when we come to think of it, goodness *is* uneventful. It does not flash, it glows. It is deep, quiet and very simple. Mere greatness offers no reward to compare with it, for greatness compels that homage which we freely bestow upon goodness. It passes not with oratory; it is commonly foreign to riches, nor does it often sit in the places of the mighty; but in may be felt in the touch of a friendly hand or the look of a kindly eye.

The doctor had an odd way of disparaging his patient's ailment. The sufferer might be pretty sick, yet, in the old doctor's dictum, he was only "somewhat uncomfortable." "Rather unwell," marked the next lower stage, plain "sick" the next, which finally evolved into "pretty sick" if the patient drew near the shadows. In the sick-room and in consultation, he scorned the big words and Greek and Latin derivatives of his profession, stabbing them with the phrase, "Dead tongues don't cure living bodies."

In night work, the abomination of the doctor's life, he seemed to take delight, and his gig, with its swaying lantern, was a kind of cherry beacon to the whole countryside. To a night call he never failed response, and tradition told of but once when his patience recoiled.

It was at two o'clock on an April morning when the tired doctor was aroused by a farm-hand, on horseback, who said curtly that his employer was very sick, then galloped away. The doctor dressed, harnessed his old mare, drove her seven miles through the dusty highway, and had just neared the home of his patient when the messenger met him with the words, "Doctor, I started to ride back to tell yer to bring yer forceps: Mr. Smith's got a bad toothache." Then for the first and last time the doctor turned homeward and spoke some words suspiciously profane.

A touch of irony ever veined the doctor's humor. It was when Levi, very aged and quite worthless, sole colored man in the village, and with a flexible biography as to marital faith and hen-roosts, fell sick with an ailment more painful than deadly and cried, "Doctor, I wish this pore old nigger was dead," that the doctor responded, "Guess 'twould be about as well, about as well."

The doctor's goodness was of the sort that reaches out its beneficence into future generations. As he drove along the country roads, he stopped here and there to plant a young fruit tree carefully taken up by the roots from his orchard. One of the beauties of the neighborhood today is the doctor's trees, now grown tall and laden with Nature's bounty.

Almost five decades of his hard country practice had gone by when the old doctor left us. He has just mounted his buggy for the far night ride to a sick-room when paralysis seized him, and next day a second attack took him away—quickly and without pain, as he had ever wished. In a brief rally into consciousness, he counted a few of his own pulse-beats, smiled, and said playfully, "Too late, the patient will die." "If doctor had only been sure of the doctrine, he'd a been jest about a saint," was pious old Phœbe Grant's comment. And he was just about that—without the doctrines.

ADDRESS AT A GIRLS' "HIGH-Y" BANQUET.

There is nothing more inspiring than to face an audience such as this, for a young girl's outlook upon life has all the keen zest of the explorer who has just set foot upon unchartered lands—and indeed each one of you is embarked upon a voyage of discovery—to discover what? Yourselves, and your relation to all life.

From every state of the United States; from the Isthmus of Panama and the Hawaiian Islands, from South America, France, Roumania, Russia, China, and the islands of the sea, girls have gathered under one banner—the blue triangle—for that voyage of discovery, the purpose of which is "to find and give the best."

One who seeks good and seeks to do good must have honesty of purpose, the sincerity that was exemplified in the character of Sir Galahad, purest and noblest of all the knights of King Arthur's Round Table, and who alone from all that sought it looked upon the Holy Grail. This thought-germ of sincerity is crystallized in your motto and slogan: "To face life squarely."

As one turns a perfectly-cut gem this way and that, and from every facet finds a new revelation of symmetry and beauty, so this motto may be examined minutely, ever unfolding new meanings, new inspiration.

What is it to be "square?" Ask the mason, as he tries the first runs of stone or brick in the building, and he will tell you that unless the foundation walls meet at right angles or squarely, the superstructure cannot be erected with any promise of permanence.

To face life squarely, expanded to all its full significance, means to be loyal to principles and to friends, earnest in purpose, reverent toward things holy, cheerful and ready to serve others, gracious in manner, impartial in judgment, eager in seeking true knowledge, dependable in small things and great, and sincere at all times.

One hundred and two thousand members of the "High-Y—what a tremendous power for good that represents! More than one-tenth of a million girls whose lives have been consecrated to noble purposes. And what are those purposes? They are to live as a Christian girl of her age should and to put into practice in her community her standards of Christian living.

The program is four-fold in its emphasis, and includes health, knowledge, service, and spirit.

Why is health important? Because a girl must be vigorously well if she expects to do her part in the world and to keep in thoroughly good spirits. The laws of health are few and simple. They may be summed up in a very few words: Breath fresh air, take plenty of exercise, eat such food as you can thoroughly digest, work regularly with body and mind, and take all the rest you need.

Knowledge means to acquire a practical education, that is, an education that will fit a girl for life. What will best fit a girl for life? First of all, a well-balanced character. The first thing we all need is to have our wills so trained that when we see the right, we may instantly do it, and we need to be taught to see clearly what is right.

But as character may be formed in many ways, why not form it by learning practical things? What, then, does a girl most need to know? To read the right kind of books, to cook healthful and tasteful meals, to make her own clothing, choosing simplicity and quality rather than display in dress, to keep a bank account and practice thrift through daily economies.

The grand aim of life should be the same for all, whether gifted or not. But the particular aim must vary with the individual. Probably with five girls out of ten the particular aim is to have a happy home. While many girls wish to be the center of a happy home, they are often careless about the means of making themselves fit for such a position.

They think that when love comes it will do everything, and it is true that it will do wonders. But suppose a girl remembers that if she is well she can make her family happier than if she is always ailing; suppose she remembers how much good housekeeping does to make a home attractive—is she not more likely to have a happy home than if her aim had been less definite?

This leads directly to the thought of service, which is really the corner stone of the Girl Reserve creed, as it is also the corner stone of national stability. Service takes nothing from the few, while it opens up to the many the opportunities for a richer, fuller, more complete life. It is the cement that binds society into a solid foundation upon which to build better places in which to live and work.

The opportunities for service are manifold. If you have ever experienced the pure delight of helping some family of poor children to have a real Christmas, you will know a joy that transmutes the dross of selfish pleasure into pure gold. If you have helped to provide a scholarship to keep some other girl in school, you will feel an inspiration that comes from constructive effort toward a noble cause.

And back of all and directing all is the animating spirit—that intangible something that binds the "High-Y" into one living, breathing entity. It is the motive power of team-work—the sort of thing that carries a victorious football eleven to success. If you have that spirit, all things are possible, for right aspirations, persistenly cherished, will surely come to pass.

IN EVERY TODAY WALKS A TOMORROW.

It is related of an Eastern magician that he discovered by his sorcery that the philosopher's stone, which was able to turn baser metals into gold, lay on the bank of a certain river, but he was unable to determine its exact location. He therefore walked along the bank with a piece of iron, which he applied successively to all the pebbles that he found.

As one after another they produced no change in the metal, he threw them back into the stream. At last he met with the object of his search, and the iron became gold in his hand; but he had become so accustomed to the movement of throwing the pebbles back into the stream, that he involuntarily tossed the precious stone away from him, and it was lost forever.

Thus in the acts that we do today is contained a prophecy of what we shall do tomorrow. Every time we perform any action, mental or physical, we have more inclination to, and greater facility for, the performance of that action under similar circumstances than we had before. A new task learned in the evening becomes easier to perform each morning than it was the night before, and easier still on Monday morning than it was on Saturday evening. The Germans go as far as to say that we learn to skate in summer and to swin in winter. What they mean is this, that having been taught to skate in the winter, the impression deepens unconsciously all through the summer, so that we find ourselves much more proficient when the next winter comes around.

How powerfully the actions of today influence the conduct of tomorrow is shown in an incident related by Harriet Mattineau. A tribe of Indians attacked a white settlement and murdered the few inhabitants. An Indian woman, however, carried away a baby from the settlement, and reared it as her own. The child grew up with the Indian children, different in complexion, but like them in all other ways. To scalp the greatest number of enemies was, in his view, the most glorious thing in the world, and he became a fearless and successful warrior.

While he was still hardly more than a lad, he was seen by some white traders, who persuaded him to accompany them back of civilized life. He showed a great interest in his new surroundings and an earnest desire for knowledge. He went through a school and college course with credit, and was ordained as a clergyman.

After a few years he went to serve in a settlement near the seat of war between Great Britain and the United States, and learning that the former had some tribes of Indians for allies, he went out to look for some of his former associates. When he returned, one of his friends in the white settlement was struck by a singular change in his manner and in the expression of his face ,and then, noticing blood on his shirt, asked if he were wounded.

He denied this, and crossed his hands firmly on his breast, but his friend, supposing that he wished to conceal a wound, unclasped his hands and was horrified to find beneath them a bloody scalp. "I could not help it," said the poor victim of early habits, and turning, ran swiftly back to the Indian camp and was never again induced to leave their tribe.

"A character," as J. S. Mill says, "is a completely fashioned will;" and a will is an aggregate of tendencies to act in a certain fixed and definite manner which has largely been established by custom. A tendency to act only becomes effectively established in us in proportion to the frequency with which the actions actually occur and the brain grows "used" to their repetition.

Could the young but realize how soon they will become mere walking bundles of habit, they would give more heed to their conduct while in the plastic state. We are spinning our own fates, good or evil, and never to be undone. The drunken Rip Van Winkle, in Jefferson's play, excuses himself for each fresh lapse from sobriety by saying, "I won't count this time!" Well, he may not count it, but it is being counted none the less. Down among his nerve cells and fibres the molecules are counting it, registering and storing it up to be used against him when the next temptation comes.

"In every today walks a tomorrow." Nothing we ever do is, in strict literal sense, every effaced. Of course, this has its good as well as its bad side. As we become permanent drunkards by so many separate drinks, so we become respected and honored in the moral world, and authorities and experts in the practical and scienific spheres, by so many separate good acts and so many hours of conscientious work.

Let no youth have any anxiety about the outcome of his education, whatever the line of it may be. If he keep faithfully busy every hour of the working day, he may safely leave the final result to itself. He can with perfect certainty count on waking some morning to find himself one of the competent ones of his generation, in whatever pursuit he may have singled out. Silently, between all the details of his business, the power of judging in all that line of endeavor will have built itself up within him as a possession that will never pass away. Young people should know this truth in advance. The ignorance of it has probably caused more discouragement and faint-heartedness in youths embarking on active careers than all other causes put together.

It is necessary, above all things, never to lose a battle. Every gain on the wrong side undoes the effect of many conquests on the right. The necessary precaution, therefore, is to so regulate the opposing forces of right and wrong that the right may have a series of uninterrupted successes, until repetition has fortified it to such a degree as to enable it to cope with the oppositiion under any circumstances with the assurance of success.

VOCATIONAL TRAINING.

The old idea of human progress was that only by slow and almost imperceptible steps can civilization evolve to its highest forms, or the inherent evils of human society be overcome. Today science has so revolutionized most of our early concepts that we find many of the things we have believed in unable to bear the clear light of critical analysis.

The early history of our country demanded the public school. Today the times demand another equally important step to accelerate the evolution of social progress, to prevent decadence, and to keep step with the rapid strides of the mechanical arts.

The people need and demand a broader, deeper, more complete education, expressed in terms of present-day conditions and made universal just as was the public school. Benjamin Franklin's father took his boy out walking to observe various tradesmen at work in order to learn the youth's particular bent or inclination. All parents do not exercise the same wise forethought, and vocational guidance is becoming recognized as a legitimate and important function of the public school.

It is said that the most dangerous point in the lives of children in the elementary school is the moment at which they leave it. Unless children are properly directed at this turning point in their lives, the knowledge and discipline acquired at school may be lost and they may become eventually unfit either for employment or for further education.

II

Boys and girls on leaving school are thrust into industry in great numbers, and are taken merely as process workers and not as apprentices. Too many boys fall into the casual employments or blind-alley jobs that drive them into the ranks of the unskilled, and later they drift along as vocational tramps. New demands are therefore made for solving the problem of vocational education.

In our colleges, seminaries and universities, where pure science should have its best expression, we too often find instead the most persistent adherence to the old and unscientific methods of memory cramning, with total neglect of hand training. This system is in direct antagonism with the teaching of Spencer, that a more scientific and practical education not only better fits for complete living, but for higher attainments and the enjoyment of all that is ethical and aesthetic in life.

It is to meet this emergency in our educational system that the vocational school has come into existence. The remark is often made that our social progress does not keep pace with our mechanical progress. To prepare for the higher civilization that is surely coming, the first and most important step is to introduce a general system of industrial and vocational education, which, as a noted expert declares, "produces a new and superior order of people."

If our civilization is to reach its highest attainment, we must come to see that no aim or object of social desire is so great as the best possible development and training of the average citizenship; and the present haste and waste of rushing immature children from the schools into bread-winning life, to become, like the machines they operate in factory and shop, mere automatons, is most harmful and ultimately destructive of national permanence.

Pupils who enter a vocational school at fourteen to sixteen years of age cannot begin life in any possible manner so hopefully, so advantageously, as in a course that from its very nature draws out and develops the thinking powers and applies the thinking to practical work with the hands. The whole effort of working to create the needs of physical life, aside from its healthful, hygienic value, is admirably adapted to develop the ability to reason from cause to effect, and thus strengthen the logical powers.

It seems unaccountable that such deference has been paid to the teachings of the great educator, Froebel, and yet that so little is known of the breadth of his philosophy of a complete educational system, of which the kindergarten, usually consider the sum total of his educational process, is only the first rung of the ladder.

In his ideal, the carrying forward of a system of handicraft and vocational training through all the subsequent processes of education was fully as essential as was the kindergarten as the first step. He looked upon man as essentially a creator, and the development of his creative faculties as a necessary part of his education. He declared that it was but little use to develop the receptive powers of the brain, without at the same time, and as a necessary reflex action, developing the active and formative powers of the mind.

He made skilled labor a part of morality and religion, and the culture of the mechanical productive faculties a portion of spiritual growth. He discredited attempts at the elevation of the race merely by storing the money with facts and literary concepts, while neglecting to develop the creative powers of the brain and the dexterity of the hand. He aimed to follow the pathway of all race progress with each individual of the race; first cultivating the hand to do; then the brain to remember how and why.

To express one's self and to develop individuality by the creative skill of the hands was with him a foundation principle; and we can best develop the latent faculties of the race by imitating his profound philosophy. Vocational training is built upon this broad and secure foundation and is allied with all that is best in the constructive ideals of our social and industrial life.

THE INFLUENCE OF MANUAL TRAINING ON CHARACTER.

The theory that the school should fit boys and girls, too, is now, more than ever before, accepted by all leading educators. It is therefore only natural that manual training has found a place in the curriculum that it is deemed important to train the hands in the use of tools and of practical grafting.

But aside from its practical utility, manual training also affects character. It is something no boy should miss. For it is here in the manual training class that he learns some of the most important lessons. It is here that he discovers that manual training is, after all, not such a tremendous hardship as he had imagined. Girls likewise, if instructed in sewing, cooking, etc., will soon be amazed at the fact that their mothers really know more than they had thought. In other words, manual training is apt to teach our American youth some respect for common labor, for the man who can not always promenade clad in a silk shirt and in clothes made according to the latest style, but who has to work in the sweat of his brow to earn a living for himself and his family.

I once heard of a high school boy who one day found himself in a manual training class. I say, found himself there, for how he ever came to be in a shop where they did carpenter work, he himself was unable to discover. His curiosity having been aroused, he stayed where he was. When evening came, he felt more tired than he had ever been before. Neither Latin, nor physics, nor algebra, nor any other of the cultural studies had ever put him in a shape like this. His limbs ached, for he had been told to use the saw and the plane, and to use them vigorously. All at once it dawned upon him why "dad" was so tired when he returned from the factory; all at once it came to him how hard his father had to work to give him and the other children an education. In this case, manual training increased the boy's self-respect, and still more, it prompted him to think more of his father.

In the next place, let us bear in mind that the direct object of manual training is not to produce an article of merit but rather to develop the power to produce. It awakens innate faculties and gives him self-reliance and courage. It brings home to him the truth of the old saying that no one knows what he can really do until he tries.

Another effect of manual training is the cultivation of habits of industry. To be industrious, thrifty, to practice economy and kindred virtues are qualities somewhat foreign to many of our American youths. Of course, manual training will scarcely change a lazy boy into an industrious one over night. But since, as psychologists tell us, repetition is at the foundation of every habit, we can reasonably assume that continuous practice in handling tools and making objects well worth the time spent in their fabrication, will, at least, gradually, beget habits of industry where they were before but little known.

Again; manual training is apt to make boys and girls more contented with their respective lots. It is a well-known fact that quite a number of youths dislike school because they are more or less averse to "book-learning." They like to "tinker" at something; to do work, in which, according to their view they find more pleasure because they consider it more useful. Many a boy has been held in school by means of putting him in the manual training class when nothing else could have kept him within the confines of the "old building." To be contented, to be satisfied and to be permitted to do what one likes to do, are great factors in the formation of character.

Furthermore, since manual training requires initative, and often even imagination, it teaches the pupil to rely on his own resources and his own ability. Moreover, let it not be forgotten that quite a number of boys have earned their first dollars by disposing of articles which they learned to make in school. Every boy feels proud when a dollar or two jingles in his pockets, even if they had been given to him by an over-indulgent uncle or aunt. But who does not recall the pleasure that was his when he earned his first few dollars. How proud did he feel. He stepped along as proudly as if he were the next person to Mr. Rockefeller or Mr. Ford. To have earned some money increases the self-respect of the boy, gives him an air of independence and a feeling of superiority. It is for this reason that manual training may be said to develop some of the most manly virtues,—provide the pupil can sell some of his handiwork.

A MESSAGE TO GARCIA.

He who voluntarily undertakes a mission in the cause of humanity, and who never hesitates or falters in his task until it is accomplished to the best of his ability, is truly a hero. The most glowing pages of history record the deeds of men and women who have been faithful even unto death and who have placed the interest of the race above that of the individual.

What matter whether such service in the cause of humanity receives public recognition or not? It was not undertaken with any such paltry end in view, and though reward may come, the world can never adequately repay the services of its great benefactors.

On one occasion, as Napoleon was riding in review down the long lines of his gallant soldiers, he passed a company commanded by an aged captain who by some oversight had never received the promotion to which he was entitled by his bravery and long service. As his commander passed by, the old soldier with eyes fixed straight ahead, said distinctly, but in respectful tones:

"Fifteen campaigns, Sire: private, lieutenant, captain."

And Napoleon, without halting his steed as he swept past the files of bronzed veterans instantly called out:

"Major, colonel, brigadier-general, marshal of the Empire."

While we recognize the justice of this swift promotion, our admiration would be deeper had the old captain served on without presenting any claim to higher rank.

Crucial circumstances in the affairs of nations often place grave responsibility in the hands of a single individual. If he fail in his courage or loyalty, history may have to be written in a minor key and great opportunities be lost beyond recovery.

It was the wise Solomon who wrote: "As the cold of snow in the time of harvest, so is a faithful messenger to them that send him; for he refresheth the soul of his masters."

When war broke out between the United States and Spain, there was urgent need to communicate quickly with Garcia, leader of the Cuban insurgents, to secure his coöperation and advice. Garcia was somewhere in the mountain fastness of Cuba—but where, and how could he be reached, when mail and telegraph services were powerless?

Someone familiar with Cuban conditions remarked to President McKinley: "There's a fellow by the name of Rowan who will find Garcia for you, if anybody can."

So Rowan was summoned, and the president looked into his clear, honest eyes and gave him a letter to be delivered to Garcia. It was a simple trust, and committed to its bearer without flourish of oratory, but as President McKinley handed the letter to his messenger, he realized the truth of the statement, "Rowan will find Garcia for you, if anybody can."

Rowan took the letter, sealed it in an oil-skin pouch, strapped it over his heart, and set out upon his fateful mission. He sailed for four days down the Atlantic seaboard, landed by night on the coast of Cuba from an open boat, and then vanished into the jungle. There were wild beasts and watchful enemies to elude, food and drink to be secured, and devious paths to be followed where an error of judgment would have meant dangerous delay, but throughout it all he kept the precious letter safely hidden in his bosom and forged steadily on toward the point where he knew that he would find the leader of the Cuban patriots.

The story of that journey has never been written in detail as was the story of that splendid and spectacular voyage of the "Oregon" from San Francisco to Key West, after a cruise of 17,499 miles on two oceans and double the length of a continent, but both were inspired by the same unwavering patriotism, and both were equally successful.

In three weeks, Rowan came out on the other side of the island of Cuba, having traversed a hostile country on foot, and delivered his letter to Garcia. His work was done ,and he sought no reward or plaudit of admiring throngs. He had been true to his country and his president, he had delivered his message to Garcia.

But the story of his deed was too brilliant and inspiring to remain hidden in the voluminous pages of official documents, and Fame paused in her record of battles to write high on her scroll the name of a simple citizen who did his duty.

After the battle of Thermopylæ, the Amphictyonic Council erected on the summit of the mountain, near the famous Pass, a plain and unpretentious column in memory of the three hundred Greeks of Sparta who gave their lives in defense of her liberty. Its inscription read: "Traveller, go tell at Sparta that we rest here in obedience to her sacred laws." There was no need to chisel upon that column the names of the three hundred patriots: they could be recited without an omission by every school child in Sparta. This was Fame in its purest and most worthy form.

And as the story of the war with Spain is handed down to future generations, the name of Rowan will be preserved beside that of Dewey and Sampson. Each gave in different degree according to his ability, but each gave from the pure fountain of patriotic devotion.

WHAT A FARM BUREAU CAN DO FOR FARMERS.

That the farmers of the country are awakening to the necessity of employing modern, business-like methods in conducting their farms if they want to secure the best results, is becoming more apparent every day. The rapidity with which Farm Bureaus are being formed all over the United States is the best proof in the world that the men who till the soil are beginning to realize that antiquated methods and old-fashioned ideas have no more place on the farm than in any other line of work.

The idea of the Farm Bureau originated in 1911, when the Crop Improvement Committee of the Council of Grain Exchanges conceived the plan of placing an agricultural expert and advisor to farmers in every county in the United States. The committee started to work to raise a fund for this purpose, and this fund received a tremendous stimulus in the shape of a million-dollar donation from Julius Rosenwald, of Chicago, who provided in the gift that one thousand dollars should go to each of the first thousand counties that were willing to coöperate in the work.

Two of the first counties to avail themselves of this gift were Kankakee County, Illinois, and Pettis County, Missouri. The farmers and business men of Kankakee County were quickly impressed with the great value of the Crop Improvement Committee's plan, and determined to win the honor of being the first county in the United States to qualify for one of the thousand-dollar donations.

A few far-sighted men behind the scheme had a dream of double crop production, and of resultant prosperity that would make Kankakee County the best place in the world to live in. The idea caught the imagination of the people of Kankakee County. Farmers, bankers, millers, manufacturers, joined hands to raise the money needed to put the bureau on a permanent basis. In less than two weeks more than $10,000 was raised, and the organization known as the Kankakee County Soil and Crop Improvement Association was incorporated with a capital stock of $50,000.

Prof. John S. Collier, of the Agricultural Department of the University of Illinois, was engaged as the Association's expert. His duties were to advise the farmers, individually and collectively, as to the best methods of cultivating their farms, to point out mistakes and prescribe the remedies, to organize clubs, associations, etc., to give practical farm demonstration in crop rotation, soil building and farm management.

Prof. Collier then started to plat every farm in the county, of which there were about 2,500, making a complete history of each, together with a soil analysis. The county authorities contributed the use, rent free, of four commodious rooms in the new half million-dollar county building as the Association's headquarters. In these were established Prof. Collier's office, a large meeting room, a library of books, a rest room for the farmers' wives and a large playground for the farmers' children. A completely equipped agricultural laboratory was also installed by the Kankakee High School.

As soon as the association was formed, work was started to secure co-workers in every township in the county. These sent in regular reports of the progress of crop improvement. Domestic science was made a part of the work of the county farm bureau, in charge of a competent woman who made a study of home life throughout the county and acted as an adviser to the farmers' wives.

The soil expert went over each field and gave advice as to its management. Another plan of the bureau was the formation of a seed testing association, which made it possible to insure clean, tested seeds for every farmer in the county. A seed house was erected in Kankakee, equipped with seed cleaning and seed grading machinery of the most approved type. It was estimated that clean and tested seed alone would add half a million dollars to the crop value of the county.

The county adviser was always on the job. He not only visited the different farms in the county during the spring, summer and fall, but gave lectures during the winter and answered all letters sent him. He brought to the county in concrete shape all the scientific facts that had so long been bottled up in our colleges and experiment stations.

Strange as it may seem, the smallest part of the county farm agent's work proved to be advisory. The farmers resent the adviser idea, and justly. No class of people likes to be the subject of definite uplift work; but the first problems to be solved in rural communities are those of organization and team-work, which make it possible to secure the results aimed at.

For instances it requires the coöperation of a neighborhood to adopt single varieties of grain and standardize the product of the community so that it can be offered in sufficient quantity to command higher prices. Hog cholera cannot be eradicated unless the community works together in reporting the disease so that serum can be promptly administered and such sanitary precautions taken as are necessary to prevent it from spreading.

One man cannot drag the roads continually. An individual farmer can hardly be expected to keep his place free from weeds if his neighbor allow the some weeds to mature just across the fence. Smut cannot be eradicated from one farm if winds from surrounding fields blow across that place, carrying the disease spores.

The county adviser takes note of the different soil types, the drainage, the fertility, the adaptability of the varieties of seeds to that particular farm; he also takes note of the position of the farm buildings, the social and economic conditions of the neighborhood, and attempts to get in close touch with the farmer and his family.

In the fall, when most of the farms have been visited and the soils analyzed, the adviser meets the farmers of each township in an all-day conference. He tells each man what is deficient in his soil, what sort of crop he had better plant for the ensuing year and the proper rotation, and advises the farmers in a multitude of other personal problems.

The farm bureau is rightly considered a business man's movement and emanates largely from commercial sources, primarily for commercial reasons. In it the farmers have been recognized in their true light as the prime movers of commerce, and, being a part of the organization, they will not only help build it up, but get their just share of the benefits.

ADDRESS AT A DISTRICT TEACHER'S ASSOCIATION.

A woman of philanthropic tendencies was paying a visit to a lower East Side school. She was especially interested in a group of poor pupils, and asked permission to question them.

"Children," she asked, "what is the greatest of all virtues?"

No one answered.

"Now think a little. What is it I am doing when I give up time and pleasure to come and talk with you for your own good?"

A grimy hand went up in the rear of the room. "Please, ma'am," said a voice, "you'se buttin' in."

I am glad to have the opportunity of "butting in" today to introduce the president of our association, whom you all know as one of the leading educators of the State. We welcome him as a leader and fellow-worker in the noble cause of education—that great army with its 680,000 members, each representing an ever-widening circle of influence.

In these days when the world is turning to the schools for the solution of many of its perplexing problems and for the quieting of its crisis of unrest, we all realize the great responsibility resting upon us, as well as the exceptional opportunities afforded us, for rendering a service that is beyond price to our community, our State, and our Nation.

The schools of America are dedicated to the transmission in their purest form of the folk-ways of democracy to the next generation. That is, it is the purpose of our schools to train the young for life in a democratic society. The traditions, the ceremonials, the habits of thought, the skill and lore, the character, the standards of social and political morality to be transmitted through American schools, are the essence of democracy. And since our children are to live their lives in these democratic folk-ways, the schools must know democracy and its characteristic life before they can set up their machinery with intelligent purpose.

The folk-ways of democracy—how do they differ from organized human society generally? They are distinctive in several ways. First and most characteristic is the ideal of liberty. Our people have liberty as a part of their being. We sometimes even forget how it was won after a mighty struggle, how our fathers endured hardship and faced death to gain it. We take liberty for granted. We demand for ourselves liberty of thought, liberty of movement, liberty of possession, liberty of speech.

And with this innate sense of liberty comes a consciousness of equality. We take without questioning Thomas Jefferson's dictum that all men are created equal. American folk have a powerful conviction that there is no rank, nobility, upper class or distinction, that is not largely assumption. Even military rank is accepted with reservation, and social precedence is but an idle and presumptuous arrogance.

Our liberty and equality express themselves in the formula of "a government of the people, by the people, for the people." The people is itself the government; the people of itself supplies the individual agents of government; and the people claims all the benefits of government.

The sanction of government lies in the consent of the governed; government is instituted to secure liberty and equality for the people. Citizenship therefore rises at once to a level with the old conceptions of royalty. The government agent is a ruler, a sovereign, yet a servant of all the people. The government rests firmly in the consent of the governed, and can have no cause for being except the welfare of the governed.

The school having these fundamental characteristics clearly in view, may now outline the quality of citizenship which it is to foster and perpetuate. Its objects will be to inculcate the virtues of the perfect citizen. Liberty calls for self-control, voluntary observance of law and order, unselfishness, a lofty deference to the rights of others. Equality calls for humility and generous regard for all good qualities in our neighbors; and our formula of government requires a ready responsiveness to all social needs.

Briefly stated, liberty, equality and individual sovereignty, the blessings of democracy, presuppose a high degree of self-control, humility and serviceableness in the conduct of citizens. Without these elements of behavior, democracy will tend to become tyranny.

And if our democracy is to endure in its present form, the schools must produce socially-minded citizens. Everything admitted to the school curriculum must have a social value, and its social significance must be set in high relief. Our teaching must have a social purpose in place of the old individualistic purpose. Instead of making the child conscious of a selfish value of skill and knowledge, we must electrify him with a consciousness of the community value of such skill and knowledge.

Democracy is an ideal organization of human society, and as such it is built on the presumption that education can eliminate the unfit of all kinds and can socialize and morally magnetize the fit. The distance between this ideal and the dead level of ordinary human ignorance and selfishness is the measure of the need of education for a democracy.

The education demanded of the schools is that which frees the human spirit and enables it to become master of itself; which trains the will to obedience; which clarifies the judgment; which purifies the emotions; and education that fits man for association with his fellows in the bonds of peace and liberty and law.

LITERATURE ON SOCIAL PROBLEMS.

When I learned from our Program Committee the subject assigned me for this paper, I confess that I felt somewhat like a certain little girl in a public library, who, after taking down from the shelf a copy of Pope's "Essay on Man," and studying its contents in great perplexity for some minutes, was heard to remark, "This may me *easy on man*, but it's hard on children."

Among the vast number of books on social problems that have appeared within recent years, one looks with some uncertainty for a few that may be taken as representative of the trend of public thought along the lines that are included in that comprehensive term "social science."

Many of the sacred formulas of the past about government, about laws, and about social conditions, are today in the crucible to find if there is any base metal in them. Modern politics has changed its character, and deals with a whole set of new questions. Economic theories on supply and demand, on competition, on the rights of property, are being examined from every angle.

The critical spirit is creating for man a new self-consciousness. Psychology works patiently to discover the nature and laws of the mind. Sociology seeks to relate the individual to the larger life of society.

There are certain broad characteristics of our age that make it peculiar. There are certain forces that are ceaselessly playing on modern life, and which may be said to be creating a new world. They are forces that make for change, and therefore produce unrest.

One is the critical movement, which began with investigating our ancient literature and traditional history, and has gone on to question all authority. The new criticism refuses to be warned off any ground, and is applying its acid-test to every institution of man.

The second is the scientific movement, which has done so much for practical life. This new science is not content with practical triumphs, but pushes its method so far as to test all truth.

The third is the democratic movement, which is changing society over the whole civilized world. The new democracy is not only making new conditions of life, but is invading the region of theory and making new conditions of thought.

One of the pioneers in the modern field of social science, and one to whom we are indebted for some of its most helpful literature, is Jane Addams, who in her "Twenty Years at Hull House" has collected many incidents of her study of social problems among the poor by what may be called the laboratory method in this most interesting of social settlements.

In her two later books, "The Spirit of Youth and the City Streets," and "A New Conscience and an Ancient Evil," she discusses with rare penetration and sympathy the inherent longing in the heart and soul of youth for the art and beauty of life—a cry for bread to which the city streets can offer no response but a stone. In her "Newer Ideals of Peace," she has taken up the problem of the worker from the standpoint of wages, hours of labor, and physical surroundings.

Several other women writers have treated the same subject with an insight born of practical experience. Dorothy Richardson, in her book, "The Long Day," relates her experiences as a New York factory girl, in which she shrank from no hardship that might bring with it the knowledge of actual conditions, thus illustrating that remarkable statement of Emerson: "There are moments in which we court suffering, in the hope that here at least we shall find reality, sharp peaks and edges of truth."

Mrs. John Van Vorst and her daughter, Marie, in their book, "The Woman Who Toils," made a similar excursion into the realm of the actual.

Social problems connected with immigration loom large in our city life, especially in that of New York, which receives 83 per cent of our new foreign population. Mary Antin, once herself an immigrant, has written luminously on the hopes and fears that fill the breast of the new arrival on our shores in her volume, "The Promised Land." Edward A. Steiner has treated the subject more exhaustively and scientifically in his two books, "From Alien to Citizen," and "On the Trail of the Immigrant."

One writer who could not be omitted from any list of books on Social problems is Jacob A. Riis. Like Mary Antin, he was one of our naturalized citizens, and he tells the story of that process of Americanization in a book that reads like a romance, "The Making of an American." One will find in that volume some pen pictures of the early public career of Theodore Roosevelt which cannot be excelled in sympathetic insight. Another book which no doubt has already occurred to your mind in connection with this one is "The Americanization of Edward Bok," which should be an inspiration to every American youth.

Jacob Riis was a lover of children, and his work for the improvement of conditions of child life in New York is set forth in "The Children of the Poor." Two other writers have covered the same field from different viewpoints, Ernest K. Coulter in "The Children in the Shadow," and John Spargo in "The Bitter Cry of the Children."

Prison reform has been treated by Maude Ballington Booth in "After Prison, What?" Lewis E. McBrayne and James P. Ramsay in "One More Chance," and by "No. 1500" in "Life in Sing Sing."

And so the list could be continued, but I must close this rambling excursion into the endless labyrinth of social problems and social reform lest I have the experience of a street speaker in one of our recent political campaigns. He shouted, "what we want is social reform; what we want is land reform; what we want is finance reform; what we want is prison reform," when a weary voice in the audience added, "What you want is chloroform."

THE VALUE OF THE FINE ARTS.

What is the true purpose of art—is its object utilitarian, or does it exist as a means of expressing the æsthetic emotions? To answer this question, let us go back for a moment to the beginnings of art. There have recently been discovered in caves in France and Spain relics of men who lived before the Ice Age, certainly more than 100,000 years before the Siege of Troy—men so far away from ourselves that scientists class them by their skulls as different species.

Yet these earliest known human beings had plainly felt this universal need of expression for many generations; they had gone far beyond the shaped arrow-heads which are the first art expression of primitive man. Engraved on pieces of bone, scratched on the walls of their cave homes, carved from the rack, painted in colors on the roof, are figures of reindeer, bison, and horses, so life-like that sportsmen today recognizes with a thrill the exact position he has seen a caribou take on the Newfoundland barrens, and sees in this inconceivably remote savage a blood-brother in feeling to the men who carved the deathless horses of the Parthenon.

Surely this is art—this giving immortality to a feeling about something by portraying the object that aroused it. One can fairly see this primeval hunter telling how he stalked the game he has brought in for food—and finding the quickest way to express his recollection simply to scratch the scene on a smooth, hard surface—for men two hundred thousand generations later to marvel at.

This particular race of artists vanishes from our meager records, and there is nothing to compare with their work for hundred of centuries. But the old instinct never dies; the man or woman capable of expressing emotion superlatively always reappears. It may be in basketry or pottery or rugs with beautiful designs, beautiful because they are fitted to their purpose, because they have symmetry and simplicity; because the decoration has a meaning traceable back through the ages.

It may be furniture made for Egyptian or Assyrian kings, or jewelry of exquisite design to hang about a woman's neck; or palaces decorated with all the skill of the age; in a myriad forms we find the artist using some daily necessity or luxury to express his sense of joy in life and its wonders, leaving these records of his emotions to startle the eye of beholders a dozen or a hundred thousand generations later.

What did the artist get out of it? A living perhaps, and a very poor one. Margaret of Austria, only a few hundred years ago, paid her chief architect-artist about half what she paid her head cook. But the real pay was the joy of expressing,—that mingled necessity and delight which is one of the most precious qualities of the children of men.

All these were craftsmen—men not separated from their fellows, but performing many different functions. A sixteenth century artist was apt to be at once a poet, a painter, a sculptor, an engineer and a decorator. Nothing by which he could express his surging emotion was beneath his enthusiastic attention.

Art could not help being vital under such conditions. And alive you will find it through all the stormy course of history; right down through those wonderful and maligned "Dark Ages," which produced some of the world's most precious treasures of the world's heritage, art "cried aloud in the streets," and was heard to some extent by all.

Then, as now, one of the most pleasurable results of any form of art was the opportunity offered for the development of the higher æsthetic faculties. All high culture serves as a refuge from the ills of daily life. If, then, there be in this world a retreat from its trials and cares, is it not well worth while to discover and cultivate it?

Art is a great deliverer. It has a purifying and liberating function. It purifies, for all true art is the outgrowth of reverence; it liberates as all beautiful forms of expression do by freeing one from serfdom, selfishness and narrow vision. As one objectifies his impressions, he realizes the true worth of life, which is to catch and hoard beautiful emotions, and by contemplating them, create them into new forms, new life. Thus he molds his sensibilities of life into new and beautiful works, and becomes a creative force.

Nor is the appreciator of beautiful creations cut off from the artist's joy of life. To keep the higher senses, sight and hearing, alive and alert, is to be more a man, to live more of life, than the stupid or the vulgar. A true love of art is as much a deliverer from selfishness and self-consciousness as love itself .

A noted art critic says: "You must look at pictures studiously, earnestly, honestly. It will take years before you come to a full appreciation of art; but when at last you have it, you will be possessed of one of the purest, loftiest and most ennobling pleasures."

It is not a little part of the artist's work that he discover and interpret to the world new beauty; and the value of his work may be estimated by the importance of his discovery. This is the rendering of objective beauty, tinctured, perhaps, by the artist's individuality, method, or feeling.

But there is a higher beauty in the subjective of which it is necessary to speak. The most perfect beauty lies not in external surroundings, but in the conception of the human mind. There is nothing in nature that can compare with it; beauty of form, texture of quality sink into insignificance beside it.

Take "The Sower" of Millet, and what is it that we admire about it? The texture and light could be equalled or excelled by a hundred living artists; the figure is of little consequence. It is the thought, the conception of heroism in daily life that is strikingly beautiful. It is here that art gives us in its truest sense a cultivated taste for the beautiful. As an interpreter of life, it opens the gateway into new realms of delight.

THE LAWYER'S CODE OF ETHICS.

Lawyers have always been and doubtless always will be subjected to criticism by those who picture to themselves a distorted type, examples of which unfortunately do exist and have existed, who use their knowledge of the law to impose upon or circumvent the innocent and ignorant. But this type is as much condemned by the profession itself as by the most severe critic; it is not in any respect representative, and where it flourishes it does so in spite of professional traditions, and because either of the secret manner in which it works, or of the absence of efficient machinery in the courts to follow up and punish professional misdeeds.

Lawyers as a body are not without a code of honor, and though the laws have not formulated and defined this code, lawyers themselves have to some extent done so, by their traditions and voluntary acts. One finds the same general outlines of ethical propriety in a lawyer's conduct expressed in the regulations of Rome, the Code of Christian V, of Denmark, the practices of the French Bar, the oaths in the German States, the oath of office in the Swiss Canton of Geneva, the statutory oath of the State of Washington, the code provisions of several western states, and the canons of ethics of the American Bar Association, adopted in 1908.

While these differ in detail, in underlying principle they are much the same, and they all alike advocate and enjoin a high ideal of conduct whose controlling motive is altruistic. Fundamentally and historically a lawyer's first duty is to his client, though he may not lawfully trangress certain other duties in his fidelity to his employer.

In the United States a lawyer now exercises the threefold function of adviser, representative, and advocate. The office of attorney, in the English courts, is said to have originated in a royal ordinance of

King Edward I, in 1295; and the reason for its creation is said to have been the hardship to the individual defendants of going personally from distant parts of the kingdom to attend the King's Court.

These attorneys appear to have been at the outset merely agents, standing in the place of their principals; and so fully was the agency recognized that it was said at one time that an infant or an outlaw might be an attorney. Starting from this basis, as an office, the function of the lawyer developed until now he must be of good moral character and learned in the law, and must be examined for competency, duly admitted to the bar, and sworn to support the national and state constitutions, and to administer his office to the best of his ability.

One of the ethical problems which is endlessly discussed, but upon which lawyers appear almost without exception to be agreed, is the duty of the lawyer in defending one accused of crime, whom he knows, or has substantial reasons to believe, to be guilty. In this one case lawyers as a class appear to be arrayed against a prevalent but superficial contrary sentiment in the community; they acknowledge and assert that such a defense may be properly undertaken. But even here, the proper ethical limits of such a defense are well understood.

A lawyer may not properly seek to divert suspicion from his own client, by pointing out another innocent individual as the offender, or by presenting false evidence in support of another theory; in each instance his only justifiable course is one of silence in regard to the actual facts, and of requiring the opposition to procure a verdict in strict accordance with law, and after sustaining the burden of proof which the law imposes upon the prosecution. Every precaution against wrongful conviction of an innocent man, which experience has demonstrated to be desirable to that end, is equally available as to the right of a man who asserts himself to be innocent.

Cases may arise in which it is the legal duty of the lawyer to defend a man whom he knows to be guilty, and in which he has no option. But ordinarily he can escape such a predicament, because in the United States he is ordinarily free to reject a case which is tendered to him, if its defense is distasteful or abhorrent to him.

It must be remembered that the criminal law is only a crude device at best. It is man-made and not divine; it is not accurate; it does not measure moral guilt; only to a limited extent does it allow for provocation or temptation; it rarely allows for ignorance, and never for training, education, or environment; it is not necessarily tempered with mercy; it makes no allowance for repentance; it is frequently cruel to the convict, not necessarily fitting the punishment to the crime or to the criminal; and it is always cruel to his dependents if he has previously met his obligations to them. Such being the defects of the law itself, is it matter for wonder that the lawyer in his interpretation should frequently be subjected to criticism?

When the lawyer's personal interest alone is considered, or he seeks to subvert the law to secure to his clients what is legally denied to them, then the traditions and common precepts of the profession speak with no uncertain voice. These traditions have been formulated in the canons adopted by the American Bar Association, as a purely voluntary statement of the more common precepts of professional ethics. Of these principles the following is an excellent summary:

"Above all, a lawyer will find his highest honor in a deserved reputation for fidelity to private trust and to public duty, as an honest man and as a patriotic and loyal citizen."

ADDRESS BEFORE THE KNIGHTS OF PYTHIAS.

Brother Knights:

The fact that our lodge is to have the honor of entertaining the Grand Lodge of the State is a matter for congratulation on the part of every Knight. This will bring together in our city a body of men who stand for the highest principles of morality, the most uncompromising integrity, and who represent the most exalted ideals of friendship. Our community cannot fail to be benefitted by their presence among us, and our lodge will receive a new inspiration toward exalted endeavor.

Pythianism represents a present total membership in the United States of 908,454. The influence exerted upon national ideals and community life by an organization such as this, numbering almost a million members, can hardly be overestimated. The vitality and rapid gain in membership of our order are proofs that it fills a distinct need in the life of men of the present day. That need is the desire latent in every man's heart for a closer bond of union with his fellow men, and for the assurance of a type of friendship founded upon true moral principles and conforming to the most lofty standards.

We have no record of any other fraternal order that can boast a more rapid growth than the Knights of Pythias. This is the more remarkable since the order was started while the nation was engaged in the deadly struggle of civil war. It would appear that its formation was like a bright star of peace come to shed its silver rays over a troubled and mourning nation, to dispel the clouds of gloom and hatred, and to gather in friendship's fond embrace the true and noble from all parts of the nation into one bond of reconciliation and peace.

As we contemplate the principles which underlie and animate the Knights of Pythias, and when we devote our minds to the study of their beautiful teachings, the spirit and sentiment which inspires them penetrates our being, and unconsciously we learn to model our lives more and more in harmony with their truths.

Toleration in religion is one of the tenets of our order, which holds that there is no partial, sectarian, or national God, but that whoever strives to do His will and obey His commandments is acceptable in His sight, no matter what his denomination or creed.

The injunction to obey the law makes every Knight of Pythias a loyal citizen, a man who upholds the honor of his country and who is willing to pay with his possessions, and if necessary with his life, for the protection it has afforded him. To be a Knight of Pythias is to be a good man, a good citizen, a good neighbor, and a good friend.

The last cardinal tenet of our order is loyalty to government. Loyalty includes faithfulness and the desire to promote everything that tends to secure the welfare of the nation. Consider for a moment what it means to have nearly a million men pledged to the loyal support of the nation and ready at a moment's notice to defend its honor and rights. The Knights of Pythias is indeed not only a fraternal but a patriotic organization.

But perhaps the one principle which represents the heart and soul of Pythianism is friendship. Founded upon the beautiful story of Damon and Pythias, the famous friends of ancient Syracuse, our order sheds its light over the somber scenes of human weakness and depravity like the tender reflections of the setting sun, and in its radiance faith is strengthened and confidence in human nature takes new heart of hope.

Fraternalism is one of the brightest stars upon the dark and troubled waters of existence. What a dreary place this world would be if we had no true friends whom we could trust, who are ever ready to protect our good name and defend our character, and who will fight for us and even die for us if necessary. Friendship, benevolence and charity, these are the cement that binds the elements of society into a solid and substantial structure that defy all the winds of heaven.

Every true Pythian should be like a great rock in a weary land, under whose shelter the way-worn traveller may rest from his toilsome journey and find new courage and refreshment for the days to come. The life of every true Knight should be characterized by deeds of friendship which shed a light on the pathway of fellow-Knights and bring them into a mutual bond of union.

There is a place for every true Pythiain beside his unfortunate brother, to guide and admonish, cheer and strengthen. If anyone has entered this order prompted by selfish motives, let these low ideals be lost and swept away in the great current of brotherly love, benevolence and charity, and let each member realize that the principles of Pythian knighthood lift him above the sordid objects of material gain.

A Pythian should endeavor to free himself from every practice which savors of immortality, selfishness or hypocrisy, and to so order his life that no one may point at him the finger of scorn. The family circle of every true Pythian should be a minature lodge for dispensing deeds of friendship, charitiy and benevolence.

The ultimate ground of all fraternity is brotherly love. The heart

that loves its fellow-man is in tune with nature and with all mankind.
And with the growth of the principles of our beloved order will come
a widening faith, enduring patience, unselfish ambition, and affection
which will bear the test of time and trial.

THE SUNDAY SCHOOL AND THE COMMUNITY.

The first Sunday school established in this country solely for moral
and religious instruction was the school at Beverly, Mass., connected
with Rev. Abiel Abbot's parish, and instituted in 1810. The second
was that of Rev. Dr. Lowell's parish, opened in 1812. Both of these
were societies or parishes of Liberal Christians. Another Sunday
school of the same denomination was established at Cambridge, Mass.,
in 1814, and another at Wilton, N. H., in 1816.

The Sunday school has for its basis the fundamental principle that
moral and religious instruction is an original and indispensable want
of the child's nature; and that other and more efficient means than
parental instruction and example and the ordinary services of the
church are requisite for his proper culture, education and development.

Once a little experiment in local philanthropy, the Sunday school
has grown until it is in America the greatest, the most momentous,
the most heroic of our social institutions. If size alone made an institution great, the American Sunday school, with its thirteen million
children, might fairly claim to be so. Every city, township, county
and state is covered by an organization uniting all the Protestant
evangelical Sunday schools; and these in turn are linked together
through the International Sunday School Association, which covers
the continent and its adjacent islands and coasts.

The Sunday school needs to be great to meet the momentous task on
its hands. Since the first Sunday school was started, the whole enterprise of public education has taken shape and direction, has become a
national institution, and has taken over that responsibility for the secular education of the children which heretofore in every age had been
a function of the church. That our boys and girls need instruction in
the fundamentals of faith, morals and religion, and that many of the
social and civic ills of the day are the result of the weakness or break-
down of the religious education of American children, few will deny.
This is the reason for the supreme importance of the Sunday school in
every community.

There was a time when the father, the mother and the minister
looked after the moral education of the child. Churches were closed
during the week with the idea that between Sundays the parents gave
religious instruction to the children. With the demands made upon
the average pastor today, there is little time to look after the children

individually, and parents who give their children religious instruction at home are the great exception.

One by one, as parents have dropped their duties, the public school and the Sunday school have taken them up. Sometimes these duties are dropped through indifference and carelessness, oftentimes through absolute inability on the part of parents to meet them. But whatever the cause, the fact is that hundreds of parents today have turned over the whole question of the moral and religious training of their children to the Sunday school teacher.

A stupendous task this is indeed. If you were given half an hour a week to teach your child morals, ethics, patriotism, Bible history, theology, purity, good citizenship, temperance, love and duty toward his fellow-man—to overcome heredity and environment, and make that child by the time he had reached the age of twenty years a stalwart Christian man, would you be equal to the task? Yet it is what you are expecting of your child's Sunday school teacher.

Now, given thirteen million children to be taught the most important truths of religion and morals, who should do this great work and who should support it? Professional teachers, say many—a force trained, paid, supervised and equipped just as teachers in our best week-day schools need to be. Not all will agree that this is the best way to handle our Sunday school problems, but few will deny that the cause is worth all this and more if its ends can thus be surely accomplished.

What, then, shall we say of the actual facts? These thirteen million children are left to the care of about fifteen hundred thousand good people who have volunteered to do this great work gratuitously. As a rule, they have had no opportunity for special preparation, and are obliged to contribute or otherwise raise all the money needed to carry on the work, and to adapt their methods to such equipment and housing as can be secured or improvised after the wants of the church have been attended to. This, it must be acknowledged, is heroic service.

Few persons would be bold enough to deny that the modern Sunday school has been a powerful agency for good. A noted educator has said that when he considers the fact that it is in session but one hour of the week, he takes off his hat in genuine respect for the army of teachers who, with a real love for the service, are accomplishing results of tremendous value.

The Sunday school is a school. It is the duty of a good school to be a part of the life around it, and to make room in its work and in its play for the beginnings of the life that its pupils are some day to live out to the full. A good Sunday school will give proper place to the teaching of temperance, honesty, truthfulness, and all the private and civic virtues. It will, through its interest in missionary and philanthropic enterprise, furnish practical expression to those impulses to do good which it is its duty to evoke and train in the hearts of children.

The modern Sunday school likewise respects the civic life and its calls to duty, and will join with the public school in impressing from time to time the duties of good citizenship. In the new regime of the Sunday school, all these topics of practical importance find their place, and the lessons are prepared with the help of specialists in temperance, civics and missions.

As a factor in influencing the mental and moral development of the child, the Sunday school stands next to the home and the public school in importance, and its equipment for this great work is constantly improving under the direction of able minds and with the aid of the self-sacrificing devotion of its splendid army of volunteer teachers.

TRADE ASSOCIATIONS.

The historian of American business must recognize in the trade association a unit which is, in these years of consolidation, as inevitably and intrinsically a part of our industrial fabric as the corporation has become. Long ago the prevailing partnership gave place to the corporation because of the obvious advantages possessed by the latter—because there were constructive activities that two or four or ten or twenty small units properly combined could do better, more economically, and more extensively than any one unit operating independently.

It must be evident that the purposes of corporations and of trade associations are different. Trade associations are corporations raised to a higher power. Corporations or firms exist to do business, to capitalize service in business, to manufacture, to sell, to distribute. Trade associations are not in business. They do not manufacture; generally they do not distribute or sell. Their aim is to facilitate these and other commercial or govermental processes.

Many trade associations came into being during or following the World War, when the War Industries Board and other governmental agencies besought all business men to join or form associations to serve as clearing houses of information and inquiry between the scattered thousands of our business public on the one hand and the government in its hour of need on the other.

For it must be remembered that the government must, in the nature of things, look upon each industry as a single permanent unit. If the government wishes to do what every government department often has occasion to do, namely, to deal with one or another industry, to get its views concerning a matter of trade strategy or trade development abroad; to inform it about this or that or be informed by it—obviously it cannot easily interview or correspond with the existing tens of thousands comprising that industry.

This would have been a comparatively simple matter a century ago, had such an occasion ever arisen. Now it is next to impossible. So the trade association, with officers in Washington or some other center, meets the need of a link serving as a means of expression of and a means of expression to an industry.

The larger view of trade associations shows that in the United States as well as in the countries of Europe, they form an indispensable link between the government and the business public. Here you find the Department of Agriculture pronouncing them invaluable, and Congress accepting them as a part of the changing scene of things in which individuals have lost their voice and representation rests with organized groups. And here again, you will find them, in coöperation with the government, accomplishing the elimination of freak varieties of production and collective wastes in industry which mean a loss of thirty per cent of our national energies.

Trade associations are doing invaluable educational work for their members. For example, many of them are doing a great service that can be performed in no other way in promoting the establishment of proper methods of cost-accounting. Clearly it is to the advantage of no one for a manufacturer to go on producing at a loss, and adequate statistics cannot be gathered in any industry without uniform methods of cost-accounting.

During the World War the trade associations become clearing houses for facts about stock of raw materials, work in process, labor employed, manufacturing processes in which waste and duplication might be eliminated, actual and potential output, and—of secondary importance then, but of very great moment later—costs of production, upon which the government based the prices it would pay. This information enabled the government to allocate raw materials and labor to the best advantage, and to buy its supplies at prices which, though higher than peace-time prices, were arrived at upon a basis of cost and not by guess-work, and were very much lower than the prices originally demanded by manufacturers.

The manufacturers themselves were vastly enlightened by this experience. Many of them learned for the first time that some of their competitors were using more effective methods, and what these methods were. Many learned for the first time how to figure their own costs of production and the real meaning of cost-accounting. And—most revealing of all—they rediscovered the fact that there in another kind of competition besides competition in price, namely, that if everybody gets the same price for his product, any individual producer can still earn more by increased production or decreased cost of manufacture.

The larger thought is that America, after a century in which the gods gave us such gifts and opportunities as were never bestowed upon any other nation in the history of the world, is entering a period in which nature no longer offers a lap overflowing with plenty. Except in the dim frontiers of science, our pioneers have for the most part completed their work. These are the days of refinement in processes, if we are to keep our place in the sun. And these are the days of consolidation accordingly.

THE ELEMENTARY SCHOOL PRINCIPAL.

As soon as the school began to be more than merely a place where one teacher instructed children of all ages in the rudimentary branches; as soon as increase in attendance made the employment of more than one instructor necessary, it was found that a ship without a captain would soon strand on the rocks. Hence the office of principal, to whom every teacher under his jurisdiction owes certain obligations and duties, chief of which are loyalty and obedience. The teacher is responsible to the principal, but his responsibility is, primarily, a responsibility for results. In other words, the instructor is answerable to the principal for the efficiency of his work. But whatever authority the principal may possess, it is delegated to him chiefly by the superintendent, who demands certain results from his principals; the latter pass on these demands to their teachers, and these, in turn, hold the class responsible for their fulfillment. Such conditions are, especially in cities, brought about by the inability of the superintendent personally to look after the welfare of every school under his jurisdiction.

While it may thus be said that the office of the principal resembles that of the superintendent, inasmuch as both are more or less supervisory and executive, yet the office of the superintendent may be said to involve more responsibility than that of the principal. Generally speaking, the principal intervenes between the classroom teachers and the superintendent. He promulgates to his subordinates all orders that may come to him from the central office. He exacts obedience from his teachers, the janitors, the engineers because he knows that the superintendent holds him responsible for the efficiency of the work done within the building. But the principal is responsible neither to the board of education nor to the community at large. Such responsibility belongs to the superintendent, who, in some states, is answerable even to the state authorities for the condition of his schools.

Whether the office of the principal is, primarily, educational, administrative, or clerical, is a question easier raised than answered. No doubt, when our school systems were small, the principal devoted at least some of his time to teaching. But wherever the systems have been enlarged, it was soon found that practically all of the principal's time was taken up by administration. This is by no means surprising, for, as Prof. William Chandler Bagley states, the principal "is responsible for everything that belongs to or goes on within the limits of his school,—for the instruction, for the discipline, for the care and condition of the material equipment." On another place we are informed, by the same authority, that "the prevailing tendency is to relieve the principal of teaching duties in order that he may devote all of his time and energy to the general welfare of the school." Of course there always is some clerical work connected with the office, but to stress this as one of the more important duties of the principal, is a gross misconception of his duties and obligations.

No doubt, relations between teachers and principal would soon become strained, should the former deny their superior's right to educational leadership, or assume an attitude of defense when directed, counselled or censured. There are still too many teachers who believe the principal's work consists chiefly in "getting ready;" in setting the machinery into motion, but that afterwards he ought to sit back in calm composure to observe with silent satisfaction the work of his teachers. Of course no principal, in his desire to lead his teachers, should go so far as in the name of system to smother the initative or override the opinions of his teachers.

As to the specific work of the principal, it may be said to cover a large variety of duties. Occasionally, he may have a weak teacher and it at once becomes incumbent on him to render any aid that may be needed and to be ready with his counsel and full support in order to teach the instructor how to sustain himself. On the other hand, the habit of some teachers for every little difficulty and annoyance to fall back on the principal, is weakening, undermining the influence of the instructor. As regards the daily routine work of the principal, much depends on local conditions, the size of the school, the character of both teachers and pupils, etc.

Since the principal is a leader in the community, he is confronted by various civic, social, and community duties. He should therefore constantly strive to acquire a thorough and definite understanding of the general operations in relation to the several departments of society. In other words, the principal, who would like for a high degree of success, must store his mind with a variety of knowledge on all subjects of social interest. The acquisition of knowledge on civic and social questions will prove highly beneficial to him, while its possession will add much to his usefulness and knowledge.

The duties as supervisor have been lessened, at least in the larger systems, where now special supervisors do the work formerly incumbent upon the principal. But wherever these special supervisors are still unknown, he must be careful not to "supervise" too much, that is, make too frequent visits, and even if his visitations should be less numerous, he must avoid everything that might tend to secure for him the reputation of a habitual critic. Criticism should be constructive, and never be bestowed in the presence of pupils. But while actually supervising, he must see to it that the curriculum is being followed and its precepts are being carried out by every teacher under his charge.

The principal's relation to the superintendent should be founded on respect, willingness to coöperate should never be wanting. To accord to the superintendent a treatment which the principal would resent from his own teachers, would be detrimental to the morale of the school.

Whether democracy in school management is possible is a debatable question. Much depends on our interpretation of democracy in relation to school administration. But even if it were possible, let us not forget that the best kind of democracy is bound to fall without loyalty and obedience.

ADDRESS PRESENTING A PICTURE OF PRESIDENT HARDING TO A HIGH SCHOOL.

In the presentation of this picture, the object sought is to bring before your minds in the likeness of our Chief Executive a symbol which will inspire your thoughts to sentiments of patriotism and loyalty to this great nation of which it is your good fortune to be citizens.

How could we fail to love our great mother—our country—to whom we owe all that we are? Our country is our larger home, and home, for every creature who is not a slave or an outcast, is a sacred abode, unlike any other, not to be exchanged for any other.

The Swiss peasant finds home in his bleak chalet, with no comforts, with many deprivations, very scantily provisioned, cut off in winter for weeks it may be from his nearest neighbors; and yet, transplant him to the city, surround him with luxury and repose, spare him from drudging for tomorrow's meager fare, and he will pine of homesickness. The Arab takes his home with him wherever he pitches his tent; and he, too, would languish were he forced to exchange his nomadic life for any dwelling, were it even a palace.

The outer habitation does not make the home, nor do the furniture, clothes and food. Home is the complex of whatever has shaped our life—in childhood, the love and discipline of father and mother, the comradeship of brothers and sisters, the intimacy of playmates, and all sights, sounds and impressions which we draw unawares from nature and the world outside of us. As we mature, home means family and friends; the dreams, the labor, the sorrows and joys that are the lot of man.

Wooden walls and plaster ceilings are but the shell that holds us while we absorb these experiences, which memory preserves when they are past. Associations almost unobserved in the making bind us forever, having become an individual part of ourselves. Not less noble and scarcely less instinctive than the love for home should be the love we feel for our larger home, our country.

In the early stages of society, patriotism, being a matter of necessity, developed as a matter of course in every one. So long as the tribal stage existed, each member of the tribe was compelled to cleave to it for self-preservation. All he was, his fortune in peace or war, depended upon the prosperity of his tribe, and his devotion to his chief was unquestioning and unreserved. The mere fact of being a stranger was equivalent to being an enemy; persons not of the tribe were outlaws, liable to be enslaved or killed.

When the smaller and often isolated state gave way to larger political combinations—to kingdoms and empires—patriotism continued to be the natural ideal of every citizen, and the ruler, who symbolized the state, received the obedience and loyalty of all. The great empire protected its members just as the small clan had done, and in return they honored and supported it and felt a pride in being under its dominion. The best service that monarchs have rendered has been to personify the state; the average human being finds it hard to burn with zeal for an abstract ideal and so easy to idealize a person.

The claim of patriotism will not be denied. Modern assailants of the family suppose that by destroying it they can emancipate the individuals who compose it. They conceive that the goal of life is the throwing off of all restraints. Normal restraints, those which built up a man and make him master of himself, are really the means by which he gets his true freedom. The man who thinks that by casting off the restraints of society he gets a larger freedom, deceived himself. At most he exchanges a higher plane for a lower and retreats toward that of the beast, out of which it has been man's mission to rise and climb. He accepts the bondage of a more insistent selfishness.

The same is true in the case of those who deny or fail to recognize the claims of patriotism. Patriotism is not an institution like the family; rather it is an emotion, a passion, the flower of man's communal life. Not to feel it is to be dead indeed; it is to suffer a loss which for the citizen is like incapacity to love for the individual.

The range of a man's sense of duty measures his level on the moral scale. Now patriotism is a duty just as love of parents or children is. The wretch who deserts his wife and children or leaves his needy parents to starve, saying that he feels no obligation toward them, can find no one to defend him except another wretch as base as himself. How shall we qualify those who declare that patriotism does not concern them? What sort of a heart—if heart he have at all—must his be who repudiates his country, his mother?

Like all other forms of devotion, patriotism is not merely a fine sentiment,—not dilating with pleasurable emotions when the American flag is unfurled; not rising to our feet when the Star Spangled Banner is sung; not sending off fire-crackers on the Fourth of July. It manifests itself in service—in service that neither doubts, nor counts the cost, nor asks recognition. In peace or in war, the patriot serves his country joyfully, because it is the natural thing to do.

Life is not worth living unless your country is founded on principles that are worth dying for. The estate which every American inherits he holds in trust. On him it depends whether his share in the Republic shall be handed on unsullied to his descendants—and not only unsullied, but increased and strengthened.

"All men on whom the higher nature has stamped the love of truth," says Dante, "should especially concern themselves in laboring for posterity, in order that future generations shall be enriched by their efforts, as they themselves were made rich by the effects of generations past."

THE PECULIAR SPIRITUAL AND CULTURAL ANCESTRY OF THE IRISH PEOPLE.

In tracing the ancestry of the Irish people, we are of course anxious to know something about the men and women who first dwelt on the island. Ancient native legends inform us that in remote times tribes called Firbolgs and Danauns inhabited the country. These are said to have been conquered by the Milesians or Gaels, who then acquired supremacy in the island. Little is known about them. In fact, the early history is shrouded in mystery until about four hundred years after Christ, when the Scoti, or inhabitants of Scotia, made their appearance. It was about that time that St. Patrick arrived, and if the reports of the Rev. J. H. Todd, his biographer, are correct, he succeeded in implanting into the hearts of those early inhabitants of Ireland no small amount of spirituality. Up to the time of his arrival, the ancient Irish system of belief and practice has prevailed, but as soon as he had entered upon his mission, a different spirit began to exert its influence. And no wonder, for we are told that he founded in Ireland over 360 churches, baptized with his own hand more than 12,000 persons, and ordained a great number of priests.

That even at that early period some culture prevailed, is exhibited by various writings still extant. One of the earliest historic pieces is a metrical life of St. Patrick, which was followed by a multitude of legends, mythological and imaginative tales.

Although from the earliest period, each province appears to have had its king, yet we should grossly err were we to assume that these monarchs ruled with an iron hand, caring but little for the welfare of their subjects. In fact, much of the king's power was delegated to chiefs selected from the most important families. Justice was meted

out not according to arbitrary notions of a king or chief, but by professional jurists called Brehons.

One of the most important factors testifying to the cultural state of
the early Irish people, is the so-called crannog or lake-dwelling. The
Celtic lake-dwellings are more or less artificial islands composed of
earth and stones strengthened by piles. The relics found in these
buildings as well as the structures themselves have thrown much
light upon the early culture prevailing on the island. The dwellings
are fully described in the proceedings of the Royal Irish Academy.

The ancient Irish were, likewise, adepts in the manufacture of
various articles. They made them of metal, stone, clay, and other
materials. A large collection of these early articles can still be seen
in the Museum of the Royal Irish Academy at Dublin. In fact, a
greater number and variety of antique golden articles of remote age
have been found in Ireland than perhaps in any other part of
Northern Europe.

While speaking of culture, reference deserves to be made to the
various institutions in which both religious and cultural aims were
zealously cultivated. Owing to the activities of St. Patrick, Ireland
soon became the seat of western learning, and its monasteries were
the schools whence missionaries proceeded throughout continental
Europe.

Among the eminent native Irish of those early times was St.
Columban, born in Leinster about the year 545. According to his
biographer, he must have been a most remarkable preacher. For, we
are told that "the flights of imagination, the pious transports, the
rigorous application to principles, the warfare declared against all
vain or hypocritical compromises, gave to his words that passionate
authority which may not always and surely reform the soul of his
hearers, but which dominates over them, and, for some time at least,
exercises paramount sway over their conduct and their life."

Another light of that period was St. Adamnan, to whom we are
indebted for nearly all the information we have about the early
Scotch-Irish Church. In fact, the 6th century is brilliant with names
proving the progress of the early Irish in matters of education and
religion.

We should, however, be guilty of self-deception were we to think
that spiritual and cultural conditions among the forefathers of the
present Irish were beyond reproach. Not only in those early days,
but even at the present time, we often find history and pagan superstition badly mixed so that it is often difficult to arrive at definite
conclusions. One example will be sufficient. We are told that St.
Kevin founded a monastery near Glendalough, to which students came
from far parts of the world. In fact, it was a seminary of Christian
teaching, from which missionaries were sent to many distant lands.
But if we were to visit the ruins of this once famous school, some old

Irish woman might insist on being our guide, and we might find some of her stories as incredible as those of the Arabian Nights or of mythology and medieval folklore.

It was Thomas Moore who gave St. Kevin a place in English literature. He tells us that the saint, in order to escape the temptations of a maiden, whom he names Kathleen, was compelled to throw her off a rock into the lake. Or, in the words of the poet—

> "With rude repulsive knock
> He hurls her from the rock.
> Glendalough, thy gloomy wave
> Soon was gentle Kathleen's grave."

But notwithstanding such and similar little incidents, the ancestors of the Irish people must be acknowledged to have made laudable efforts to rise above the common level of the times. If, at any later period, literature, among the Irish, began to decline; if the people, as a whole, failed to come up to accepted standards, the fault lies, not so much with the people themselves, but with the conditions surrounding them and the trials to which they were subjected. Let young Ireland therefore make strenuous efforts in the right direction in order to redeem what may have been lost.

MEDITATIONS OF AN EMPLOYEE.

There are still too many employers who consider themselves lions when it comes to dividing the profits. They want them practically all, leaving only a paltry, measly share to their employees. They clamor for coöperation on the part of their men, but are themselves unwilling to attract them by means of wise and unselfish management. It is usually that kind of employers who constantly encounter difficulties in the solution of labor problems and who decry the profit-sharing plan as an industrial "soothing syrup."

But no matter what some employers may think of the fifty-fifty plan, it remains certain that, wherever it has been adopted, it has shown itself to be a great incentive to those who assist in the manufacture of certain products. Every factory that has instituted the profit-sharing plan, reports greater coöperation on the part of employees, a higher interest in the business with which they are connected, and a larger profit through the elimination of waste of both time and material. In the National Cash Register Company, of Dayton, Ohio, every worker is made to realize that he is working for his own business. Through the profit-sharing plan he is made a silent partner in a gigantic enterprise, without investing any capital. J. H. Barringer, the General Manager of that vast factory, is being actuated by the philosophy of the Great Teacher, and not by that of materialism and greed. The Benjamin Electric Company of Chicago, too, is a firm believer in the Golden Rule in business. That firm has but one rule, viz., always do unto the employee what he should do unto them.

True, these outstanding examples of true philanthropy in business have had some imitators, but the plans inaugurated by them are deficient, taking but little, if any, cognizance of fundamental principles. If profit-sharing plans or other improvements for the amelioration of material conditions are being made, profits or benefits should not be distributed equally to employees regardless of the importance of their positions or their length of service. As Derick S. Hartshorn rightfully says, "seniority means length of service, rather than the order in which the employees were hired. As a usual thing even the experienced mechanic needs to be broken in on the new job and the green man requires months and even years before he is competent. Labor turnover is one of the banes of the employer and recognition of a substantial kind should be made for long service."

In many instances, it is the old employee that helped to make the business. He stayed with the firm though he might have received better compensation somewhere else. Some employers are still too quick in making changes. The names on their pay-rolls are constantly changing; they are unmindful of the fact that breaking in new men means loss of time, material, and output. Quite frequently the quality of the product is also endangered. But that is not all. For the worst is really yet to come. For all the time spent in breaking in newcomers has quite often been expended in vain. As soon as another firm offers a slight increase in salary on easier hours, the "floater" turns his back on the man that employed him last. It is the man that "sticks" to his job, that is regular and steady, that is most valuable to an employer, and not the "floater" who is here today and somewhere else tomorrow, or the fellow who comes to work when he pleases and stays at home when he feels like resting.

The old employee instead of being rewarded is often neglected. The foreman, the boss, or whatever his superior may call himself, thinks of him as a man afraid to "kick" and always willing to do a lot of work at low wages. In more than one factory the old employees are looked upon as fellows constantly afraid of being "fired," and therefore always ready to undergo the worst hazards.

If the services of old employees would be appreciated better than they often are, many firms would succeed better than they do. The controlling interest in one of the large factories of the central states had been owned by a friendly, warm-hearted old gentleman, who was always ready to retain a man as long as he possibly could. Advanced age made it advisable for him to sell out to a western capitalist. One of the first things the new management did, was to "lay off" practically all old employees, some of whom had been with the concern for 20 or 30 years, and to hire an entirely new set of hands. The result was ruin. Business dwindled down to almost nothing because the new workmen were less experienced and less skilled. The product was inferior in workmanship and material.

The writer knows of a man who had been in the employ of a certain firm for 16 years. No one paid any special attention to him. He was always on the job and rarely laid up. His work was satisfactory; had it not been, he would not have been kept on the pay-roll for 16 years. One day an old acquaintance of the boss, who had been away for a number of years, visited the establishment, and noticing the old employee still performing his duties, he extolled the faithfulness of the "old timer." The remark proved to be an eye-opener. At once the employer realized that he had so far failed to appreciate the services and help of old employees, and therefore concluded to give to each a substantial present. The whole procedure had a twofold effect. In the first place, the old employees felt that they had been rewarded for their faithfulness with which they had served the firm, and, in the second place, the action of the employer served as an advertisement and increased the sales of the firm.

Only a short time ago, the press reported that 400 employees of H. A. Dix and Sons, dress and uniform makers in New York, have become the owners of a business with an income of $1,000,000 a year as a reward for building it up. H. A. Dix, Sr., who came to America as an immigrant from Russia and built up a vast fortune, announced that he had turned the firm over to the workers because he and his sons had made enough money out of it to last them the rest of their lives. He declared he always believed that employees should be compensated other than by mere wages. Mr. Dix, after legally making the transfer, loaned the employees a quarter of a million of dollars to operate the business, which is to be run by seven workers.

If there were more employers like H. A. Dix and Sons, industrial warfare would soon be a thing of the past, and the faithful worker would feel himself amply rewarded for having been both industrious and persevering.

MAYOR'S ADDRESS OF ACCEPTANCE OF NEW ARMORY.

Ladies and Gentlemen:

The history of a free people is largely written in their institutions, and in accepting from the Governor and on behalf of the people this splendid armory which is to be the pride of our city, I realize as do all of you that it typifies the power and stability of that great Republic of which we are so fortunate as to be citizens.

The National Guard has proved itself to be a bulwark of American liberty, and in thorough keeping with the true ideals of American military policy. Shortly after the disastrous battle of Camden, General Washington wrote to the president of Congress, ''What we need is a good army, not a large one.''

It does not require a close study of the military policies of the American people to discern that they are by tradition and custom opposed to a large standing army, and that in times of war or other emergency, when the civil government can no longer enforce the laws, they place their main reliance upon what may be broadly termed the citizen soldiery of the Republic. Centuries of oppression suffered by their European ancestors, traceable to irresponsible power backed by the force of arms, have taught them to safeguard their liberties by limiting the size of the nation's standing army, and reserving to themselves in their sovereign capacity the right to keep and bear arms.

In the Declaration of Independence we find one of the principal complaints of the colonists against Great Britain was that the latter maintained large standing armies in times of peace to overawe the people. And when that declaration had been made a living reality by an appeal to arms extending through eight long years of suffering and death, and a strong, centralized, constitutional government had sprung from the weakness and inadequacy of the union under the Articles of Confederation, we find the fears of the people crystallized in the second Amendment to the new Constitution of the nation:

''A well-regulated militia being necessary to the security of a free state, the right of the people to keep and bear arms shall not be infringed.''

This was a constitutional expression of the right which the people then enjoyed, and which they not only reserved to themselves, but . made its abuse on the part of the new government impossible by this constitutional prohibition. So long, then, as our government is a government of, by, and for the people, so long must its ultimate reliance repose on the intelligence, integrity, and patriotism of its citizen soldiery.

John Quincy Adams, in his message to Congress, March 4, 1825, referred to the militia in these terms:

''The organization of the militia is yet more indispensable to the liberties of the country. It is only by an effective militia that we can, at once, enjoy the repose of peace, and bid defiance to foreign aggression; it is by the militia that we are constituted an armed nation, standing in perpetual panoply of defense, in the presence of all the other nations of the earth.''

It is true that the people conferred upon the Federal government the power to raise and support aries distinct from those that might be formed by calling forth the militia, but they hedged it about with limitations, and their representatives have always jealously opposed any attempt to augment the standing army beyond the number that to them seemed imperatively necessary.

But consider for a moment the military power of the Federal government in regard to the militia. It can provide for organizing, arming, and disciplining this force equally in times of peace or war. This means that every able-bodied citizen in this broad land may be enrolled in the militia, and that this force may then be organized, as Congress may deem advisable, into infantry, cavalry, artillery, or other branches of the military service, and then armed and trained until the whole becomes an efficient military machine, and that the revenues of the nation may be used for these purposes.

But owing to the neglect or laxity of the provisions of the individual States for the support of an adequate body of citizen soldiery, the experience of a century and a half of our national existence showed the militia, upon which the country depended for defense during that period, to be seriously insufficient for the great tasks which devolved upon it. However, experience is the great teacher, and today our people seem to realize that the military profession is indeed a profession, and that soldiers cannot spring into existence panoplied for war, as did Athena from the forehead of Jupiter.

From untrained militia, the States have gradually evolved the splendidly trained forces of the national guard, which in reality has become the national guard of the Republic. Our experience in the World War has taught us new standards of preparedness, and by destroying our dream of security and isolation has made us indeed a power to be reckoned with in the councils of nations.

In this substanital and well-equipped armory, therefore, and in the efficient organization of the National Guard which will make it their headquarters, is the promise of a new era in American military policy, and of a national security based upon genuine principles of preparedness. Our city sees in this building not only the emblem of a powerful commonwealth, but of a Union of States amply able to meet its needs for defense in times of peace as well as war.

IS THE MORAL SIDE OF THE SCHOOL RECEIVING PROPER ATTENTION?

The demands upon moral character were never so great as now; but what of the *emphasis* upon moral character in our educational system? No one would be inclined to deny that character is the aim of education. This axiom is still a part of our formal pedagogy, and by many it is supposed to govern our practice; it is proclaimed at educational gatherings, and appears regularly in books and articles in our magazines. But in the woof and warp of educational thought and teaching, it has no such place as it had in former ages.

13

The pages of Plato, Aristotle, Comenius, Montaigne, and Milton, which deal with education, are dominated by the moral element. One of the most striking passages of Plato's "Republic" is the one which insists that the literature selected for the curriculum shall be adapted in the most perfect manner to the promotion of virtue."

Does any school or college today choose its classics with this primary regard for the promotion of virtue? Montaigne would have history taught in such a way that the teacher "imprint not so much in his scholar's mind the date of the ruin of Carthage, as the manners of Hannibal and Scipio." Milton's definition of education in his "Tractate" magnifies the moral aim: "I call, therefore, a complete and generous education, that which fits a man to perform justly, skilfully, and magnanimously, all the offices, both private and public, of peace and war."

With Doctor Arnold of Rugby, one ideal is always supreme, that of moral thoughtfulness and devotion to duty; all else is auxiliary and subordinate. The key to Horace Mann's self-abnegation in the cause of the schools was his belief that education is the only force that could elevate character; his labors, his public addresses, and his writings, are all inspired and penetrated by the moral aim.

When we come to current educational discussion, we find a surprising change of emphasis. The reader who will make comparison between the earlier writers and the leading formal treatises on education of our own time, will agree that far less stress is laid upon the moral element.

Our textbooks themselves mirror this neglect of the moral phase of teaching. In Murray's English Reader, one of the most used readers of the early nineteenth century in America, out of eighty-four prose selections, fifty-four are distinctly moral; eighteen others are religious; of the remaining twelve, nearly all have a moral or religious motive.

Now examine a typical modern reader, and the contrast will be striking. The distinctly and avowedly ethical and moral is conspicuous by its absence. The great majority of the selections are non-moral; narrative to entertain or amuse, historical matter to inform or instruct, essays to cultivate the literary taste, and a goodly admixture of the humorous.

But not only has moral training been crowded out, as it were by indirection, through the pressure of the intellectual burden of the schools: it has also suffered many direct attacks. The chief of these may be summed up as a reaction against the strictness of earlier periods, and an emphasis upon the right of the child to grow up in accordance with the leanings and impulses of his own nature.

This gives point to the suggestive gibe that there is just as much family government today as ever, but that it has passed from the hands of the parents into the hands of the children. In our recoil from the harshness and pietism of the days of our great-grandfathers, and our enthusiasm for the rights of the child, have we not drifted into a policy of *laissez-faire* in moral training? Young people now-adays must not be preached to; even the sermon for children is so completely sugar-coated with humor and entertainment that our ancestors would never have called it a sermon at all.

America today has the only great school system the world has ever seen which does not include a definite and formal instruction in religion—with the single exception of France, which relinquished it in 1882; and France has put in place of its religious instruction the most systematic and thorough moral instruction ever taught in a national system of education, and is today working with unflagging zeal to make the moral instruction the most efficient and vital part of its whole curriculum.

This, then, is the educational emergency as it exists today: increased demand upon character, and diminished care for the cultivation of character in our public school system. As M. Marion, French Minister of Education, has said: "The truth is that we have not yet seriously comprehended that the whole political and social problem is one of education. Henceforth education alone can rescue our modern societies from the perils that threaten them."

Fortunately signs are not wanting of a widespread awakening to the seriousness of the situation. We are beginning to realize that what has been merely an article in our educational creed must become a working principle in our educational practice; that the final question regarding education is whether it avails to produce the type of character required by the republic and the race.

To accomplish this we need, not less clearness and accuracy of thought, nor any sacrifice of the true interests of the intellectual life, but more warmth of genuine and appropriate feeling, and more stimulation and guidance of the will. In brief, we must fit our practice to Herbart's great formula, that the chief business of education is *the ethical revelation of the Universe.*

THE BOY AND HIS GANG.

The belonging instinct seems to be natural to boys between the ages of twelve and sixteen, and the majority of boys belong to gangs at some period of their career.

In its essential characteristics, the gang is a real social body, animated by a common consciousness, with a completeness hardly found in the associations of later life. It is the budding of the human faculty of membership; the boy is coming to himself as the destined member of a social organization.

Team play is the highest expression of membership in the gang, the most whole-hearted surrender to the belonging instinct. The player learns that the team is, in the first place and always, a work of faith. It grows as its members have power to imagine it, and faith to maintain, and act upon, the reality of that which they have imagined.

Next to team games come the more direct and primitive expressions of the instincts upon which these are based. The instinct of tribal war, which forms the basis of football, and to a less extent of baseball, hockey, and many other games, finds satisfaction in fights with rival gangs, the preferred weapons being stones, sticks and snowballs.

Then there are actual raids in obedience to the instinct that prescribes the raiding games: the robbing of cellars and greenhouses; swooping down on gardens, orchards, and fruit stands; smashing windows and the glasses of street lamps; stealing street signs, gates, and barber's poles; engaging the groceryman in conversation while a companion makes off with a bunch of bananas; escaping down dark alleys and over roofs; breaking, harrying, pillaging, and carrying off.

Boys at this age are overborne by their own undirected and misguided energies. A mere temperamental outbreak in a brief period of obstreperousness exposes a promising boy to arrest and imprisonment; and accidental combination or circumstances, too complicated and overwhelming to be coped with by an immature mind, and may condemn a growing lad to a criminal career.

In the life of each boy there comes a time when primitive instincts urge him to action, when he is himself frightened by their undefined power. He is faced by the necessity of taming them, of reducing them to manageable impulses, just at the period when "a boy's will is the wind's will." That the boy often fails may be traced in those pitiful figures which show that between two and three times as many cases of incorrigibility occur between the ages of thirteen and sixteen as at any other period of life.

Take the petty crime due to the sheer spirit of adventure. Many boys in the years immediately following school find no restraint in either tradition or character. They drop learning as a childish thing and look upon school as a tiresome task that is finished. They demand pleasure as the right of one who earns his own living. They are constitutionally unable to enjoy anything continuously, and they follow their vagrant wills unhindered.

Unfortunately, the city lends itself to this distraction. At the best, it is difficult to know what to select and what to eliminate as objects of attention among its thronged streets, its glittering shops, its gaudy advertisements of shows and amusements.

There is an obligation resting upon parents at this critical period of their children's lives to exercise patience, tact, and the wise method of adroitly substituting innocent amusements for those of more dangerous tendency.

One exasperated and frightened mother took her boy of fourteen into a police court on the charge of incorrigibility. She accused him of shooting craps, smoking cigaretts, idleness, and keeping bad company. She later acknowledged her regret upon finding that taking a boy into court except as a last resort only gives him a bad name, and that the police are down on a boy who has once appeared in court, which makes it harder for him to keep a straight course. She now finds in her once troublesome charge a steady young man of nineteen who brings home all his wages and is the pride and stay of her old age.

In the final analysis, the chief factor in juvenile delinquency is not vicious tendencies, but wrong environment. The first factor in this dangerous environment is the inefficient home. According to estimates made in numerous racial surveys, 20 per cent of parents lack the proper qualifications for parenthood, 10 per cent are immoral, and 7 per cent of homes have been deprived by death of one or both parents. Public education must be looked to as the principal means of combatting the tendencies of the inefficient home.

The second factor in wrong environment is the public arena. This includes the street, billiard rooms and dance halls, and moving picture theatres. The city which permits these places to be the acme of pleasure and recreation for its young people commits a stupid and grievous mistake. It is almost as though the adult population assumed that the young men are able to grasp only that which is presented to them in the form of sensation. It is as though we were deaf to the appeal of these young creatures claiming their share of the joys of life, flinging out into the dingy city their desires and aspirations after unknown realities, their longings for companionship and pleasure. Their very demand for excitement is a protest against the dullness of life to which we ourselves instinctively respond.

Heretofore, it has been almost impossible to remove the vice-breeding factors in the community, because the dollar has been the standard. Recreation and amusement for the young have been in the hands of men who care not how many souls they send to destruction so long as they can line their pockets with unholy gain. Our boys must have social and recreational activities. The only question is: shall we furnish them under the proper control, or shall we continue to permit the commercially minded to traffic with their souls?

THRIFT FROM THE BANKER'S STANDPOINT.

It has been estimated by the American Society for Thrift that 95 per cent of the men in the United States who reach the age of sixty are still dependent upon their daily earnings or upon the means supplied to them by others. Moreover, not one man in thirty who retires on a competence proves able to retain that competence to the end of his life.

The reason for thrift is plain. It is simply that if we do not have thrift we shall not have a margin of production over consumption— that is we shall not have capital. If we do not have capital, we cannot have progress, for we shall have no means to make improvements in existing facilities. There is the danger of extravagance. And it is a very real danger.

We often get a wrong start on thrift. We think of it only as buying less, whereas we should think of it as buying more wisely. We know that buying less does not increase production, but on the contrary decreases production because the demand fails. If we should stop all buying for a time, undoubtedly a great number of stocks held in weak hands would have to be sold off, but more probably the stocks would be bought by the stronger merchants and all prices advanced in order to cover the necessity of holding, and the only thing that would drop would be production. That is, we should not add to the wealth of the country; we should only go into a period of national hibernation.

It is a tribute to the economic sense of the American people that appeals to cease buying on the ground that prices will thereby drop have usually fallen upon unheeding ears.

There is another class of argument met with now and then that would encourage the accumulation or hoarding of money for one grand whirl of spending. There is a certain humanness in this idea which in a way makes it less objectionable than the economic fallacy just mentioned. But intensive preparation for periodical spending debauches is not thrift.

There is a reason for thrift as a positive and not a negative habit. Thrift is not opposed to silk shirts and automobiles. It is opposed to giving something for nothing; and we might almost define thrift as consuming less than one produces for the purpose of being able to produce more. If a nation consumes all that it produces it cannot go forward. A community is but a collection of individuals. Therefore, thrift is an individual affair.

Thrift can be considered as a social question, but its present-day importance is economic and not social. Its economic side is of paramount import. For the purpose of thrift is to provide more working capital so that the means of adding to the wealth of the nation may be augmented.

Adding to the productivity of the nation increases the stock of goods for distribution and not only increases the buying power by lowering the price of commodities, but also actually increases the wage of the worker by increasing the demand of capital for labor. This is the big fact in thrift.

Thrift followed by investment is simply common sense. Thrift has not been popular because it has been represented solely as a kind of morality which might be achieved by sufficient chastisement of the soul. It has rarely been impressed upon the minds of any body of workers that they could raise their wages more quickly by investing in industry than by striking against industry. Few workers have ever considered this economic equation, and also few employers. The primary thought in the majority of stock-purchasing and compulsory saving plans is not to raise the wages of the worker by providing more efficient means of production, but rather to chain the worker to his job by representing that he will lose something concrete if he leaves.

This may be disguised under the declared motive of anxiety that the worker does not waste his money. And probably because there has been no public instruction in the real efficacy of thrift, and of the real part that it plays in the capitalistic system, there has been practically no provision for anything in the nature of systematic national thrift, no positive systematized force whose slogan will not include anything retroactive such as decreased buying or hoarding.

Everybody, without exception, would like to live better from day to day. And that is what national thrift can accomplish if it be systematically and intelligently put forward. Deprivation, the doing without things that ought to be had, is not thrift, but a peculiarly vicious form of thriftlessness, for then thrift, as far as that individual is concerned, is a taking away and not an adding to.

To what extent does thrift actually prevail in this country? Savings-bank deposits show steady increases, small in individual amount, but vast in the aggregate. However, the excess of deposits over withdrawals remains relatively too small. Besides this index as to the state of thrift, there are the coöperative building and loan associations which in many parts of the country have become very popular. Again there is the increase in life insurance policies which has been extremely rapid in the past twenty years. Furthermore, we have the item of investment buying, which absorbs an immense volume of annual savings. An estimate once arrived at by Elmer Atkinson would indicate that the nation is putting aside for rainy days about two billion dollars a year.

It it an evident fact that the banks are the great teachers of thrift. The banker is becoming more and more the financial adviser to his community. And in proportion as he uses his influence in behalf of the general prosperity of the community will that general prosperity react to his own advantage.

THE NEW GENERATION MEETS THE OLD.

It is always an encouraging sign when people are rendered self-conscious and forced to examine the basis of their ideals. The demand that they explain them to skeptics always makes for clarity. When the older generation is put on the defensive, it must first discover what convictions it has, and then endeavor to present them convincingly.

One of the basic grievances of the older generation against the younger of today, with its social agitation, its religious heresy, its presumptive individuality, its economic restlessness, is that all this makes it uncomfortable. When you have found growing older to be a process of the reconciliation of the spirit to life, it is decidedly disconcerting to have some youngster come along and point out the irreconciliable things in the universe. Just as you have made a tacit agreement to call certain things non-existent, it is highly discommoding to have somebody shout with strident tones that they are very real and significant.

Through much of the current writing runs this subtle note of disapprobation. These agnostic professors who unsettle the faith of our youth, these intellectuals who devote themselves to the cause of social justice, these remorseless scientists who would reveal so many of our reticences—why can't they let well enough alone, and see that God's in His heaven and all's right with the world?

This older generation has succeeded in straining away by a slow process all the repellant attitudes in the old philosophy of life. It is unfair to say that it believes in dogmas and creeds. It would be more accurate to say that it does not disbelieve. It retains them as a sort of guarantee of the stability of the faith, but does not make more than a feeble effort to interpret them in the light of modern knowledge.

The foundations of its beliefs are mainly ethical, and based on the fundamental principle of good conduct. By good conduct is meant that sort of action which will least disturb the normal routine of modern middle-class life; common honesty in business affairs; ambition in business and profession; filial obligation; the use of talents, and always and everywhere simple human kindness and love.

Now one would indeed be churlish to find fault with this devout belief in simple goodness which characterizes the older generation. It is only when these humble virtues are raised up into an all-inclusive program for social reform and into a philosophy of life, that one begins to question, and to feel afar the hostility of the older generation to modern standards of belief.

If there is any one characteristic which distinguishes the older generation, it is the belief that social ills may be cured by personal virtue. Its highest ideals are sacrifice and service. But while these ideals enhance the moral value and satisfaction of the doer, what of the person who is served and sacrificed for? If the feelings of service and sacrifice were genuinely altruistic, the normal enhancement of the receiver would be the object sought.

Can it not be said that for every individual virtuous act on the part of a doer, there is a corresponding depression on the part of the receiver? It is exactly those free gifts, such as schools, libraries and hospitals, which are impersonal and social, that we can accept gratefully and gladly; and it is exactly because their ministrations are impersonal and businesslike that they can be received willingly and without moral depression by the poor.

The ideal of duty is equally open to attack. The great complaint of the younger against the older generation has to do with the rigidity of the social relationships into which the younger find themselves born. One is "supposed" to love one's aunt or one's grandfather in a certain definite way, at the risk of being "unnatural." These restrictions often liberate those forces of madness and revolt which bewilder spiritual teachers and guides. It is these dry channels of duty and obligation through which no living waters of emotion flow that it seems the object of the younger generation to break up. They will have no network of emotional canals which are not brimming, no duties which are not equally loves.

It is the same thing with service. The older generation has attempted a compromise with the new social democracy by combining the words "social" and "service." The assumption is that by doing good to individuals you are thereby becoming social. But to speak of "social democracy," which of course means a freely coöperating, freely reciprocating society of equals, and "service" together, is a contradiction of terms. For when you serve people or do good to them, you thereby render yourself unequal with them. If the service is compulsory, it is menial and you are inferior. If voluntary, you are superior.

No church in which this exaggerated ethic is enshrined can escape from paying the price of this assumption of ethical power. The church which saves men as members of the Beloved Community will flourish, and it will save men to a spiritual democracy, not a spiritual aristocracy. The older generation is slow to recognize that suberb loyalty that is loyalty to a community—a loyalty which, paradoxical as it may seem, nourishes the true social personality in proportion as the individual sense is lessened.

I then object to the ethical philosophy of the older generation on the ground that it is too individualistic, and under the guise of altruism, too egotistic. Its world is too hardened and definite. All the weapons with which the younger generation attacks the world,—enthusiasm, passion for new ideas, religious fervor,—seem only to make it uneasy. It has failed to broaden its institutions and ideas for the larger horizon of the time, and in this sense it has signally failed to lighten, cheer and purify the moral atmosphere of today.

ADDRESS AT OPENING OF NEW MUNICIPAL BUILDING.

Ladies and Gentlemen:

This is a proud day for our city for it represents the successful completion of a project which has been near to our hearts and uppermost in our minds for many months. Everyone who has the welfare of our city at heart rejoices today at the opening of this beautiful building, with its modern appointments and attractive architecture, the future civic center in which will be grouped the various activities of city government and welfare.

This building represents an ideal which has already existed in the minds of our citizens. That ideal is the ideal of the city beautiful, a home adorned with the hand of industry and art, in which men may live and work and hope. In olden days costly structures were erected to commemorate the deeds of some king or warrior, but now we erect buildings and dedicate them to the advancement of the arts of peace and the upbuilding of the mass of the people.

As you pass through this splendid building and note its ample and well-planned provisions for the comfort, health and convenience of those who will work within its walls, you have good reason to be proud of that ideal which has herein become embodied in brick and stone.

And back of that ideal is the thought which has been the foundation of this great republic of ours, the secret of its permanence and power, as well as the prophecy of its future advancement—the aspiration toward good citizenship.

Empires have risen and fallen, dynasties have been established and endured through generation after generation only to sink at last into the gulf of oblivion, but the only foundation yet discovered for an enduring state is a citizenship enlightened, honest, industrious, frugal and God-fearing.

It was for the realization of such an ideal that our forefathers established the Plymouth colony and endured the hardships of the wilderness, and that William Penn formed his holy experiment and laid the foundation of a mighty commonwealth.

In the feudal state, the citizen was nothing more than the vassal or serf of the overlord; in an absolute monarchy, the life and property of the citizen are subject to the disposal of the ruler. In a republic, however, citizenship becomes clothed with many of the attributes elsewhere vested in monarchs. The vote of the citizens chooses the head of the government, makes or unmakes constitutions, amendments and laws; and his voice in local government determines the conditions which most nearly affect him as a citizen.

For his protection, courts decree justice; police and fire departments protect his life and property; schools and colleges educate him and his family; and religious tolerance guarantees him the right to worship God according to the dictates of his own conscience. A powerful army and navy exist to protect him from the dangers of foreign invasion and conquest, and embassies at the courts of all nations represent his interests with dignity and power.

He is the heir to the greatness of a Washington and a Lincoln, he shares the glorious traditions and protection of a flag that has never known defeat or dishonor; and for him inventive genius has harnessed the lightning of the clouds, covered the continent with a network of steel highways, and made the air the carrier of his messages and a thoroughfare of communication and travel.

But privilege invariable carries with it obligation, and the ideal citizen is the one who realizes that as he has freely received the benefits of a representative government, he must freely give his best in thought, word, and deed to preserve that government intact.

A man becomes a citizen in the true sense of the word only when he recognizes his responsibility to his government and to his community. A citizen is one who shares the burdens of his nation and of his city, cherishes its interests, supports its institutions, protects its good name, and contributes to the richness of its life.

The chief concern of the ideal citizen is to aid his community in developing the higher civic life, which is the source of man's highest efficiency and of his more enduring influence. For him, citizenship means broadmindedness, tolerance with the faults of others, optimism which puts to shame the critics of honest effort and the enemies of progress, and a mind ever open to investigate any proposal for the good of the community.

The ideal citizen ought not only to have care to further legislation for the well-being of the people by giving them beautiful buildings, clean streets, pure air, wholesome water, and the best food supplies; but to train them to love the best things in the best forms.

He will ever be vigilant to maintain the higher civic life of the community, which means the expression of its collective ideals. It involves civic order and civic beauty as well. It means well-kept streets, and it also means spacious, well-ventilated and well-governed schools. It means capable government, and it means also museums, libraries, art galleries, restful parks, and beautiful architecture.

It was the pride and boast of the Emperor Augustus that he found Rome built of brick and left it built of marble. Something of the same aspiration is found in the mind of every true citizen—he desires to leave his community a little better than he found it.

In this new municipal building is the evidence that our citizens are awake to the responsibilities of civic duty in the world's greatest republic. And from this civic center will radiate lines of power and influence that will make this a greater city and its people better fitted for the privileges and duties of twentieth century citizenship.

FORMS OF INTRODUCTION FOR SPEAKERS AT OPENING OF NEW MUNICIPAL BUILDING.

"These exercises would not be complete without a few words from our mayor, whose interest in this building has been manifested from its earliest inception, and I therefore have pleasure in introducing Mayor ――――――――."

"Our worthy architect has given us such evident proof of his constructive genius in this beautiful building that I feel sure that you will welcome a few words from him regarding its plan and interior appointments."

"Our bankers are intensely interested in our new building for the reason that it will advance the interests of trade, facilitate the transaction of business and attract new residents to the community. I therefore take pleasure in calling upon ―――――――― who will speak on some of the financial aspects of our new venture."

THE VALUE OF THE BIBLE AS LITERATURE.

The study of the Bible from the point of view of English literature shows at once how deeply it has embedded itself in the substance of that literature, while at the same time retaining its own individual character. It is unlike any other book because it has been and is recognized as the Word of God, and in its thought and purpose it is different from any other work in the language. This unique position of the Bible in English literature springs from the essential character of the Book itself, and not merely from the attitude of its readers toward it.

A moment's consideration will show anyone how naturally he thinks of this book as the sum of the actions and sayings of men of another region and age of the world; and whether these men of Palestine come from the time of David or from the time of St. Paul, they lie together in one's mind as belonging to a single land and a single marvellous period of the world's history. Moreover, the whole substance of the

Book is imbued with a directness and freshness of inspiration which
are unique. It is a right instinct which places the sayings of Isaiah,
St. Paul and St. John on a higher level than the sayings of Socrates
and Marcus Aurelius, and the words of Jesus on a plane apart and
above them all.

This essential unity of quality is even more apparent in the style,
which in its directness and its simple nobility is the one standard
which we have in English to control the development of our language.
The phrases from the Bible which have grown into our everyday
speech spring impartially from the Old and New Testaments: we use
"the son of his old age," or "the valley of the shadow of death," or
"the pure in spirit," or "lilies of the field," without thinking whether
they come from one part of the Book or the other. This unity of style
is largely due to the fact that the whole book was translated at the
same period into a language of unsurpassed and unfaded vigor, which
now has enough tinge of the archaic to give it a color of its own.

It was Tyndal's great achievement that once for all he fixed the
language of the whole Bible; and under the anxious and inspired care
of the revisers who followed in his steps, the style has been brought to
a point of simplicity and dignity, of strong feeling expressing in the
rich sonorous prose, of stateliness and directness, which set it apart
from the style of any other book in the language.

In material, there is an endless variety. There are scraps of folk-
songs of war and victory, early legends and myths, histories based
on contemporary records and full of the vigor of a most vigorous
time, great bodies of laws which reflect important changes in civilization, highly developed schemes of liturgy and ecclesiastical law, col-
lections of proverbs so pithy and closely wrought that they still hold
their truth, psalms of pious and collected meditation or of jubilant
expressions of faith, the soaring messages of prophecy, the mystical
visions of the apocalypse, the simple, everlasting stories and teachings
of the gospels, the fiery and eloquent arguments of St. Paul.

In the Old Testament, all this material is Oriental. But it has
preserved for us the history, the poetry, the wisdom, the religious
ideals and national hopes of a people whose individuality and tenacity
of thought are perhaps the strongest known in history. The poetry
is marked with a singular concreteness both of idea and of idiom, and
by a freedom of form otherwise unknown in English. The books of
wisdom are shrewd and at times soaring, but they never reason in the
modern sense of the word.

In the New Testament, side by side with the Oriental simplicity
of the first three gospels and of the later book, there is a new element,
and an approach to modern modes of thought in the fourth gospel,
in the epistles of St. Paul, and in Hebrews. In these three works we
find the first efforts to formulate a theology, to philosophize religion.

Yet all this diversity has grown together into the unity of our

English Bible. The seeds of this unity were already sown in Old Testament times in the gradual advance of the people of Israel to higher and purer ideas of the nature and majesty of Jehovah. In each age their books of history were subject to a constant revision which selected and moulded the material with a strongly governing purpose.

In the times of Ezra and Nehemiah, the Law in the form of the Pentateuch became a definite book, venerated above all other books in existence. Then the prophetical books, which for the Jew included the historical books after the Pentateuch, followed the Law to a separate place in their esteem, and finally the Old Testament was completed by the addition of the other books.

When the devoted labors of William Tyndale, his scholarship and genius had set the style of the English, the later revisions merely corrected the detail without altering the strong characteristics which he had stamped upon it. Moreover the language of England in the sixteenth century had the vigor which belongs to the vernacular freshly turned to purposes of literature, and its comparative poverty in abstract and learned words separate it from our language today and set the Bible a little apart from other books.

Thus the work came to its full growth in the English language in a form which, in spite of its foreign origins and the diversity of its sources, makes it a single Book, and the Book which of all books in English is the most native and the most deeply ingrained in our literature and our language. Its influence upon English literature is so profound and universal, that like the scarlet thread in the British cordage, it can be traced in the works of every important writer. That influence is still powerful today, and in the Bible we have a standard of thought and expression which make it the great literary model of the ages.

PROBLEMS OF THE INDUSTRIAL WORKER.

"Labor is an anarchist whose sole aim is the crushing of the labor-giver!" Such is the accusation hurled against the workers by capital that grows fat on the heart's blood of the poor. Each side makes its complaints, but the plaints of the worker are the saddest of all.

It is true that wages are higher than they were a decade ago, but the increase is only nominal, for the demands are higher and the means of existence are far more expensive than they were ten years ago. With all their "high" wages, what is the lot of most of the laboring men today? Life for most of them is a hand-to-mouth existence. Only a few of them can lay by anything for old age. In most industries, if not in all, the worker is at the complete mercy of his employer. Only last year a vast number of bituminous coal miners in the Hocking Valley, Ohio, were near starvation, and they and their families would have had to face death with unerring certainty had it not been for the assistance rendered by some philanthropically inclined individuals and societies. And what brought those miners into this precarious condition? Why did this happen? It was because the operators had them working only part of the time at low wages, and then closed the mines altogether in order to keep the output below normal and the prices high.

Whenever some mechanics complains of their meager incomes, the public is quick to remind them of the high wages received by masons, carpenters, bricklayers, etc. But it is well to state that the wages paid in these industries are high only in appearance, and by no means above normal. All those employed in the building industries have only a comparatively small part of the year during which they may find ample opportunities for renumerative work. Many, if not most, of them must depend on summer to earn enought that will pay for the support of their families during the long months of winter.

No man, unless he is an industrial worker himself, can fully realize what it means to work long hours at low wages, and, at the same time, be exposed to all sorts of dangers, hazards, and injury. Almost daily the press reports accidents in mines, factories, and quarries. Neither are these accidents confined to any one locality. They are of common occurrences in all sections of the country. According to the latest available statistics, as compiled in the World Almanac for 1923, 24,643 men lost their lives in the coal mines of the United States within ten years; during the same period 1,551 men were killed in quarry accidents. Accordinig to the same authority, during one year the number of those maimed in a single industry (quarrying) was 11,217.

Such are the working conditions of men; those of the women are not much better. According to the last Census Report, there are 8,540,511 women employed in gainful occupatiohs, most of whom may be classed as industrial workers. Let us look at a few of the industries employing chiefly women and see how they fare. In the cigar factories and tobacco shops the work is done almost exclusively by women. It is of a sedentary nature, and therefore unhygienic. But this is not the worst. As soon as the factory system had fully developed, the sweating system came into vogue, compelling thousands of poor women to spend the day in filthy, ill-ventilated work-shops and the night under the most distressing conditions in garrets and cellars. Wages are always excessively low, no matter whether the work is done in the home or in the shop.

But what should be done to remedy existing evils? Some advocate the Golden Rule as an efficacious remedy. No doubt, its universal application would be of immense benefit. But since the suggestions as to the adoption of the Golden Rule come mostly from the employers, we have good reasons to assume that the worker would be the fellow who would be expected to follow it, especially when it comes to dealing with his employer. The latter would scarcely consider himself bound by its precepts. At any rate, as long as trusts and operators make strenuous efforts to crush every labor union and stamp out every right and liberty of the union man, we can not believe that capital would be inclined to follow the dictates of the Golden Rule.

There will be no industrial peace until every industrial worker receives an adequate share of the profits of his labor. It is unjust that the lion's share should be swallowed up by capital, while labor, the equal producer, should content itself with the leavings. Moreover, the worker must no longer be placed in competition with steel and machinery. He must be guaranteed hours of toil that will not impair his health and undermine his strength. He must have sufficient time for rest, recreation, and amusement, in a word—he must be put above machinery.

ADDRESS FOR FLAG DAY EXERCISES.

We are here today for the purpose of honoring the emblem of our national sovereignty, expressing in symbols the principles for which our Nation stands and for which it will shed its blood. It is a sacred emblem to be held in reverence.

We are glad that we as members of the Benevolent and Protective Order of Elks can thus fittingly honor the Stars and Stripes, so closely connected with our history. In fact, our history is written on our flag. No state, however great, however prosperous; no organization, no matter how influential or how powerful, should forget the debt owed to those thirteen English colonies that made this great Nation possible. It is this feeling of gratitude which led to the establishment of Flag-raising Day, which was first recognized on June 14, 1894, when at the request of "The Sons of Revolution" and "The Colonial Dames of America," the Stars and Stripes were raised on all public buildings.

Our first flag had thirteen stripes and in the canton where now appear the stars, was placed the Union Jack of England. This was the flag that Washington raised in 1775 over his camp at Cambridge. This was the flag that John Paul Jones hoisted, not over the Bonhomme Richard, but over his first naval ship, the Ranger.

This flag, bearing the British Union Jack, was not altered until the Declaration of Independence, nearly one year later. The Union Jack was at first replaced by a single five-pointed star on azure ground. It was not until July 14, 1777, that Congress replaced the single star by the constellation of thirteen stars. The Treaty of Paris, in 1783, by which Great Britain acknowledged each one of these thirteen colonies by name, to be a free, sovereign and independent state, admitted this, our national flag, to the august company of the historic banners of the Old World. There is today one of those great

banners older than ours. This one is the white cross, on a field of
red that represents the free confederate states of Switzerland.

Let us never lose sight of the debt the whole world owes to these
thirteen colonies. Those thirteen stripes stand to Europe and the
world as the sign and token of a free people requiring of their government a charter of liberty, a written contract, limiting the power
of rulers and reserving to themselves all the powers not granted to
those rulers. Not until a bill of rights was embodied in the first ten
commandments, did the colonies agree to a ratification of their constitution. And since that time, every state, without exception, has
repeated in her own constitution, this guarantee of the personal,
religious, and intellectual freedom of man.

Whenever we fling our banner to the breeze, we are apt to speak
of it as "Old Glory." No doubt, this is done partly on account of
its age, because our flag is twenty-three years older than the present
flag of Great Britain, seventeen years older than that of France,
nearly one hundred years older than the tri-colors of Germany and
Italy, and eight years older than the flag of Spain.

But the chief reason why we speak of our national banner as "Old
Glory," is its glorious history. Wherever it was hoisted, tyranny had
to give way to freedom; despotism was superseded by liberty. It had
its origin in that long and tedious conflict that brought independence
to the colonies. In 1812 it demonstrated to the world that American
seamen can not be compelled to serve on foreign ships. In 1845
"Old Glory" gave liberty to Texas. In 1861, it carried freedom to
4,000,0000 slaves. In 1898, it spread abroad the spirit of true liberty
in Cuba and the Philippines. What the Stars and Stripes achieved
during the World War, is scarcely necessary to recount. You are
acquainted with the facts. We all know that it led our armies onward to victory. Moreover, Captain C. P. Hall carried our national
emblem into the Arctic regions; Rear-Admiral Peary hoisted our
national colors at the north-pole, and in 1909-1910, the Smithsonian
African Expedition, under the direction of Col. Theodore Roosevelt,
carried the American flag into the Dark Continent.

In view of these facts, how appropriate that we, as a lodge, should
show our appreciation of our national blessings and our triumphant
banner. Of course, a true American always honors his national emblem and all that it stands for, but it is only proper that our lodge
should at least once a year assemble in a body, for the express purpose
of giving due respect to our flag. We are not only members of a
lodge, but also citizens of a great commonwealth, and as such it behooves us to honor the flag that protects us.

It is a most gratifying thought that the Order of Elks, from the
time of its incipency in 1868 to this very day, has always responded
to all calls of the country. Unlike some, the Elks have done more
than merely "spouting" patriotic oratory. They have shown by their

actions that they are willing to follow the flag whatever its destination. It has led many of our young men into the battlefields of Europe, where they have acquitted themselves nobly and creditably. The Elks Support Fund has provided vocational training at a cost of $69,000 to 106 disabled American boys. Moreover, the total receipts of the War Relief Commission, from June 5, 1920 to June 15, 1921, were $422,010. I am glad I can mention these facts because they make it plain that our patriotism is more than mere verbiage.

Let us then renew our pledges of loyalty, allegiance and obedience. Let us think of what it really means to be an American at this advanced stage of our country's history. Let us be mindful of America's blessings and opportunities, and, with Lowell say:

> "Our hearts, our hopes are all with thee,
> Our hearts, our hopes, our prayers, our tears,
> Our faith triumphant over our fears,
> Are all with thee, are all with thee!"

THE WORLD IS CALLING FOR MORE STATESMEN.

On the banks of a noble river, overlooking a splendid city which bears his name, stands a lofty shaft of purest marble, reared by a grateful people in memory of a simple Virginian gentleman. They rise heavenward from the dust—the monument from that of earth— the man from that of history—pure, serene, sublime.

The monument stands, as the man once stood, in the broad open daylight, challenging criticism. The cenotaph is man's best work; the man, God's. This stately column, marked by simplicity, solidity and grandeur, is a fit memorial to him whose life was given as the foundation stone of American manhood. Its marble blocks, a tribute to his greatness from states and nations in every clime, speak with dumb but eloquent lips of the glory and majesty of Washington.

But that great life is closed—the pure patriot, the lofty statesman, the broad-minded, unselfish, courageous man is gone. His mantle lies where it fell. And with him has fled from our council chambers those qualities which made him the noblest figure that ever stood in the forefront of a nation's life.

His death brought sorrow to every fireside in his native land; it lowered to half mast the flags of England's triumphant fleet; it furled the proud banners of the victorious army of France, and draped them in black. The civilized world, moved by common impulse, testified to the loss humanity had sustained when the silken cords that bound him to those shores were snapped, and his soul drifted out beyond the bar into the unknown ocean of eternity.

But what of conditions in our legislative halls today? It has well said that "the practice of party intrigue is unfavorable to the development of a statesman. It narrows a man's mind and distorts his vision." ¡His eye, accustomed to the obscurity of committee-rooms, cannot range over the wide landscape of national questions.'' And again it has been truly said, that ''a great empire and little minds go but ill 'together.''

. From the moment a man abandons the retirement of home for the public walks of life, throughout his entire career he is set upon by knaves whom the public suffers to infest the road along which he must pass. Here he finds he cannot proceed until he yields implicit obedience to some irresponsible, unprincipled, and despotic party boss; there he is robbed of his money, and yonder of his morality.

The baneful effects of this degrading system are everywhere apparent. Virtues, public and private, have been corrupted, national honor tainted, the whole tone of our government—municipal, state, and federal—conspicuously lowered. No political character is deemed above suspicion—I had almost said deserves to be, when we see the most courageous men in our public life today stooping from their high office to pay a campaign debt by a political appointment.

For generations we have been deeply interested in pulling down kings from their thrones and in devising forms of government that would not require personal leadership. The constitutional fathers had a profound respect for people in general, but they were afraid of individuals in particular. It was a machine they wanted: one that automatically held everybody in a fixed orbit or immediately restored anyone who went tangent to it to his proper place.

They failed to realize that in society, as well as in mechanics, the power which runs a machine must come from some source outside of it. No machine will run itself. Our ''invisible government'' is only the natural leadership which our form of government does not provide for in visible form.

The so-called ''political machine'' is misnamed. It is quite the opposite of a machine in that it constitutes the power of leadership which the real machine must have in order to operate. Constitutions and laws will not direct and govern the affairs of society any more than the bridle on a horse will direct the horse where his master wants him to go.

In our political affairs we worship the cult of mediocrity. James Bryce wrote a chapter in his ''American Commonwealth'' on why great men do not become presidents. At a time when the best brains in the nation are needed in public life, we see to it that these men follow other pursuits of a private nature. Great ability ought to be harnessed and made to work for the common good. This is all the more true when we consider the fact that it is going to require a great deal more ability to handle the affairs of this nation in the future than it has in the past.

Never were we in greater need of men with strong minds, brave hearts and far-reaching vision—men with brains enough to see the right and courage enought to do it. On every hand momentous questions press for solution. The problems growing out of the World War alone are staggering in their magnitude and complexity. They must be settled if the future of this nation is to remain secure—but it will require statesmen, not mere politicians, to furnish these solutions and to apply them fearlessly.

A republican form of government presupposes an intelligent people, jealous of their right, ready and willing to discharge those functions which must, of necessity, fall upon them. If they are unwilling to perform those duties, then a republic is an idle and dangerous dream, which soon will resolve itself into a hideous nightmare.

We in America are heirs of a government which has won the praise of the world, and which, if properly preserved, will bestow the greatest blessing upon ourselves and those that come after us. But, for its preservation, in view of the fact that a large number of our voters are far below the democratic standard of intelligence, it is imperative that we have good leaders—that the race of statesmen shall not perish from the earth.

RESPONSE TO ADDRESS OF WELCOME TO WOMEN SOCIAL WORKERS.

In acknowledging the cordial and gracious welcome to your capital just extended to this convention, I feel sure that I speak for every delegate present in saying that we are glad to be here and to experience that charming hospitality and true friendliness for which this city and the state have ever been noted in history, song and story.

We are tempted to linger beyond the time at our command among the abundant memorials of an age of romance and chivalry, of knee-buckles, powdered hair, and fine manners, and we pause as we see through the crepe myrtle and magnolias some old colored mammy standing in a colonial doorway and rubbing our eyes, wonder whether an illustration from Thomas Nelson's pages "In Ole Virginia" has suddenly taken life.

None of us have failed to admire the stately beauty of this typical southern city, with its magnificent distances, its beautiful monuments to Washington, Lee, Jackson, and the Confederate soldiers and sailors, and surely not one of us will wish to go away without standing for at least a moment in the pew in old St. John's Church, where, in 1775, Patrick Henry made his stirring address which ended with the immortal words, "Give me liberty or give me death."

The cause which brings us together here is in striking contrast to these momentoes of a day when not even the term "social service" had been coined, for, in its present significance at least, social service has been the development of very recent years.

It cannot be denied, to be sure, that "in business and in politics we are still individualists," but there is much evidence that even in these fields concern for the common welfare is coming to be a determining influence, while in the field of "social work," which means merely the organization of the social spirit for effective expression, there has within the past ten years such expansion and deepening as scarcely has a precedent.

There is a church in an eastern city which has a legend carved in a stone arch over its front entrance that reads: "This church is conducted for the benefit of the people outside." This is the spirit of social service; it is forgetfulness of self.

The growth of social consciousness in America is not the perquisite of any one political party, nor is it manifested only in govermental action. It can be traced in the platform of all the parties, in presidents' and governors' messages, in acts of legislatures, in judicial decisions, and in the conduct of municipal affairs.

But it is seen also in the efforts that are being made by the churches of all denominations to meet the needs of the present day; in the gradual remodeling of the curricula of the public schools, so that children will be fitted for life, and not merely for college; in the many books on social problems which are printed every year, and still more in the intelligent discussion of social questions in the popular magazines and the daily press. Most of all, perhaps, it is manifested in the growing number of persons who are definitely engaged in social work, either as volunteers, serving on committees and boards of directors and giving their time and thought in many other ways, or as paid workers making this their profession and daily occupation.

The social spirit in America has expressed itself variously as organized charity, housing and public health movements, settlements, municipal and social research, experiments with new criminal procedure and prison reform, playgrounds and recreation centers, religious and medical social service, industrial commissions, and public welfare departments.

These diversified and yet, in essential aim and motive, allied activities, have given rise to a new vocation, to a profession in the making. This calling, from the very nature of the work it is to do, and from the character of its leaders, makes an extraordinary appeal to the missionary spirit of young men and women in and out of our colleges and universities, who have seen the vision of a new social order in which poverty, crime and disease, if now wholly banished, will certainly be vastly diminished, and at any rate will not exist as the result of social neglect.

These associated activities of the new social reform have caught up and as it were assimilated many of the old established agencies for relieving individual distress and misfortune. The hospital is no longer merely a refuge for the sick, but also a health center. From it radiate preventive and educational influences as important as the bedside ministrations to the sick.

The orphan asylum is no longer a place to keep a few orphans alive, but a child welfare station, in which the whole problem of organizing the educational, moral, economic and recreational life of the child may be studied, in some respects even to better advantage than in the necessarily more complex normal home life.

The relief society is no longer solely to supply food and fuel and clothing to the "worthy poor," but it is to improve their condition, to re-establish their earning capacity and independence. For these reasons, the men and women who are employed in relief societies, children's institutions, and hospitals find themselves in close sympathy and accord with the social workers who are securing new housing and compensation laws, promoting instructive nursing and medical inspection, or revising a discredited penal system.

The things which social workers do in common—their difficulties, obstacles, and discouragements, as well as their purposes, ideals, and achievements, unite them in one great family despite great differences in their training and education.

We have already been made to feel that your citizens are in sympathy with the great cause of social service, and especially from our gracious hostesses have we received a welcome which has warmed our hearts and inspired us with fresh enthusiasm for our tasks. To them and to all your good people of   we give assurance of an appreciation deep and sincere.

SPEECH FOR RETIRING PRESIDENT OF KIWANIS CLUB.

Across the entire northern expanse of the continent of Africa, broken only here and there by limited regions of fertility, stretches an arid waste of shifting sand, continually in motion like the waves of the sea, and like the sea, obliterating and swallowing up all traces of human effort and human ambition.

Did I say all? That statement must be modified by a notable exception, for beyond the western banks of the Nile, rising sheer out of the desert sands to a height of from 300 to 450 feet, rise those sublime sentinels of the ages, the Pyramids, that already have looked down upon the changing scenes of fifty centuries, and probably will remain as they are until the last human being disappears from the earth and the cold and lifeless planet falls back into the luminary from which it came.

No living man can say how those vast blocks of granite, which in the Great Pyramid aggregate 89,000,000 cubic feet, with a mass of 6,848,000 tons, were transported across the yielding sands, or how they were raised to their positions and joined with a cement that outlasts the stone itself, but one thing we do know, and that is that their creators belonged to the great craft of builders, who in every age of the world have wrought in clay and bronze and iron and brick and marble and steel, and whose works do follow them.

But the members of this noble craft do not work in material things alone. The great epochs of history are marked by their achievements in the invisible realm of thought, wherein some Newton reasons out a universal law from the fall of an apple, some Watt sees in the moving lid of a tea-kettle the imprisoned giant of steam, or some Franklin employs the humble medium of a kite string to harness the thunder-bolt of the clouds.

Our forefathers were builders in the truest sense, when in Inde-pendence Hall on July 4, 1776, they affixed their signatures to an immortal document which declared that "all men are created free and equal," and that "governments derive their just powers from the consent of the governed." And the visible evidence of their inspired labor is a nation set upon a hill, whose light cannot be hid.

But with the growth of our nation have come problems inseparable from an experiment in civilization upon a scale so vast. The operative organs of society have grown faster than the regulative organs, hence the opportunities for the unscrupulous to fight their way to success and power are magnificent.

If the microbe of self has sufficiently poisoned their world, the thing is easy. It is simply a matter of *using* the institutions around them instead of suspecting and conforming to them, of making every economic, political, or legal organization a mere rung on which to set a resolute heel and swing nearer to the goal.

Against this false standard of values the voice of a new giant in the industrial and commercial world of today has raised an emphatic protest. The Kiwanis Club declares that material gain, either to an individual or to a community, is too poor a thing to win at the ex-pense of losing the best gifts of life.

When it is sought narrowly, life *is* lost. When a city glories in its great mills and factories and the dividends they earn, and boasts of its bank accounts and its balance in trade, and is blind to the broken lives on which these things are built—blind to the men and women imprisoned, body and mind, in exhausting toil; blind to the children taken from the school and from God's out-of-doors to grow shrunken and pallid in somber mills; blind to the dreary wretchedness of its tenements and the sordid alleys where its workers herd—than that city is dead to much that ought to constitute its life—dead to sym-pathy, to pity, and to that high sacrifice that might glorify its soul.

The message of the Kiwanis Club and the message which such men as are gathered here must be proclaiming always is the high supremacy of life. Prosperity is good and material success is good, but higher than these is the need that life be honored and exalted. That man is greatest and that community is greatest which has—not most possessions—but most of life; most points at which it is alive to human needs, to human values, and to the rights of every human soul.

"We Build," is our terse and expressive motto, but the essential meaning of Kiwanis is not found in the material results of its building. The organization that devotes itself solely to material accomplishments, and that leaves behind a record of work done for the material welfare of its community, deserves well of its time and place; but that organization whose ideal of service creates in its membership a higher conception of individual responsibility to the community; a conception of neighborliness as expressed in the spirit of service in the ordinary every-day affairs of life, that organization earns the lasting gratitude of men.

No one can leave an office such as the presidency of a Kiwanis Club without a sense of the high privilege of having been permitted to preside over the councils of such an organization. If I were asked what I consider the greatest benefit I have received while occupying this office, I should answer: "the revelation in other men's souls of what my own is striving for." Builders are we all—builders of thought, builders of business, builders of institutions, and though we labor with different materials and in various ways, the work of each is essential to the completed structure.

As I lay down the duties of this office, it is with the confidence that other hands will carry forward its requirements with an increasing measure of success, and to the new president of the Club I extend not only a cordial greeting but congratulations upon an opportunity for service that will enlist the highest capabilities of mind and heart.

www.ingramcontent.com/pod-product-compliance
Lightning Source LLC
Chambersburg PA
CBHW030448250626
47154CB00003BA/1185